KU-699-455

FRENCH BLOCKBUSTERS

Traditions in World Cinema

General Editors
Linda Badley (Middle Tennessee State
University)
R. Barton Palmer (Clemson University)

Founding Editor
Steven Jay Schneider (New York
University)

Titles in the series include:

edinburghuniversitypress.com/series/tiwc

FRENCH BLOCKBUSTERS

Cultural Politics of a Transnational Cinema

Charlie Michael

EDINBURGH
University Press

Edinburgh University Press is one of the leading university presses in the UK. We publish academic books and journals in our selected subject areas across the humanities and social sciences, combining cutting-edge scholarship with high editorial and production values to produce academic works of lasting importance. For more information visit our website: edinburghuniversitypress.com

© Charlie Michael, 2019

Edinburgh University Press Ltd
The Tun – Holyrood Road
12 (2f) Jackson's Entry
Edinburgh EH8 8PJ

Typeset in 10/12.5 pt Sabon by
Servis Filmsetting Ltd, Stockport, Cheshire
and printed and bound in Great Britain

A CIP record for this book is available from the British Library

ISBN 978 1 4744 2423 3 (hardback)
ISBN 978 1 4744 2424 0 (webready PDF)
ISBN 978 1 4744 2425 7 (epub)

The right of Charlie Michael to be identified as author of this work has been asserted in accordance with the Copyright, Designs and Patents Act 1988 and the Copyright and Related Rights Regulations 2003 (SI No. 2498).

Every effort has been made to trace the copyright holders of the illustrative material in this book, but if any have been inadvertently overlooked, the publisher will be pleased to make the necessary arrangements at the first opportunity.

CONTENTS

FIGURES

ACKNOWLEDGEMENTS

Retracing the origin story of this book is a humbling exercise. Numerous kind souls have helped to sustain *French Blockbusters* along its meandering path to publication. To all of those people I mention here, and to any others I regrettably forgot to include, I extend my most heartfelt gratitude.

I have been fortunate to have the support of multiple institutions over the years. At UW-Madison, a Vilas Travel Grant and a Dissertation Completion Fellowship played crucial roles in my initial research. A Foreign Languages and Area Studies (FLAS) Fellowship was a godsend during the early stages of writing. Later, various sources of departmental travel funding from the University of Miami and Emory University helped me to continue my summer research trips to Paris, as did the amazing support I received from the Borchard Foundation for my contribution to 'French Cinema and the Crises of Globalization' – a phenomenal conference that took place at the Château de la Bretesche during the summer of 2012. Everyone I have worked with at Edinburgh University Press also deserves mention. Gillian Leslie believed in this project from the moment I pitched it to her at SCMS, then offered glasses of wine and pep talks as it morphed from dissertation to proposal and, eventually, to its current form. My writing also benefited from the thoughtful feedback offered by the two anonymous reviewers and the enthusiastic support of my series editors, Barton Palmer and Linda Badley. As the manuscript entered production last year, Richard Strachan and Eddie Clark provided much-needed guidance, as did Ruth Swanney, my copy editor, and Samantha Clark, who compiled the index.

Some of the ideas expressed in these pages are published elsewhere. The second half of Chapter 1 first appeared as 'Historicizing Contemporary French Blockbusters' in *A Companion to Contemporary French Cinema* (Wiley-Blackwell, 2015). Segments of Chapter 2 and 6 originated with a stand-alone article called 'Interpreting *Intouchables*' that appeared in a special issue of *SubStance: A Review of Theory and Literary Criticism* (Johns Hopkins University Press, 2014). Finally, a variant of Chapter 5, to be entitled 'EuropaCorp and the Landscape of Contemporary French Action Cinema', will soon appear in a special volume of *Cahiers des Champs Visuels*, forthcoming in 2019 with L'Harmattan. I am grateful to the editors of these and other collections who have supported my work and encouraged me to publish it even before the book itself was ready: Gaspard Delon, Alistair Fox, Graeme Hayes, Raphaëlle Moine, Michel Marie, Martin O'Shaughnessy, Nathalie Rachlin, Hillary Radner, Rosemarie Scullion and Ana Vinuela.

The bulk of my revisions and rewriting took place in Paris during the 2017–2018 academic year. That endeavor would have been far more difficult without the friends and colleagues who supported me most during the final push. Mary Harrod has been a constant source of intellectual support and also went out of her way to help me promote my work – housing me on multiple conference jaunts to London and even sponsoring my rewarding stint as a Visiting Fellow at the University of Warwick in the spring of 2018. During my visits to England, I was also fortunate to meet two other sage researchers – Hugh Dauncey and Christopher Meir – who provided helpful suggestions and editorial comments during the book's final stages. While in Paris, I was thrilled to cross paths with an intrepid trio of scholars from Paris 3 – Mélanie Boissoneau, Quentin Mazel and Thomas Pillard – who welcomed me to their regular gatherings at the 'Cinémas de genre' seminar. Meanwhile, whenever I was desperate to locate statistical records or old press dossiers, Susane Rodes of the CNC Resource Center was more than ready to help, as were the always friendly and helpful staff at the Bibliothèque du Film (BiFi) at the Cinémathèque Française. I also want to recognize the French media professionals who took time out of their busy schedules to speak with me about their experiences working in the industry: Mathieu Béjot, Rodolphe Buet, Brahim Chioua, Dider Dekeyser, Gilles Granier, John Kochman, Marc-Antoine Robert, Patrick Sobelman, Jacques-Eric Strauss and François Yon. All of them offered their varying views of French cinema 'on the ground', and their generous counsel helped me to piece together the account I present here.

I have learned from many brilliant teachers over the years. The late Vern Bailey's heartfelt film history lectures remain some of my most indelible memories from Carleton College, where I was also inspired by courses I took with Chiara Briganti, Leigh Kane, Susan Jaret McKinstry, Mike Kowalewski, Jim McDonnell, Kofi Owusu, John Schott, Dana Strand and Connie Walker. My first, formative taste of Parisian film culture came on an incredible study abroad programme led by Carl and Ruth Weiner in the spring of 1995. As an MA student at the University of Iowa, I studied with a group of thinkers who continue to influence my work to this day – Dudley Andrew, Rick Altman, Garrett Stewart, Angelo Restivo and Steven Ungar. At the University of Wisconsin, the ideas that eventually became this book began to germinate in a term paper I wrote for David Bordwell, whose enthusiasm and encouragement has never waned in all the years since. While a doctoral student on the isthmus, I was lucky to learn from numerous other first-rate researchers on film and media history, including Tino Balio, Michael Curtin, Lea Jacobs, Shanti Kumar, J. J. Murphy and Kristin Thompson. I am particularly grateful to the quartet of dedicated scholars who also agreed to serve as readers for my dissertation committee – Laird Boswell, Vance Kepley, Ben Singer and Jeff Smith.

My peregrinations from graduate school to the conference circuit, the job market and beyond have been filled with sympathetic fellow travelers. Two of my former Wisconsin classmates, Colin Burnett and Tim Palmer, are now indispensible colleagues in the field, offering me expert feedback at multiple stages of my writing process. Several other notable members of the UW 'filmies' network – Matthew Bernstein, Richard Neupert and Greg Smith – have become invaluable mentors in my ongoing search for a permanent academic home. I am also grateful to many other card-carrying members of the North American 'film studies mafia', whose kindness and collegiality over the years have helped nourish my work more than they could ever know: Ernesto Acevedo-Muñoz, Tanine Allison, Jay Beck, Maria Belodubrovskaya, Vince Bohlinger, Nsenga Burton, Maria Corrigan, David Gillota, Ethan de Seife, Maggie Flinn, Kaitlin Fyfe, Heather Heckman, Tim Holland, Alison LaTendresse, Jason Livingston, Paul McEwan, Mark Minett, Rielle Navitski, Mike Newman, David Pettersen, John Powers, Thomas Prieto, Dave Resha, Dan Reynolds, Brad Schauer, Michele Schreiber, Chris Sieving, Gerald Sim, Jake Smith, Kat Spring, James Steffen and Jennifer Wild. Special thanks are also in order here for Chris Holmlund, whose encouragement and positivity continue to light my way, and for Frédéric Gimello-Mesplomb, whose enthusiastic reception of my work gave me newfound confidence in the latter stages of writing. Finally, words alone cannot express my thanks to Kelley Conway, my one-time dissertation advisor, current colleague and close friend. I am tremendously lucky to have found such a bright and benevolent kindred spirit to guide my intellectual path these past fifteen years.

Last mention here goes to the many friends and family who have supported my quixotic quest to become a film professor. To my late Grandpa Jim Michael, my first and finest model of professorial wisdom and sartorial cool. To Sridhar Pappu, John Nimis and Ephraim Zimmerman, who played *Star Wars* with me long before I knew 'film studies' was a thing. To Amy Borden and Kathleen Man Gyllenhaal, my original grad school partners-in-crime. To Adam Malka, Tony Sullivan and Tom Yoshikami, who make fantasy sports far more stressful than any book project could ever be. To Bob Ash and Molly Michels, whose late-night sympathy is so welcome on those rare instances when all of our kids actually go to bed. To Crissy Arcé, Carlos Fernandez, Sweta Oza and Krishna Srivinasan, friends whose very presence helped sustain me through those stormy years in South Florida. To Sonya Barbezat, Joey Meyer, Keith Sklar, Dinesh Xavier and Nav Xavier, who bring me the fresh life perspectives only siblings in-law can provide. To Chandranee Xavier, who amazes me with her quiet resilience and selfless generosity. To Calvin Meyer, Nate Meyer and Nora Sklar, who make the present so much more adorable and the future so much more exciting. To my sisters, Katie and Eleanor, who remain constant wellsprings of empathy, even in the face of my most angst-ridden self-doubt. To my parents, Jim and Sarah, for their unwavering support, love and encouragement through all of my life phases. To Jeevan and Avi, whose exuberance for watching movies now nearly matches my pride at being their father. And finally, to my soul mate, Subha, whose luminous intellect and boundless love make every day more worth living and every film more worth discussing. This book is for her.

TRADITIONS IN WORLD CINEMA

General editors: **Linda Badley and R. Barton Palmer**
Founding editor: **Steven Jay Schneider**

Traditions in World Cinema is a series of textbooks and monographs devoted
to the analysis of currently popular and previously underexamined or under-
valued film movements from around the globe. Also intended for general interest readers, the textbooks in this series offer undergraduate- and graduate-level
film students accessible and comprehensive introductions to diverse traditions
in world cinema. The monographs open up for advanced academic study more
specialised groups of films, including those that require theoretically oriented
approaches. Both textbooks and monographs provide thorough examinations
of the industrial, cultural and socio-historical conditions of production and
reception.

The flagship textbook for the series includes chapters by noted scholars
on traditions of acknowledged importance (the French New Wave, German
Expressionism), recent and emergent traditions (New Iranian, post-Cinema
Novo), and those whose rightful claim to recognition has yet to be established
(the Israeli persecution film, global found footage cinema). Other volumes
concentrate on individual national, regional or global cinema traditions. As the
introductory chapter to each volume makes clear, the films under discussion
form a coherent group on the basis of substantive and relatively transparent, if
not always obvious, commonalities. These commonalities may be formal, sty-

listic or thematic, and the groupings may, although they need not, be popularly identified as genres, cycles or movements (Japanese horror, Chinese martial arts cinema, Italian neorealism). Indeed, in cases in which a group of films is not already commonly identified as a tradition, one purpose of the volume is to establish its claim to importance and make it visible (East Central European Magical Realist cinema, Palestinian cinema).

Textbooks and monographs include:

1. An introduction that clarifies the rationale for the grouping of films under examination
2. A concise history of the regional, national or transnational cinema in question
3. A summary of previous published work on the tradition
4. Contextual analysis of industrial, cultural and socio-historical conditions of production and reception
5. Textual analysis of specific and notable films, with clear and judicious application of relevant film theoretical approaches
6. Bibliograph(ies)/filmograph(ies)

Monographs may additionally include:

7. Discussion of the dynamics of cross-cultural exchange in light of current research and thinking about cultural imperialism and globalisation, as well as issues of regional/national cinema or political/aesthetic movements (such as New Waves, postmodernism or identity politics)
8. Interview(s) with key filmmakers working within the tradition.

FOREWORD

Frédéric Gimello-Mesplomb

The year 1985. It is the mid-80s and US audiences flock to cinemas to see the latest blockbusters by Spielberg or Lucas – films by now so emblematic of the decade. Geopolitical ironies abound in these years, caught between the post-traumatic stress of Vietnam's aftermath and the unexpectedly abrupt end of the Cold War. For a moment, President Reagan's 'Star Wars' defence agenda even blurs the line between Hollywood effects and a 'real' spectacle about to take place at Cape Canaveral. Meanwhile, in France, the years of President Mitterrand and his proactive Minister of Culture, Jack Lang, are upon us. Together they launch an ambitious Gallic response to increasing transatlantic calls for 'free trade' – a controversial movement they call *le Tout Culturel*. Since David L. Looseley published his synthesis of Langian cultural policy in *The Politics of Fun* (1995), few works have studied the reform's longer-term consequences.[1] Fewer still have considered whether they could have engendered productive new forms of French cinema. Instead, scholars most often defer to a more cynical view, as if France's waning cinematic influence must be inevitable, allied somehow with the death of so many other 'master narratives' decried by French philosophers of the late twentieth century.

There have been exceptions to this story, of course. In 1997, for instance, Laurent Jullier of the University of Lorraine brought the work of Christian Metz and Serge Daney to bear on theories of digital art in order to highlight what he called a 'postmodern cinema.'[2] Outlining a contemporary style that revels in new forms of abstraction and 'visual fireworks,' Jullier pointed to the features of American blockbusters like *Star Wars* or *Raiders of the Lost Ark*, but also to the so-called *cinéma du look* from France. Already noted by critic Raphaël Bassan in 1989, this relatively short cycle of films by three young directors – Luc Besson (*Subway, Le Grand Bleu*), Jean-Jacques Beineix (*Diva, Betty Blue*) and Leos Carax (*Mauvais Sang*) – signalled a 'neo-baroque' aesthetic that combined a commercialised, MTV-inspired style with erudite cinematic influences (Truffaut, Godard, Renoir) to create a fantastic form of visual poetry.[3] While the *look* films remain a reference point for academics and critics alike, they often only get cited as an influence on later directors (Jean-Pierre Jeunet) or as a sort of cautionary parable about the dubious consequences of aestheticisation. Moreover, undue focus on the *look* may also prove to be a case of hiding a forest with a few trees.

This exciting new book by Charlie Michael proposes a counter-narrative to those who continue to reproduce what he calls '*a priori* assumptions about what the [French] industry's role on the international scene *should* be' as 'an artisanal, aesthetic alternative to Hollywood hegemony.' By focusing on just one ideological framing of these matters, Michael argues, we occlude the more complicated story of what the Gallic production sphere actually looks like today. Drawing on a broad range of research materials – from attendance data to archival documents and from film reception to interviews with industry professionals – Michael builds his hypothesis in several stages. His first move involves folding recent popular comedies (*Bienvenue Chez Les Ch'tis, Intouchables*) into an expanded generic definition of what he calls the 'local blockbuster.' But the most interesting part of the case study he performs here has to do with the tensions that his provocative concept ('French blockbusters') continues to generate, as each new success (or ambitious failure) spurs symptomatic quarrels of legitimacy between those who endorse the commercial prospects of 'big' French cinema and those who dismiss it with equal fervor. Indeed, these observations echo in numerous other artistic disputes of the 2000s, which lately seem to crop up almost every time a French director seeks to produce a popular genre film.[4]

By grouping numerous different studios (StudioCanal, EuropaCorp, Studio Orange, Gaumont) as contributors to one period of sweeping strategic change, Michael's account brings together – without *a priori* judgments about quality – an entire genealogy of French 'event films' of the past thirty years: *Cyrano de Bergerac* (Rappeneau 1989), *Germinal* (Berri 1993), *Les Visiteurs* (Poiré 1993), *La Reine Margot* (Chereau 1994), *The Fifth Element* (Besson 1998), *Amélie* (Jeunet, 2001), *Qu'est-ce qu'on a fait au bon dieu?* (De Chauveron 2014), *La Famille Bélier* (Lartigau 2014), the *Astérix* films. All of these, in their own way, serve as different iterations of the phenomenon he calls the 'French blockbuster.' Obviously, if we reduce the blockbuster to a question of profit margins, then membership in such a group would be rather easy to define. However, this book cannot be summarised as a simple rehabilitation of commercial films wrongly disparaged by French criticism.

Instead, Michael sketches the genealogy of the French blockbuster as a nascent cultural form. He notes that the year 2004 might constitute the swell of a movement that has only grown louder with each passing year, cresting perhaps in 2014, and featuring an entire decade of high-grossing films with international distribution. The titles are too numerous to list here: *Les Choristes* (Barratier 2004), *Un Long Dimanche de Fiançailles* (Jeunet 2004), *L'Enquête Corse* (Berberian 2004), *Les Bronzés 3* (Leconte 2006), *Arthur et les Minimoys* (Besson 2006), *Bienvenue chez les Ch'tis* (Boon 2008), *OSS 117* (Hazanavicius 2011), *Intouchables* (Tolédano and Nakache 2011). In 2007, director Pascale Ferran sounded the alarm bell for the French industry during the live broadcast of the *Césars* award ceremony, pleading for public support for a more robust 'middlebrow' cinema (*les films du milieu*) to mediate the ground between this new class of big budget films and ultra-subsidised small-scale projects.

It would seem, in fact, that the mainstream, 'globalised' French cinema of years past, which used to feature films by directors like Bernardo Bertolucci, now resorts most often to comedy. Another rewarding aspect of this book is that it allows us to re-assess the roles of Besson and Jeunet thirty years after their start in the 1980s. The former has become the most visible mogul in what Michael calls a new 'oligopoly' of French production as the head of his independent company EuropaCorp, while the latter ranks as a star of what we might call a new sort of 'mainstream quality' global cinema. Two directors that used to be models for an alternative sort of independent French art cinema in the 1980s are thus now prototypical business entrepreneurs. In two full chapters devoted to the debates that emerged during the releases of *Amélie* (Jeunet 2001) and *Valerian and the City of a Thousand Planets* (Besson 2017), Michael offers context for the ideological cleavages that these films exacerbated among French and American intellectuals as part of the rhetorical place that two directors now occupy in the landscape of transnational French film production. The final two chapters then evoke two other symptomatic tendencies of contemporary popular French cinema writ large: action and spectacle (Chapter 5) and comedy (Chapter 6). In each case, Michael notes how the stylistic features of recent French genre films reflect and refract the rapidly changing cultural politics of the period.

For sure, Michael's work is not for readers who cling to the clichéd myth of a French cinema where small, independent (and technically imperfect) art films battle against the Hollywood goliath. Nor is it for those who refuse to view each new student at *La Fémis* as anything but an inheritor of the French New Wave. Instead, this is a book that confronts economic reality with clear eyes, showing how an industry has succeeded in adapting, albeit with great difficulty, to a model for generating its own form of blockbuster cinema. Balancing an array of historical influences, Michael gives us a new language for navigating the internal conflicts that have marked a period of dynamic change, and when the intermittent success stories of 'big' films became fodder for debate about what forms of recognition (both economic and symbolic) are most appropriate for a national industry with transnational ambitions. Written briskly like a behind-the-scenes saga, this original book will challenge the preconceptions of anyone who thinks that notions of 'French cinema' and 'blockbusters' should remain diametrically opposed.

Avignon, April 2019

Text translated from French by Frédéric Gimello-Mesplomb and Subha Xavier

NOTES

1 David L. Looseley (1995). *The Politics of Fun: Cultural Policy and Debate in Contemporary France*. Oxford and Washington, DC: Berg.
2 Laurent Jullier (1997). *L'écran post-moderne: un cinéma de l'allusion et du feu d'artifice*. Paris: L'Harmattan.
3 Raphaël Bassan (1989). 'Le cinéma du look'. *La Revue du Cinéma* 448: May 1989. Translation in English 'Three French neo-baroque directors: Beineix, Besson, Carax from *Diva* to *Le Grand Bleu*.' *The Films of Luc Besson: Master of Spectacle* (2007). Susan Hayward and Phil Powrie, eds. Manchester: Manchester University Press: pp. 11– 23.
4 Frédéric Gimello-Mesplomb (2012). 'Produire un film de genre fantastique en France, entre hétérotopie artistique et quête de légitimité. Analyse d'une tension identitaire dans le champ de la creation' in Frédéric Gimello-Mesplomb, ed. *Les cinéastes français à l'épreuve du genre fantastique. Socioanalyse d'une production artistique* 1 (1), Paris: L'Harmattan: pp. 9–72.

INTRODUCTION: FRENCH BLOCKBUSTERS?

The first two words in the title of this book may seem an unlikely pairing. Granted, the French film industry does not actually produce blockbusters very often – at least not in the inflated budgetary sense most associated with global Hollywood. In 2015, the average Anglo-American film budget was $60 million, while the average budget for a French production barely crossed the $5 million mark (*World Film Market Trends*). The gap between these two figures is also likely understated, as it excludes promotion and marketing costs, which recent estimates put at an additional $35 million for an average major North American release; summer tent-poles like superhero franchises are usually far more than that. Due in no small measure to the reach of these enormous franchises, Hollywood currently hovers around 65% of Europe's annual market share while relegating all EU films combined to just 30% of their home turf and a miniscule 2% of the North American market (*World Film Market Trends*). Inextricable from major distribution companies and omnipresent on other media platforms, blockbusters are by now a mundane reality of North America's screen presence as it plays out in France and Europe more generally. Given these brutal inequities, the field of film studies often regards blockbusters as something like a conceptual equivalent for the booming soundtracks that so often accompany them – disrupting other cinemas with the constant drone of cultural disequilibrium.

However, if we can bracket the routine caveats about economic scale and cultural hegemony for just a moment, there is also substantial evidence to suggest that other film industries have recently been rather ambitious in seeking ways to flip the script. Scholarly attention in this regard tends to gravitate more frequently to the robust popular traditions currently flourishing across the Global South – from India, Korea or Brazil, for instance – while overlooking the corresponding shifts that have taken place in venerable cinemas from the 'old' continent. Moreover, among those, France has consistently been a leader among its comparable regional neighbours, annually producing the most films of any European cinema, showing those films on the largest number of screens, and drawing the largest number of people to see them (*World Film Market Trends*). In the process, a startling plurality of creative tendencies from France has begun to coalesce, attaining intermittent international visibility. From prestigious award winners like *The Artist* (Hazanavicius 2011) or *La môme / La vie en rose* (Dahan 2008) to English-language genre films like *Lucy* (Besson 2014) or *Taken* (Morel 2008) and to intermittent 'breakout' comedies like *Bienvenue Chez les Ch'tis / Welcome to the Sticks* (Boon 2008) and *Intouchables* (Toledano and Nakache 2011), something of a 'new' tradition of popular French cinema seems now to be appearing, seducing audiences on a surprising variety of commercial registers even while it provokes predictable cries of cultural 'homogenisation' from critics.

Proposing such intuitively different films as parts of an evolving tradition of popular filmmaking presents certain conceptual obstacles. Most obviously, that is because they tend to be indexed by media and scholarship as isolated or idiosyncratic endeavours – more the result of a bombastic mogul (Luc Besson) or an unpredictable flight of audience fancy (*Les Ch'tis*) than any concerted change in industrial strategy. Yet there are also ample reasons to consider these various titles – and the mutual distinctions among them – as the collective aesthetic outcome of a vigorous and ongoing campaign to foster a more competitive, commercialised Gallic production sphere. By amplifying this slant on recent industrial history, we give voice to the strategic concerns of an entire generation – executives, policymakers, producers, lobbyists, critics and creative personnel – who have worked diligently to find ways to counter Hollywood blockbuster franchises which, until the arrival of Netflix and other streaming platforms, ranked as the most significant structural challenge to their industry in recent memory. Since the mid-1980s in particular, French producers have responded not just by doubling down on the modestly priced art-house films that their national traditions remain best known for elsewhere, but also by paving the way for a fresh, vigorous and variously 'home-made' brand of crowd-pleasing entertainments. In its current form, this impulse dates to the reforms that occurred on the watch of François Mitterrand's high-profile Minister of Culture, Jack Lang, who oversaw a period in the 1980s and early 1990s when the Gallic media industries began to reformulate their strategic ambitions in response to a newly aggressive and globalised Hollywood. Its primary offspring today are French-made films with a glossy finish, focused on franchising and special effects, conceived by talent frequently culled from television and advertising. As a group, these are films that in some ways tend to evade easy classification, as they derive from a loose and still evolving group of three overlapping production tendencies: English-language, Hollywood-style genre films (usually from one of two studios, EuropaCorp and StudioCanal); pan-European co-productions (particularly big endeavours like the *Astérix* franchise, but also smaller ones); and a re-packaged French-language main-stream cinema that trades in a variety of different ways on what Raphaëlle Moine has called a 'neo-globalist' film aesthetics (Moine 2007: 39).

The 'cultural politics' most associated with this diverse set of titles derives from the historically specific and often paradoxical blend of forces lying behind a collective French impulse to 'take back' screens. Although they bubble with the enthusiasm of a revived popular tradition, these are also creative products conceived with an endemic awareness of how their approach to the cinema complicates the longer-standing convictions of a domestic film industry better known for other kinds of filmmaking. With a mind to capture the fraught dynamics that often greet such efforts, this book adopts a self-consciously multi-perspectival approach. In doing so, it parts company with numerous other strands of contemporary criticism and scholarship on French cinema, which tend to either reproduce or take for granted a set of *a priori* assumptions about what this particular national industry's role on the global scene should be: a bastion of artisanal, aesthetic alternatives to North American hegemony. While a certain narrative of social and political-economic resistance to globali-sation continues to play an undeniable role in the recent trajectory of French filmmaking (and arguably film history as a whole), we find that it also actively coexists, frequently conflicts and intermittently co-conspires with other atti-tudes about transnationalism that are every bit as 'French' in origin, yet receive far less coverage in the critical literature on France's filmmaking traditions.

In other words, these pages document the disruptions brought about by a recent swath of popular films that are changing what it means to make (or see) a 'French' film today. Evolving with the caprice of market demand, responding to the pull of new media platforms, and signalling the influence of changing cultural tastes, the diversely affiliated 'French blockbusters' featured in these pages brim with cultural contradictions, but also with authentic convictions about how a revamped approach to mainstream filmmaking might change the face of one of Europe's most vaunted culture industries. Theorising and historicising the emergence of this revitalised tendency – and its discontents – is the subject of this book.

A QUESTION OF HISTORY

French cinema's push for new strains of commercial success has intensified in the current millennium. Although numerous 1990s titles presaged recent tendencies, from the comedy *Les Visiteurs* (Poiré 1993), to the heritage epic *La Reine Margot* (Chereau 1994) and the science fiction thriller *The Fifth Element* (Besson 1998), reports about a rejuvenated popular French film tradition crested in 2001, when French productions surged to near 40% of their domestic market share for the first time in fifteen years. The success of that year was not limited to the most visible film – Jean-Pierre Jeunet's *Le Fabuleux Destin d'Amélie Poulain / Amélie* (8 million tickets sold) – but also to a striking variety of other titles, including a brazenly fantastic period-horror-martial arts hybrid, *Le Pacte des Loups / Brotherhood of the Wolf*; bawdily honest comedies (*La Verité si je mens 2 / The Truth if I'm Lying 2, Le Placard / The Closet*), a technically groundbreaking bird documentary (*Le Peuple Migrateur / Winged Migration*), and an action film for kids (*Yamakasi*). David Kessler, then president of the Centre National de la Cinématographie (CNC), was ebullient about these new developments: 'This is a revelation: it demonstrates the popular potential of our national cinema, contrary to this fatalist discourse that we've been hearing for so long: 'French cinema no longer attracts the public, it is too egocentric, etc.' (De Baecque and Bouzet 2001). In line with this enthusiasm, mainstream French media coverage tends to dote on commercially successful French-made films of any sort, suggesting that box office numbers portend a valuable role for mass-audience filmmaking, wherein savvy investment becomes a rampart of the renewed French charge against North American imperialism.

This narrative seems to be at least partially true. The sheer mix of titles that grace the top of the domestic French box office in recent years suggests the fruit of a collective push to find crowd-pleasing forms of cinema. In 2014, for instance, French productions commanded nearly half of their domestic market (44.4%) on the shoulders of four films at the top of the rankings, with nine in the top twenty (see Table I.1). They included the boldly irreverent breakout comedy *Qu'est-ce qu'on a fait au Bon Dieu? / Serial (Bad) Weddings* (over 12 million tickets sold) but also two rather different English-language films (EuropaCorp's *Lucy* and StudioCanal's *Paddington*) and a number of other titles that aim for success via various generic formulae: two domestic comedies (*La Famille Bélier* and *Babysitting*); an adaptation of a classic children's book (*Le petit Nicolas*); an updated animated makeover for Europe's most famous gaul (*Astérix*); and new starring turns for established box office draws Dany Boon (*Supercondriaque*) and Omar Sy (*Samba*). Though they disagree on the ultimate ramifications of the films, almost all recent analysts agree that these results evidence a domestic industry newly capable of attracting audiences and consolidating a strong commercial base.

Table I.1 Statistics compiled by European Audiovisual Observatory (*World Film Market Trends*)

Top Twenty Films – French Box Office – 2014				
Title	Country	Dir.	Distributor	Admissions
1 *Qu'est-ce qu'on a fait au Bon Dieu?*	FR	Chauveron	UGC	12,350,945
2 *La famille Bélier*	FR/BE	Lartigau	Mars	7,699,735
3 *Supercondriaque*	FR	Boon	Pathé	5,230,493
4 *Lucy*	FR	Besson	EuropaCorp	5,191,692
5 *The Hobbit: Battle of the Five Armies*	US/NZ	Jackson	Fox	8,848,676
6 *Dawn of the Planet of the Apes*	US	Reeves	Fox	3,752,285
7 *How to Train your Dragon 2*	US	DeBlois	Fox	3,297,551
8 *X-Men: Days of Future Past*	US	Singer	Fox	3,285,298
9 *Rio 2*	US	Saldanha	Fox	3,233,293
10 *Hunger Games: Mockingjay Part 1*	US	Lawrence	Metropolitan	3,228,248
11 *The Maze Runner*	US	Ball	Fox	3,127,112
12 *Samba*	FR	Nakache/ Toledano	Gaumont	3,110,070
13 *Astérix: Le domaine des dieux*	FR	Astier	SND	2,996,194
14 *Paddington*	FR	King	SudioCanal	2,782,959
15 *Interstellar*	US	Nolan	Warners	2,640,439
16 *Les vacances du Petit Nicolas*	FR	Tirard	Wild Bunch	2,372,389
17 *Guardians of the Galaxy*	US	Gunn	Disney	2,324,634
18 *Babysitting*	FR	Benamou/ Lacheau	Universal	2,307,652
19 *Transformers: Age of Extinction*	US/CN	Bay	Paramont	2,343,100
20 *Penguins of Madagascar*	US	Damell/ Smith	Fox	2,327,491

These returns also seem to reinforce the French industry's rarity among comparable neighbouring economies (see Table I.2). Since 2000, France has averaged just shy of 36% of its own market share, significantly outpacing Spain (15.7%), Germany (20.1%), Italy (26.1%) and even the UK (24%), which enjoys a conspicuous advantage due to a majority Anglophone audience and the collaboration on prominent Anglo-American franchises like *James Bond*, *Harry Potter* and *Kingsmen*.

A look to other recent yearly returns also makes the 2014 pattern look less like an anomaly. 2004, for instance, witnessed the cultural phenomenon of *Les Choristes* (8.5 million viewers) along with *Un Long Dimanche de Fiançailles*

Table I.2 Statistics compiled by European Audiovisual Observatory (*World Film Market Trends 2000–2018*)

Domestic Box Office Share for National Films (2000–2017)

	2000	2001	2002	2003	2004	2005	2006	2007	2008	2009	2010	2011	2012	2013	2014	2015	2016	2017
FRA	28.9	39.0	34.0	34.8	38.4	36.8	44.7	36.6	45.4	36.8	35.7	40.9	40.2	33.8	44.4	35.5	35.8	37.4
ITA	17.5	19.4	21.8	22.0	23.8	24.7	26.2	33.0	29.3	24.4	32.0	37.5	26.5	31.0	27.8	21.3	29.0	18.3
ESP	10.3	18.0	14.0	15.8	13.4	17.0	15.4	13.5	13.3	16.0	12.7	15.0	19.5	13.9	25.5	19.2	18.5	17.0
GER	12.5	16.2	11.9	17.5	20.3	17.1	25.8	18.9	26.6	27.4	16.9	21.8	18.1	26.2	26.7	27.5	22.7	23.9
UK	21.0	11.7	15.4	11.9	12.4	33.0	19.0	28.0	31.0	16.5	24.0	36.2	31.9	21.5	26.0	44.5	37.0	37.4

(Jeunet's *Amélie* follow-up again starring Audrey Tatou) and a gaggle of other titles – Jean-Jacques Annaud's tiger adventure film for kids, *Deux Frères*; comedian Michael Youn's Biblical send-up *Les Onze Commandements*; and *L'Enquête Corse*, a buddy film reuniting *Les Visiteurs* stars Jean Reno and Christian Clavier. In 2006, it was *Les Bronzés 3* that generated 10.2 million viewers, joined by an animated film (*Arthur et les Minimoys*), a fish-out-of-water farce (*Camping*), a romantic comedy (*Prête-moi ta main*), a surveillance thriller (*Ne le dis à personne*), a revisionist war film (*Indigènes*), and a spoof remake of a classic television show (*OSS 117: Le Caire, nid d'espions*). Similar depth and variety reinforced the record-breaking runs by *Bienvenue ches les Ch'tis* in 2008 (20 million tickets sold) and *Intouchables* in 2011 (19.4 million sold) as well as other years in the past decade and a half. And while not all years feature a breakout winner, almost every one places a handful of titles in the top 20 for national box office tickets sold. This happened again in 2017, led by the combined domestic returns of Besson's sci-fi epic *Valerian* (a disappointing but still consequential 4 million tickets sold), Boon's spoof action heist film *Raid Dingue / R.A.I.D Special Unit* (4 million tickets sold), and notable performances by three other comedies: the most recent offering from *Intouchables* co-directors Nakache and Toledano – *Le sens de la fête / C'est la vie* – at 3.5 million tickets sold, and two entries from a dynamic group of young comedic performers informally called 'La Bande de Fifi' – Philippe Lacheaux's *Alibi.com* (3.5 million tickets sold) and Tarek Boudali's *Epouse-moi mon pôte / Marry Me, Dude* (2.5 million tickets sold). Notwithstanding the expected cycle of unpredictability and seasonal variation, we are seeing what certainly looks to be an emerging tradition of competitively commercialised French filmmaking with verifiably national – and intermittently international – success to its credit.

Not everyone reads these trends with optimism. A strong set of counter-arguments has also emerged since the elation around 2001, offering broad skepticism about what the success of recent popular French films means for the creative capacities and cultural relevance of the French film industry. In the aftermath of the success of 2001, *Cahiers du cinéma* devoted an entire special report to the advent of new popular genres, warning about their imminent artistic consequences and the lurking threat of stylistic 'uniformity' ('Cinéma Français: la face cachée de l'embellie' 2002). Over the past decade and a half, a legion of specialised reports from the CNC and the Ministry of Culture, along with frequent scathing articles, reviews and op-eds in numerous major periodicals pose a set of larger questions about the wisdom of trying to generate a cinema that can in any way compete 'head-to-head' with Hollywood. A troubling side effect of the push for bigger films in France has been budget inflation. As Laurent Creton suggests in a similar recent analysis, the average and the median French film budgets during the same period traced above tends to reinforce the impression that the push for competition with

Hollywood is costing the industry elsewhere. The average (*moyen*) French film budget (*devis*) produced over the last thirty years has nearly tripled in cost – from €2 million in the mid-1980s to between €4 million and €5 million in the 1990s, and to above €5 million in the 2000s with a peak of €6.4 million in 2008. Meanwhile, the median figures during that same period stay relatively constant – starting around €2.5 million in the mid-1980s but then levelling out, rarely passing the threshold of €4 million over the next three decades (Creton 2012; Creton 2014). What this means is that the films at the top of the scale now receive an increasingly disproportionate amount of resources – a hallmark of an industry increasingly driven by the strategic push for commercial practices, perhaps not in a positive sense. For when it invests in larger films, the French industry must deal with the endemic unpredictability of the 'boom or bust' model, but without the generous financial cushion the major Hollywood studios enjoy as a result of their distribution advantages and marketability in Europe and elsewhere.

Debates about how to interpret these trends have animated French film culture of late – in the process rehashing philosophical rifts that date, in many ways, to earlier decades. Budget inflation and fluctuating production levels are, by themselves, nothing new to the industry. As Susan Hayward points out in the concise 'Eco-History' that leads off her seminal book *French National Cinema*, a longer view of French film economics shows a tendency to move in budget cycles, alternating between growth in budget size and growth in the overall number of films (Hayward 2005: 17–76). Some might further argue that the current situation has its roots much earlier. During the *nouvelle vague* of the 1960s, for instance, it was not low-budget art house films that propelled the French industry, but rather mainstream genres (comedies, *polars*, literary adaptations) that provided the stable base. Moreover, as Ginette Vincendeau frequently reminds us, French cinema has always also been a popular film tradition worth reckoning with on its own terms (Vincendeau 2000a: 56). However, most contemporary economic accounts also agree that there is a reason to set aside the recent trends in French commercial cinema as a new and rather uncharacteristic phenomenon.

France's 'mixed economy' approach to cinema has long been a model for other industries across Europe and the world. Since 1946, Gallic film policy has been orchestrated by the CNC, an independently run, government-affiliated body that oversees the *compte du soutien* (cinema support fund) which in its first incarnation derived from a tax on cinema admissions that were then rerouted to support indigenous cinematic production in a fragile post-war French exhibition market. Finding a fruitful balance between two basic funding principles has been the CNC's remit for the past half century. The *soutien automatique* (automatic support fund), first instituted in 1948, rewards commercially successful French films by allocating 'advance on takings' loans (*avances sur recettes*) to French producers for their subsequent projects. In 1959, the CNC was moved from its home in the Ministry of Communication to the Ministry of Culture under André Malraux – venerable author and filmmaker. That year, the *soutien sélectif* (selective support fund) was added as a way to complement automatic subsidies by supporting films with 'artistic or cultural merit'. Together, these two programmes gave material reality to Malraux's often cited call for a balance between 'art' and 'industry'. As the media landscape for French cinema changed over the years, the CNC's automatic support mandate rapidly expanded beyond film production – first to film exhibition (also 1959), then to distribution (1977), and later to export (updated in 2017).

Intensified global competition and new media platforms provoked sweeping reforms in the 1980s. French filmmaking of the 1960s and 1970s had reached a sort of plateau stage, consistently drawing more than half of its domestic audience during a period when there were only three French television stations (TF1, Antenne 2, FR3), all state-owned and regulated. That status quo changed abruptly in the 1980s, when the Hollywood majors found a lasting antidote to their own attendance ills by concentrating their investments on a handful of larger-than-life 'event' films. Building on the successful runs by *Jaws* (Spielberg 1975) and *Star Wars* (Lucas 1977), the strategy behind these 'blockbusters' amplified previous successes – combining foreign distribution deals, huge production budgets, and saturation marketing campaigns to generate maximal box office returns in a short time span. This aggressive new aesthetic and economic maximalism had a huge impact on the French market, flooding it with advertising, coercing cinemas to show its films on multiple screens at once, and appealing to the programming needs of the nascent television industry, which had just been privatised in 1982, and would soon be in need of prime time audience draws.

In response to the ensuing crisis, Jack Lang and other like-minded reformers at the Ministry of Culture introduced an aggressive new agenda as part of what David Looseley terms the 'politics of fun' (1995), pairing the commercial needs of television with the new deficits in film financing by prompting an industry-wide move towards televisual sources of revenue that could combine with existing state subsidy programmes. These new incentives included a system of tax shelters (SOFICAs), a government-backed risk-sharing agency (IFCIC), and – most notably – a pay-tv cable station, Canal+, that would be positioned at the centre of a new status quo. In exchange for having sole priority on film releases to television, Canal agreed to invest 20% of its profits back into French and European film production. As these initial plans became law, the crisis only escalated. France had managed to fend off the damage a few years longer than its European neighbours, but by 1986 French films dipped below 50% of their domestic share for the first time since Malraux's system was put in place.

By 1989, France's market share had slumped below 30%, primarily as a result of a slew of Hollywood franchises, led by *Batman*, *Indiana Jones and the Last Crusade* and *Lethal Weapon 2*. The next year, Lang added another major reform, announcing the creation of a government-run 'Investors Club' capable of encouraging independent French producers to make their own 'blockbusters' to win back audiences in cinemas and on television. The Club itself was formally discontinued only two years later, but its philosophical strategy for supporting a crop of big budget films largely remains in place today, as do the bulk of the other programmes intended to support them.

Lang's reforms continue to anchor the commercial ambitions of an audiovisual industry now concentrated around a few large firms, and dedicated to collectively producing a class of ambitious genre films. In recent years, a landslide of reports, articles and research initiatives have linked the former minister's legacy to the current political-economic climate and the changed production culture of French cinema. In 2006, audiovisual economist René Bonnell (himself a crucial figure to whom we will return in Chapter 1) sounded the alarm anew, observing that the period between 1975 and 2000 could also be viewed as a singular moment of drastic expansion, when 'the cost of French films literally multiplied by twelve' (Bonnell 2006: 59). Bonnell suggests that the situation since the mid-1990s deserves special attention, as film budgets increased by 50% in the space of one decade alone. Not only that, but the skyrocketing numbers – unlike intermittent production bubbles of years past – were not driven primarily by European co-production agreements, but by projects financed and masterminded by a small number of concentrated, French production studios. By 2000, Bonnell writes, the numbers had actually stabilised into something like a new normal, wherein '10 to 15% of the films are made for two to three times the average cost while about a third are made for less than a quarter of the average' (Bonnell 2006: 59).

This shift in emphasis can be seen in the extensive yearly documentation of production trends by the CNC. Table I.3 demonstrates the evolving tendencies of budgetary categories since 2000. First, French producers today are making more films overall – with a rather steep incline that starts at a low of 148 in 2000, rising to a peak of 234 in 2015 and settling in at just above 200 for the past five years. Second, French resources are responsible for making more big films these days – the category above €10 million doubles in the first decade of the 2000s, reaching a high point of 33 in 2012 before a slight recent regression. Finally, the industry has apparently begun to allocate its remaining resources more to the extreme bottom of the chart than to the middle echelons, with films below €1 million almost tripling between 2000 and 2016 while the middle budgets stagnate. Film critics, scholars and industry insiders regularly cite these three dynamics as evidence for the growing 'bipolarisation' of the contemporary French film industry. Skeptics of the new dynamic describe a

Table I.3 Statistics compiled by Centre National de la Cinématographie (CNC *Bilans* 2000–2018)

Film Budgets – 'French Initiative' Films (2000–2017)

M€	2000	2001	2002	2003	2004	2005	2006	2007	2008	2009	2010	2011	2012	2013	2014	2015	2016	2017
>10	14	20	14	18	24	22	24	28	35	25	28	28	33	19	17	27	24	22
7–10	12	14	12	12	9	17	21	21	25	21	24	24	22	29	19	24	16	27
5–7	14	15	31	20	33	21	12	20	11	30	26	22	22	17	22	26	37	35
4–5	18	9	9	17	16	7	7	9	17	9	16	12	3	11	3	7	6	14
2–4	44	40	35	38	32	46	37	43	41	45	47	41	46	47	61	50	43	52
1–2	21	32	21	37	33	33	35	29	23	18	29	25	32	22	22	36	28	24
<1	22	42	41	41	20	41	28	35	44	28	40	46	58	53	59	64	67	48
Total	148	172	163	183	167	187	164	185	196	182	203	206	209	208	203	234	221	222

new status quo that stretches resources in an unhealthy manner leaving out the 'mid-range' films that used to be the system's strength, and a haven for its most prestigious auteurs. While the gap between large and small has become a common condition across modes of cultural production these days, including Hollywood, the French film industry remains remarkable for the sheer amount of documentation and discussion it has recently generated on this topic – and for its constant search for ways to remedy the situation through the legislative powers of the nation-state.

A growing source of optimism for some and of fatalism for others, homemade blockbusters from France sit at the heart of one of the more disputed narratives in contemporary French film culture. Anti-commercialist views reached an apex during the César awards ceremony in 2007, when director Pascale Ferran voiced displeasure during her acceptance speech for her film *Lady Chatterley*, decrying the 'vanishing middle' of French film production, and warning about dire consequences for the industry. Over the following year, she and twelve concerned colleagues from across the industry met for several months during off hours at the CNC. Together they coordinated and co-authored the 'Club of Thirteen' report, a widely-circulated two hundred-page document – part polemic, part prognostic – citing budget polarisation as its primary concern. Behind its coyly poetic title – *Le milieu n'est plus un pont mais une faille* – lies an impressive 'transversal study' (*étude transversale*) of an industry it claims sits on the verge of a painful schism between (increasingly) big-budget entertainment and (increasingly) low-budget art house films (Ferran 2008). Yet as Jonathan Buchsbaum documents extensively, the Ferran report was just the most visible intervention in a French debate that has actually been raging on similar terms over thirty years now (Buchsbaum 2016).

A Question of Hegemony

Perhaps no single phenomenon better encapsulates the uneven cultural dynamics of globalisation than Hollywood blockbusters. Along with Coca-Cola and McDonald's, the biggest of Anglo-American film franchises are often characterised as a sort of universalised, mono-cultural takeover – 'a kind of cultural smoke rising from a US-led struggle to convert the world to capitalism' (Miller, Goval, McMurria, Maxwell and Wang 2005: 51). A common intellectual approach to these films in France – as well as to a lot of American commercial culture in general – has been to view them as mercilessly 'top-down' phenomena, steamrolling indigenous creative practices by buying up distribution outlets and duping European audiences with the allure of mindless, capitalist consumption. Yet even if we grant the necessary credence to a caricature like this one, it stands to reason that not all localities could possibly have the same relationship to the presence of blockbusters, wherever they are produced.

There is then another perspective worth considering – namely that the story of the localised responses to Hollywood's recent 'bigness' is often quite a bit more complicated than we first think.

We can begin by observing that the word 'blockbuster' itself cannot be ruled synonymous with America or even with Hollywood. It is rather a concept de-linked from nationality or place-ness, designating a type of filmmaking that arose over the past four decades to exceed national specificities by design, often doing so through ties to corporate business culture, formulaic and 'universalist' themes and digitised special effects. At the same time, the mobility of this form that French critics often call *le cinéma-monde* also engages by definition with other cultural formations, often in quite indeterminate and contingent ways. Such matters circulate on the often paradoxical path of defining what Julian Stringer calls 'local blockbusters' (Stringer 2003: 9), a form of expression and a source of conflict that animates the current dynamics of global media capitalism, making the very generic status – and the 'bigness' – of certain films 'something to be fought over' (Stringer 2003:8). These investigations only begin with surface observations about economic inequity. We need an account that extends beyond one-dimensional claims about dominance or aesthetic homogeneity, and instead searches for an understanding of how global media forms circulate and inhabit the many, varied auspices of the 'national'– and vice versa.

These theoretical exchanges in film and media studies are subtended by larger recent debates across the humanities and social sciences. In the 1990s, sociological and anthropological studies of global cultural formations pushed back against the largely political-economic angle taken by the first wave of work on globalisation. Not coincidentally, the new conceptual terrain of 'cultural globalisation' coincided with a series of high-profile returns to the concept of the nation itself, as well as with widespread reconsideration of the historical and philosophical conditions that gave rise to national 'containers' in the first place (Anderson 1983; Gellner 1983; Hobsbawm 1990). Eventually, a body of literature emerged to complement the top-down slant of 'world-systems' (Wallerstein 1983) and 'cultural imperialist' models (Schiller 1976) of years previous, as theorists of global culture interrogated the play of difference that could animate various localised contingencies of the 'global' – figuring the cultural forms that dealt with new dimensions of 'time-space compression' (Harvey 1990), the imaginative 'disjunctions' of 'ethnoscapes' (Appadurai 1996), the resonance of the 'glocal' (Robertson 1995), the subversiveness of 'hybridity' (Pieterse 2004), the networking of 'complex connectivity' (Tomlinson 1999), and the 'expedience' of culture as a unique form of capital (Yudice 2004) among many others.

Academic studies of national cinema during the 1990s generally followed these trends. Moving away from the largely unexamined geographical and essentialist definitions of the past, these accounts held, as Andrew Higson puts it, that any film should be studied as a product that can 'pull together many diverse and contradictory discourses' (Higson 1989: 44). Tom O'Regan's *Australian National Cinema* usefully expands and defines this palette, proposing a 'pluralist' view that conceives of national cinema as an 'assemblage' of discourses – 'the accumulation of its various (stylistic, critical, political) tendencies, the elaboration of its incommensurate (aesthetic, political, intellectual) values, its competing (filmic and social) identities and the contradictions, disjunctions and complementarities of these' (O'Regan 1996: 40). A number of later theorists espouse similar methodologies, proposing various habile metaphors for what O'Regan calls the dynamics of 'cultural exchange' (O'Regan 2007). Other theorists of these matters caution, however, that any form of methodological pluralism must be grounded in the material realities of unequal exchange. John Hill's often cited response to Higson reformulates an argument similar to many 'cultural imperialist' critics before him – that Hollywood's overwrought influence requires a form of national filmmaking that 'recognizes that its economic ambitions will have to be more modest' and that its cultural components should be 'correspondingly more ambitious' (Hill 1992: 21). In a later account with similar leanings, Michael Wayne largely concurs, citing the savage inequalities between North American and European distribution networks as a limiting horizon for any discussion about the cultural heterogeneity that filmmakers might otherwise seek to stage in response to Hollywood blockbusters (Wayne 2002). A similar spirit of nationalist resistance serves as the organising principle of *Exception Taken*, where Buchsbaum cites Hill's essay as a sort of call-to-arms at the end of his introduction. Revelatory in its fine-grained focus on policy and politics, the book is rather adamant in its focus on how '[France] financed and promoted a "certain idea of cinema" that made it the art form of the twentieth century' (Buchsbaum xxvi). Building on Buchsbaum's account in certain ways, this book highlights a set of ambitious films that nevertheless complicate the most familiar accounts of how the French film industry has sought to 'defy' Hollywood hegemony over the past three decades.

In response to these very concerns, film theory has tried on a series of compelling modifiers in recent years, from 'global' to 'world', and from 'post-national' to the prevailing current choice, 'transnational' cinema. In the process, the field has arrived again at a sort of fraught taxonomic stage, in part launched by Higson's reflection on the limits of his own much-cited essay (Higson 2000). Obliged to take stock of multiple cinematic formations but vexed by how to ground them amidst the ethical considerations of unequal cultural exchange, film theorists frequently find themselves challenged by the methodological responsibility of what Randall Halle calls 'comparing like with like' (Halle 2008: 29). In the inaugural edition of the journal *Transnational Cinemas*, Will Higbee and Song-Hwee Lim map the genesis of this conversation, closing their essay with the suggestion that the most responsible methodologies – what they call 'critical' transnationalism – should be able to both account for different modes of filmmaking and make careful evaluative judgements about a film's political-economic possibilities (Higbee and Lim 2010: 17). Not coincidentally, this second component is where pushback against the study of blockbusters most frequently resides – at the intersection of materialism and ethics. For instance, while outlining eight intriguing transnational forms of cinema, Mette Hjort echoes Hill in her claim that the most 'valuable' approaches among them are those that feature 'a resistance to globalization as homogenization' and 'a commitment to assuring that certain economic realities [. . .] do not eclipse the pursuit of aesthetic, artistic, social and political values' (Hjort 2010: 15). Though her flexible categories do not preclude the possibility of worthwhile commercialised pursuits, Hjort expresses reservations for what she calls the 'globalizing transnationalism' of films like the Chinese blockbuster *Hero* (Zhang 2002). In a pair of schematic responses to Hjort's value judgment about commercialised cinema, Deborah Shaw holds that 'questions of artistic integrity are more complex than they first appear' (Shaw 2013: 62) and that the scholarly privileging of 'marginal productions as properly transnational' has the paradoxical effect of 'marginalising mainstream works from the discussion' (Shaw 2017: 294). This argument is perhaps not surprising given Shaw's intellectual investment in recent Hollywood films by the extravagantly successful 'Three Amigos' (Cuaron, Del Toro, Inarritu). Moreover, as her book-length study of that enterprising Mexican trio demonstrates, current debates about how recent practices of commercial filmmaking influence the 'artistic integrity' and 'quality' of national forms can have an ambivalent – and fascinating – historical dimension worth exploring on their own (Shaw 2015).

In an influential summation of how these and related issues circulate in the European cultural context, Thomas Elsaesser suggests that film culture of the 'new' old continent demands a more polyvalent approach:

> the old Hollywood hegemony argument (whether justified on economic or stylistic grounds) and the 'postmodern' or 'pragmatic' paradigm ('it is what audiences make of films that decides their identity and value') tend to hide a perhaps more interesting relationship, namely that of national cinemas and Hollywood not only as communicating vessels, but (to change the metaphor) existing in a space set up like a hall of mirrors, in which recognition, imaginary identity and mis-cognition enjoy equal status, creating value out of pure difference. (Elsaesser 2005: 47)

Along these lines, transnational research on contemporary media industries can also move to allow theorists and historians space to probe how mutually implicated senses of the 'transnational' come to cohabit and imbricate the historical account itself.

This need for conceptual malleability also derives from the Hollywood strategy itself. As Stringer puts it, 'some movies are born blockbusters; some achieve blockbuster status; some have blockbuster status thrust upon them' (Stringer 2003: 10). In an early synoptic look at the period of global Hollywood, Thomas Schatz cites 1990 as an important turning point in this realisation by the industry itself, when three lower-budget hits (*Home Alone*, *Ghost* and *Pretty Woman*) reminded studio executives that other types of films could become hits. For every massively calculated *Titanic* (Cameron 1997), there is a lower-budget project that attains similar returns for just a fraction of the overall cost – a *My Big, Fat Greek Wedding* (Zwick 2002) or a *Paranormal Activity* (Peli 2007) – so planning a number of 'calculated blockbusters' (pre-planned tent-pole event films) has to be supplemented by a slate of possible 'sleeper hits' (carefully chosen films that could eventually attain 'blockbuster' results) (Schatz 2003: 33). As Schatz suggests, these films can eventually prove fit to be called 'blockbusters' – especially if they surpass the hallowed (yet arbitrary) benchmark of $50 million in profits (for his part, Arthur De Vany suggests that $100 million is now a more appropriate figure) (De Vany 2004: 243). Weekend release patterns by the majors now allow not only for a concentration around so-called 'tent-pole' pictures, but also for the alternative success stories of smaller films distributed alongside the larger franchises. This diversity of practices helps the majors infiltrate other markets at multiple levels, cross selling between platforms and exerting financial influence over other markets. In this context, then, even the smallest American film might become a 'blockbuster'– comparatively speaking – on a smaller domestic market. This space for a more flexible, mobile and 'bottom up' view of Hollywood's cinematic 'bigness' has more recently been confirmed by Justin Wyatt in his influential theorisation of what he calls 'high concept' marketing and aesthetics (Wyatt 1994), by Geoff King in a pair of authoritative works on contemporary Hollywood (King 2000, 2002) and by Steve Neale and Sheldon Hall, whose co-authored book traces the contingent yet consistent role of 'big' productions from Hollywood's first commitment to feature-length cinema in the teens all the way to its present global dimensions (Neale and Hall 2010).

As a result of these potential complications, Stringer suggests, it is useful to consider the word 'blockbuster' in a similar light to how Rick Altman proposes his influential methodology for approaching film genre (Stringer 2003: 2). Altman suggests that there are three basic dimensions for studying the meaning generated by generic forms. The first two derive from his earlier work on *The American Film Musical* (1987), which makes an analogy to Saussurian linguistics to highlight the slippery duality of generic signification, turning on both a 'semantics' (the stylistic and/or thematic 'building blocks' of form) and 'syntax' (the way that those components are strung together in terms of plot or thematic signification). With his third 'pragmatic' dimension of genre, added in his more lengthy exposition in *Film/Genre* (Altman 1999), Altman openly responds to the influence of the field's concurrent move towards cultural studies, making space in his terminology for different types of audience uptake and the relativity of cultural contexts. Genres thus become discursive 'sites of constant struggle', acquiring meaning only at the intersection of combative rhetorical claims, overlapping interest groups, and historical change writ large or small. In the end, for Altman (and Stringer) the friction between different appropriations of generic formulae ultimately warrants more targeted inquiries into the dynamics of classification itself as a problem of history and culture. Along these lines, the strategic distinctions that initially separate 'calculated blockbusters' and 'sleeper hits' can also be complicated via the consideration of other national – or nationalist – frames of reference, which themselves harbour the possibility for differences of opinion about incipient global forms. As Chris Berry puts it in his compelling case study of Asian blockbuster variants, 'the blockbuster is made sense of and practiced according to local cultural and filmmaking contexts' (Berry 2003: 218). And in many cases, as the collective authors of *Global Hollywood 2* put it, we find these are 'cases of strategic making-do, not of being overwhelmed' (Miller, Goval, McMurria, Maxwell and Wang 2005: 79).

In order to make sense of one way the French film industry has tried to 'make do' in the era of the Hollywood blockbuster, the current account brings together political-economics, film criticism and aesthetics in ways that few works in the current body of scholarly literature attempt. Despite the increase in interest in commercial and popular French cinema over the past thirty years or so, scholars still generally avoid drawing connections between the industrial factors that drive new commercial trends and the narrative and aesthetic features of the films themselves. Hayward's *French National Cinema* broke new ground in this direction, bringing together a critical perspective on economics and aesthetics to formulate the 'national' as a bundle of discourses that arise from diverse sources. Since then, the academic literature tends to filter the stylistic features of popular French cinema through other critical frameworks – stars, genres, auteurs – that engage problems of cultural politics, but do so through the legitimation of individual agency or stylistic particularity rather than acknowledgment of the systemic socio-cultural conditions that inform all of the above. Meanwhile, a burgeoning body of work on Franco-European media industries and political economy sheds welcome light on recent political-economic trends, yet most often refrains from making meaningful commentary on the films themselves.

In the interest of breadth, the few scholarly approaches that do attempt to combine a political-economic account with aesthetic analyses in their work on popular French cinema tend to avoid speculating at much length about how the films resound in terms of cultural politics (Austin 2009; Lanzoni 2015).

Among the notable exceptions to this is a series of articles by Martine Danan, which proposes a fissure between two distinct modes of contemporary French filmmaking: the 'national' and the 'post-national' (Danan 1996; Danan 2000; Danan 2006). In the second and more recent of her two modes, Danan argues, we see a cinema that 'erases most of the distinctive elements which have traditionally helped to define the (maybe) imaginary coherence of a national cinema against other cinematographic traditions or against Hollywood at a given point in time' (Danan 2002: 238). While her astute combination of aesthetics and cultural politics remains a crucial move for the field, Danan's model also falls somewhat short of acknowledging the variegated and often quite idiosyncratic cultural resonances of commercial French filmmaking since then – especially in the present era.

Across the various topics explored in this book, an over-arching suggestion will be that ambitious commercialised French films of today share a particular history that conditions their rhetorical place in contemporary Franco-European film culture. Bringing a number of contextual factors into play, I argue that the enduring significance of recent 'local blockbusters' from France lies not so much in any fixed reading of their origins or unrecognised innovation of their stylistic features, but in how their various attributes both derive from and spur conflicts between the palpably different worldviews and interpretive sensibilities that comingle in what Tim Palmer calls the creative 'eco-system' of contemporary French cinema (Palmer 2011). In this respect, the book performs an in-depth study of the factors behind what Isabelle Vanderschelden describes as the 'combination of national, international and post-national elements' that characterises recent popular French filmmaking (Vanderschelden 2007: 37). It also aligns with other revisionist trends in the study of French cinema: Ginette Vincendeau's foundational research on popular traditions in French cinema – from her conceptual work in the 1990s (Vincendeau and Dyer 1992; Vincendeau 2000a) to her many other recent trajectories on stardom, authorship and the industry (Vincendeau 1996; Vincendeau 2000a; Vincendeau 2000b; Vincendeau 2003; Vincendeau 2014); Phil Powrie's exploration of the aesthetic and socio-cultural resonances of French film texts and contexts (Powrie 1997) and his auteur study of Jean-Jacques Beineix (Powrie 2001); Frédéric Gimello-Mesplomb's interventions in favour of the overlooked legacy of the French fantasy film (cinéma du fantastique) (Gimello-Mesplomb 2012a; Gimello-Mesplomb 2012b); Laurent Jullier's inquiries into the various taste economies and aesthetic histories of contemporary French cinema (Jullier 1997; Jullier 2012; Jullier 2014); and Moine's ongoing research agenda, which probes the interface between French cinema and genre history by expanding Altman's model and clarifying its consequences for the sorts of frameworks that have to this point dominated Gallic film studies (2005, 2007, 2015).

Moine's work deserves particular recognition here, because her approach has cleared the way for the gradual cleansing of conceptual terms that still elicit frequent grumbling about American imperialism. Her work calls for broader discussions of popular forms of filmmaking in the French academy, as well as provides a valuable interface for the research methodologies that now flow more frequently between France, the US and the UK. As she puts it in the introduction to the second edition of *Les genres du cinéma*:

> The act of categorising and recognising genres – and of denying them sometimes – by different agents in the world of cinema (producers, directors, critics, ordinary spectators ...) is just as important in the study of genericity [*généricité*] as the comparison of filmic texts. Film genre is not just a question of identifying the genres of individual films, but a question of production and interpretation. From this perspective, a study of cinematographic genres must approach the subject from both a textual and contextual angle. The strong distinction between these two types of analysis in the French context generally explains the resistance to re-examining the concept of genre in a way that recognises its role as a creator of value in a complex set of interactions between films and their production and reception contexts. (Moine 2015: 4–5)

This intervention for the field of French film studies fits in quite well with a larger recent view propounded by economists, historians, sociologists and cultural theorists who research changing cultural countenance of post-war France (Schwartz 2007; Kuisel 2011; Martel 2006, 2010). Indeed, several recent anthologies share this book's fascination with countering a French academic heritage that has often balked at research terms that might threaten its cherished traditions with new modes of popular culture (Vanderschelden and Waldron 2007; Looseley and Holmes 2013). Collectively, such claims amount to a view of the Hexagon as a nation-state embroiled in a prolonged transitional period, caught between the state-centric models that made way for its post-war return to prominence (*les trentes glorieuses*) and the urgent need to adapt to more recent economic trends. For co-authors Phillip Gordon and Sophie Meunier, this dynamic amounts to 'the apparent paradox' of France's position in an increasingly globalised economy – as it is 'resisting globalization (sometimes loudly) and adapting to it (far more than people realize) at the same time' (Meunier and Gordon 2004). In Gordon and Meunier's sense, adaptation means having to accept the shifting rules of the market economy, to change practices to better conform to them and, ideally, to maximise profit from those changes.

The recent French struggle with global identity thus becomes a complicated one, as the country tries to forge a place in a new international order while also salvaging its long-term role as a dignified model of national cultural production. In light of this backdrop, it is understandable how 'blockbusters'

– whether they fit more snugly into a 'calculated' or the 'sleeper hit' category – might become a lightning rod for controversy about what role a rejuvenated French commercial cinema can (or should) play in the process. So while some onlookers view successful French films as healthy symptoms of an industry pursuing a combination of survival strategies, others see them as harbingers of destruction, wherein an infatuation with corporate success could eventually destroy the distinctive qualities of a culture and its cinema from the inside. It is a debate that has wracked French film culture in recent years, mobilising widespread fears of cultural homogenisation while pitting interpretive communities against one another. In the process, a rather diffuse diplomatic term has emerged to form a sort of uneasy truce among them: 'cultural diversity'.

A QUESTION OF FRAMING

If this book embraces the paradoxical possibilities of its title, that is not only to theorise a nascent genre, but also to capture the fraught dynamics of an emergent site of struggle and cultural exchange. In so doing, it offers its own rendition of the sort of mobile, discursive practice of criticism favoured by scholars of cinematic transnationalism, who urge us to explore cultural formations in terms of the different thought trajectories generated by contemporary film-making practices. Recent inroads in the broader sociological literature analyse how the linguistic variations within interpretive communities generate different frames for how to interpret the localised contingencies of globalisation (Fiss and Hirsch 2005). In his book *Language and Globalization*, for instance, Norman Fairclough calls attention to the 'distinctive vocabularies' that circulate around keywords like 'free trade' or 'terrorism' – 'differ[ing] in grammatical features' and 'forms of narrative, forms of argumentation and so forth' depending on context (Fairclough 2005: 4). Rooting out this sort of evidence lays bare the play of *disjunctions* that are created by global pressures as they appear within various contingencies of the 'local', the 'regional' and the 'national'– to invoke Arjun Appadurai's still prescient term (Appadurai 1990: 295).

To Fairclough's point, a particular challenge for theorising and historicising the transnational activities of French cinema remains the vehement incongruence of different opinions expressed in the industry, both about political-economic strategy and about the films themselves. In their exhaustive survey *The French Challenge: Adapting to Globalization*, Meunier and Gordon single out the French film industry – among all the cultural areas they cover – as home to some of the greatest debates about globalisation and French cultural identity (Meunier and Gordon 2004: 48). One of the most memorable moments in this regard occurred at the 1993 Uruguay round of the General Agreement on Tariffs and Trade (GATT) negotiations, which saw a unified European contingent resist North American free trade proposals by arguing for an audiovisual 'cultural exception' to the liberal exchange of goods and services. Back in Paris, thousands of demonstrators, including hundreds of film industry professionals, hit the streets to show solidarity. Though this type of collective action does remain a significant animus for French cultural policy, historians like Meunier and Gordon are quick to point out that the Hexagon is also brimming these days with a renewed push for cultural and economic power. We are remiss to highlight French resistances to globalisation, they argue, without also showing how the country is actively adapting to and, in many cases, finding creative ways to profit from the new trajectories of global media capital. Moreover, if the past thirty years of French film history has witnessed the emergence of a new (or at least massively recalibrated) type of mainstream filmmaking, it is a development that can only be fully grasped as a product of extraordinary dissent, where heady days of commercial success invariably mix with widespread anxiety about an uncertain future. This account seeks to give those mixed emotions full voice – and indeed to make them a structuring principle of how its ideas are organised. The contention in doing so is methodological. For only by embracing the multiplicity of critical vantage points that currently animate the French film landscape can we begin to appreciate how recent trends in popular filmmaking are read and, in many cases, even make themselves readable in terms of the larger 'conversation' that is occurring across different levels of both the media industry and film culture at large.

In summary, this outlook offers a way to read the heightened commercialist tendencies of contemporary, mainstream French filmmaking as a product of antagonisms in a local community that entertains very different, ongoing viewpoints about what a 'globalised' national cinema means and what it should look like. For some, the very prospect of a new *cinéma de genre* – and its attendant push for 'big' films – is symptomatic of a regrettable double failure that results in films neither economically capable of competing with Hollywood, nor culturally significant enough to offer lasting value. Taken to the extreme, this view might see any placement of the word 'blockbuster' next to the word 'French' as an inevitable (yet quite depressing) endgame with rules rigged in favour of more powerful players. We need not deny this vantage point, however, to embrace a more multi-dimensional one as proposed by film scholars like Stringer, Altman and Moine, or put in practice by sociologist Olivier Alexandre in his recent landmark study (Alexandre 2015). This alternative research programme could ask, for instance, from what historical circumstances this new type of French productions initially sprang in the 1980s and 1990s. It could also suspend value judgments long enough to root out the varying, contingent senses of identity that have been attached to the recent and variously 'big' forms of commercial cinema in France.

To approach film history in this way is to re-immerse oneself in the bundle of theoretical insights initiated by theorists like Higson, O'Regan and Hayward as well as to draw anew on the sociological caveats that drive recent cultural theories of globalisation. Along these lines, any informed sense of 'national' culture must be an incipient, moving target, composed of the competing discourses and rhetorical positions that cluster around all sorts of cultural production – even the overtly commercial ones. What we find when we do so is an entire set of generative mechanisms, often underplayed in accounts of the past thirty years of French cinema. And along with them comes a history of rampant internal disagreements, especially post-Lang, about how to preserve the hallowed Malrauvian balance between 'art' and 'industry' while coping with the intensified pressure generated by Hollywood blockbusters and their attendant strategies.

It turns out that the flirtation with making a more competitive popular cinema has been a persistent subplot of the French media industry's more general conversation about how to establish a viable 'cultural exception' to Hollywood. Moreover, the continual, collective effort to do just that makes the history of France's diverse and intermittent 'local blockbusters' a yarn filled with frequent strife and periodic consensus – one well worth spinning on its own merits. The six main chapters of this book sketch the contours of what that story might look like. The first two provide historical and theoretical backdrops for the material to follow. Drawing on research at the CNC, the *Bibliothèque du Film* (BiFi), the French Ministry of Culture, trade press publications like *Le Film Français* and *Ecran Total*, and interviews with film professionals from various levels of the industry, Chapter 1 relates a condensed history of the industry's gradual investment in a yearly crop of big-budget films over the past thirty years. A look at the variety of reforms instituted by Lang between 1981 and 1993 shows how Socialist policies often entailed compromise between competing viewpoints, ending in a commitment to pursuing ambitious budgets while promoting an increased 'audacity' in commercial cinema that could complement art house fare both financially and culturally. The second half of the Chapter then surveys the many 'unintended consequences' (*effets pervers*) of Lang's plan since then, including the industry's concentration around a small number of big production companies and its ongoing attempts to adapt – this time to the new digital technologies and revenue streams that arrived when streaming services like Netflix became powerful new players in content creation in the past several years. Following this historical account, Chapter 2 proposes a method for charting how successful French films – in their various generic affiliations and stylistic guises – have become the fodder for an ongoing debate about the artistic legitimacy of globalised popular culture.

A dominant tendency in film criticism today remains a view of French cinema as the self-proclaimed European leader of a global auteur movement against Hollywood dominance. Broad mistrust of popular genre cinema frequently serves as a corollary to what I call the *exceptionalist* framing of the EU's mandate for pursuing 'cultural diversity', which retains both the word choice and the ideological bent of Lang's original usage. Aligning with an attitude similar to those of the GATT demonstrations, this perspective of the industry and its proponents tend to draw taste-based lines between film 'art' and 'commerce', connecting them to the project of a united European front for supporting an independent, artisanal cinema focused on the creativity and authenticity of local forms of expression. Such views also tend to regret the current consequences of Lang's reforms, which they now see contributing to heightened commercialist practices, to the detriment of auteur filmmaking. On this view, the malleability of the most recent international rhetoric used by the CNC and other outward-looking institutions in France also becomes a tactical error – the 'acceptance of a logic that is clearly a neoliberal one' (Poirrier 2006: 16).

Whereas many prevailing conceptions of Franco-European cinema focus on preserving its cause as a viable alternative to global media forms in France and elsewhere, they are often counteracted by what we term here a *professionalist* view of the same set of factual information. This second perspective suggests that state support mechanisms can only accomplish so much amidst the current accelerating financial and technological conditions of the world economy. No less committed to the survival of the industry in a certain sense, this viewpoint insists that any path to a sustainable 'cultural diversity' must remain grounded in the realities of a competitive, changing industry. Less obviously militant (though no less political) in its stance, it takes its name from the places it appears most often – statements by industry professionals who speak across global frameworks, referring both to French and to Hollywood filmmakers on a craft-based level, and embracing the work of 'making films' without necessary reference to the systemic inequalities of the global industry. On an executive level, this rhetoric often accompanies investment in corporate forms of creative practice, primed to compete within the logic of global flows and to respond quickly to the advent of new media platforms. On a critical one, it dovetails with the views of many critics and filmmakers who grew up in the 1980s, watching as Hollywood blockbusters dominated the market, and wishing that their own national cinema could muster a more direct response along similar lines. Denizens of this view tend to characterise themselves as 'realists' about what the industry faces. Not surprisingly, they also read Lang's mixed-economy legacy rather differently to their exceptionalist peers, emphasising the wisdom of his choice to wed French film culture with incipient forms of media entrepreneurship (initially cable television) and to accept the Hollywood challenge as a mandate for catering to popular taste in more effective ways.

Finally, between these two tendencies lies a mediating move – perhaps the most common, frequently the most vexed. In its *pragmatist* support for commercialist and auteur cinema alike, this third tendency falls back on a gradual renewal of existing public-private policies, making concessions to both 'popular' and 'elite' forms of filmmaking. Embracing the complex socio-politics of French film policy as it works to adapt progressively to the numerous challenges of the digital era, this third framing also frequently proffers a relativist aesthetic sensibility, highlighting the value of all types of films and visual media to the publicity of a national media industry fighting for visibility in a global capitalist economy.

An approach like this one is by no means exhaustive. It does, however, offer a useful heuristic for reading how various entities – films, filmmakers and state institutions, as well as critics and scholars – can be drawn into larger political-economic debates about how to articulate the wellbeing of contemporary French cinema. As we shall see later in case studies of individual films and film genres, these three extant framings of the same material, while separable in theory, are not always so in practice. Yet it is in the places that they overlap or run up against one another – the strategic rhetoric of individuals, the ambivalent aesthetics of films, or the unfolding practices of institutions – that we find our most fruitful junctures for extended analysis. For although the language that circulates in and around recent French films are always case-specific to some degree, they also display the friction between several positions that have by now become quite familiar, each encrusted in its own way with the hopes and frustrations of a three-decade entanglement with the challenge of global Hollywood.

To further elucidate how these terms play out in debates about the many and various 'globalised' qualities of contemporary French filmmaking, the following four chapters demonstrate how and where these long-standing ideological divisions – already a factor in Lang's negotiations with trade unions and industry professionals two decades prior – ripple to the surface of discussions about the diverse filmmaking practices of contemporary France. First, we consider two films that serve as bookends of sorts for the primary period of most interest here. Chapter 3 returns to the often cited debate about the aesthetics of Jean-Pierre Jeunet's *Amélie* (2001), a benchmark case study for outlining how three broad rhetorical frames traverse the trade press coverage, policy reports and critical polemics that initially surrounded the film, as well as how similar disagreements continue to make it a vital node for discussions about the 'globalised' aspirations of French cinema. Chapter 4 performs a similar analysis on *Valerian and the City of a Thousand Planets* (Luc Besson 2017), which nearly two decades later became the most expensive French-made film in history. Here a look at the production and reception of one ambitious film also allows us to reflect back on the career arc of its director, Besson, who has been the most consistent – and controversial – contributor to the Gallic attempts to 'beat Hollywood at its own game' since Lang.

The last two full chapters then look at how several different characteristics of popular filmmaking have come to straddle the transnational dimensions of the industry in provocative ways. Chapter 4 enlists the cause of action cinema, perhaps the most visibly 'globalised' aesthetic ingredient of contemporary Franco-European cinema. Initially left to Hollywood in the era of the tent-pole blockbuster, action scenes have enjoyed a recent renaissance in French studios. Using recent industrial history and the formal analysis of individual films combined with their reception, the chapter shows how contemporary French-made action films traverse the ideological gaps between different approaches to one of the most visible components of 'globalised' cinema. In Chapter 6, we then consider the concurrent proliferation of 'localised' French comedies, which in an industrial sense often seek more limited regional audiences, yet also play formally with the broad cultural attitudes about transnationalism sketched earlier in the book. An analysis of three titles – *Intouchables* (Toledano and Nakache 2011), *Qu'est-ce qu'on a fait au bon dieu?/ Serial (Bad) Weddings* (de Chauveron 2014) and the three-deep franchise *Les Tuche* (Baroux 2011, 2015, 2017) – suggests that recent comedies, noted frequently for their 'politically incorrect' depictions of race and class, also work to caricature the discrepancies between the different faces of 'local' French identity that confront one another in an age of encroaching cultural globalisation and blockbuster cinema.

Finally, the conclusion offers a brief reflection on perhaps the most unlikely blockbuster of the bunch. *Of Gods and Men / Des hommes et des dieux* (Beauvois 2010) is a sedate, nuanced, quasi-documentary re-creation of the events leading to the tragic deaths of a group of French Trappist monks during sectarian conflicts in Algeria in 1996. A decorated auteur entry from the Cannes festival the previous May, the film sold a surprising three million tickets in France, setting records for a Cannes release and holding its own amidst the annual fall parade of North American Oscar contenders. Celebrated by critics as a slow-paced rejoinder to digitally enhanced Hollywood fare, the film also suggested a radical revamping of the Langian genre that started it all some thirty years prior: the heritage film. In so doing, *Of Gods and Men* also renewed once more an ongoing debate about the unfolding fate of a country's cinematic heritage, stylistically countering the crop of differently affiliated genre films that continues to redefine the stakes of cultural legitimacy in a national film industry engulfed in an energetic, unruly period of transition.

WORKS CITED

Alexandre, Olivier (2015), *La règle de l'exception: écologie du cinéma français*, Paris: Editions l'EHSS.
Altman, Rick (1999), *Film/Genre*, London: British Film Institute.
Anderson, Benedict (1983), *Imagined Communities: Reflections on the Origins and the Spread of Nationalism*, London: Verso.
Appadurai, Arjun (1990), 'Disjuncture and Difference in the Global Cultural Economy', *Theory, Culture & Society*, 7, pp. 295–310.
Appadurai, Arjun (1996), *Modernity at Large: Cultural Dimensions of Globalization*, Minneapolis: University of Minnesota Press.
Austin, Guy (2009), *Contemporary French Cinema: An Introduction*, 2nd edn, Manchester: Manchester University Press.

Berry, Chris (2003), 'What's Big About the Big Film?: De-Westernizing the Blockbuster in China and Korea', in Julian Stringer (ed.), *Movie Blockbusters*, New York: Routledge, pp. 217–229.

Bonnell, René (2006), *La vingt-cinquième image: une économie de l'audiovisuel*, 4th edn, Paris: Gallimard.

Buchsbaum, Jonathan (2016), *Exception Taken: How France Has Defied Hollywood's New World Order*, New York: Columbia University Press.

De Baecque, Antoine and Ange-Dominique Bouzet (2001), 'Entretien avec David Kessler', *Libération*, 30 May, 2001.

'Cinéma français: la face cachée de l'embellie' (2002). *Cahiers du cinéma*, 564: January.

CNC (2000–2018), *Bilans*, Paris: CNC Editions.

Creton, Laurent (2012), *L'Economie du cinéma en 50 fiches*, 3rd edn, Paris: Armand Colin.

Creton, Laurent (2014), 'The Political Economy of French Cinema: Attendance and Movie Theaters', in Alistair Fox, Raphaëlle Moine, Michel Marie and Hilary Radner, eds. *A Companion to Contemporary French Cinema*, London: Wiley-Blackwell: 15–44.

Danan, Martine (1996), 'From a "Prenational" to a "Postnational" French Cinema', *Film History*, 8:1, pp. 72–84.

Danan, Martine (2000), 'French Cinema in the Era of Media Capitalism', *Media, Culture and Society* 22: pp. 355–364.

Danan, Martine (2006), 'National and Post-National French Cinema', in Paul Willeman and Valentina Vitali (eds), *Theorising Transnational Cinema*, New York: Routledge.

De Vany, Arthur (2004), *Hollywood Economics: How Extreme Uncertainty Shapes the Film Industry*, New York: Routledge.

Elsaesser, Thomas (2005), 'European Culture, National Cinema, the Auteur and Hollywood', *European Cinema: Face to Face with Hollywood*, Amsterdam: Amsterdam University Press.

Fairclough, Norman (2006), *Language and Globalization*, London: Routledge.

Ferran, Pascale *et al.* (2008), *Le milieu n'est plus un pont mais une faille: Rapport de synthèse*, 27 March, <https://www.afcinema.com/IMG/pdf/Le_Club_des_13_rapport_3_.pdf> (last accessed 6 August 2018).

Fiss, Peer C. and Paul M. Hirsch (2005), 'The Discourse of Globalization: Framing and Sensemaking of an Emerging Concept', *American Sociological Review*, 70, pp. 29–52.

Gellner, Ernst (1983), *Nations and Nationalism*, Ithaca: Cornell University Press.

Gimello-Mesplomb, Frédéric (ed.) (2012a), *Les cinéastes français à l'epreuve du cinéma fantastique*, vols 1 and 2, Paris: L'Harmattan.

Gimello-Mesplomb, Frédéric (2012b), *L'invention d'un genre: le cinéma fantastique français*, Paris: L'Harmattan.

Halle, Randall (2008), *German Film After Germany: Toward a Transnational Aesthetic*, Chicago: University of Illinois Press.

Harvey, David (1990), *The Condition of Post-modernity: An Enquiry into the Origins of Cultural Change*, London: Blackwell.

Hayward, Susan (2005), *French National Cinema*, 2nd edn, London: Routledge.

Higbee, Will and Song-Hwee Lim (2010), 'Concepts of Transnational Cinema: Toward a Critical Transnationalism in Film Studies', *Transnational Cinemas*, 1:1, pp. 7–21.

Higson, Andrew (1989), 'The Concept of National Cinema', *Screen*, 30:4, pp. 36–47.

Higson, Andrew (2000), 'The Limiting Imagination of National Cinema', in Mette Hjort and Scott Mackenzie (eds), *Cinema and Nation*, New York: Routledge, pp. 63–74.

Hill, John (1992), 'The Issue of National Cinema and British Film Production', in Duncan Petrie (ed.), *New Questions of British Cinema*, London: British Film Institute.

Hjort, Mette (2010), 'On the plurality of cinematic transnationalism', in Kathleen

Newman and Natacha Durovicova (eds), *World Cinema, Transnational Perspectives*, New York: Routledge, pp. 12–33.

Hobsbawm, Eric J. (1990), *Nations and Nationalism since 1780: Programme, Myth, Reality*, Cambridge: Cambridge University Press.

Jullier, Laurent (1997), *L'écran post-moderne*, Paris: L'Harmattan.

Jullier, Laurent (2014), 'Post-modern Hi-fi vs. Post-Cool Low-fi: An Epistemological War', in Annie van den Oever (ed.), *Technology, 'The Key Debates: Mutations and Appropriations in European Film Studies'*, Vol. IV, Amsterdam: Amsterdam University Press, pp. 154–165, 309–311.

Jullier, Laurent (2012), *Qu'est-ce qu'un bon film?*, Paris: La Dispute.

King, Geoff (2002), *New Hollywood Cinema: An Introduction*, New York: Columbia University Press.

King, Geoff (2000), *Spectacular Narratives: Hollywood in the Age of the Blockbuster*, London: I. B. Tauris.

Kuisel, Richard (2011), *The French Way: How France Embraced and Rejected American Values and Power*, Princeton: Princeton University Press.

Lanzoni, Rémi Fournier (2015), *French Cinema: From its Beginnings to the Present.* 2nd edn, London: Bloomsbury.

Looseley, David L. (1995), *The Politics of Fun: Cultural Policy and Debate in Contemporary France*, London: Berg Publishers.

Looseley, David L. and Diana Holmes (eds) (2013), *Imagining the Popular in Contemporary French Culture*, Manchester: Manchester University Press.

Martel, Frédéric (2006), *De la culture en amérique*, Paris: Gallimard.

Martel, Frédéric (2010), *Mainstream: Enquête sur la guerre globale de la culture et des médias*, Paris: Flammarion.

Mazdon, Lucy (2000). *Encore Hollywood: Remaking French Cinema*. London: BFI Publishing.

Mazdon, Lucy, ed. (2001), *France on Film: Reflections on Popular French Cinema*, London: Wallflower Press.

Meunier, Sophie and Phillip Gordon (2004), *The French Challenge: Adapting to Globalization*, New York: Brookings Institution.

Miller, Toby, Nitin Goval, John McMurria, Richard Maxwell and Tina Wang (2005), *Global Hollywood 2*, London: British Film Institute.

Moine, Raphaëlle (ed.) (2005), *Le cinéma français face aux genres*, Paris: Broché.

Moine, Raphaëlle (2007), 'Genre hybridity, National Cinema, Globalised Culture' in Isabelle Vanderschelden and Darron Waldron (eds), Translated by Jonathan Hensher, *France at the Flicks: Trends in Contemporary Popular French Cinema*, Manchester: Manchester University Press, pp. 36–50.

Moine, Raphaëlle (2015), *Les genres du cinéma*, 2nd edn, Paris: Armand Colin.

Neale, Steve and Sheldon Hall (2010), *Epics, Spectacles and Blockbusters: A Hollywood History*, Detroit: Wayne State University Press.

O'Regan, Tom (1996), *Australian National Cinema*, New York: Routledge.

O'Regan, Tom (2007), 'Cultural Exchange', in Toby Miller and Robert Stam (eds), *Companion to Film Theory*, pp. 262–295.

Palmer, Tim (2011), *Brutal Intimacy: Analyzing Contemporary French Cinema*, Middletown: Wesleyan University Press.

Pieterse, Jan Nederveen (2004), *Globalization and Culture: Global Mélange*, Oxford: Rowan & Littlefield.

Powrie, Phil (ed.) (1999), *French Cinema in the 1990s: Continuity and Difference*, Oxford: Oxford University Press.

Powrie, Phil (2001), *Jean-Jacques Beineix*, Manchester: Manchester University Press.

Poirrier, Philippe (2006), 'Introduction' in Philippe Poirrier and Geneviève Gentil (ed), *La politique culturelle en débat: Anthologie, 1955–2005*, Paris: Comité de la Ministère de la Culture, pp. 1–18.

Robertson, Roland (1995), 'Glocalization: Time-Space-Homogeneity-Heterogeneity', in Mike Featherstone, Scott Lash and Roland Robertson (eds), *Global Modernities*, London: Sage Publications, pp. 25–44.

Rowden, Terry and Elizabeth Ezra (eds) (2006), *Transnational Cinema: The Film Reader*, London: Routledge.

Schatz, Thomas (2003), 'The New Hollywood', in Julian Stringer (ed.), *Movie Blockbusters*, New York: Routledge, pp. 15–45.

Schiller, Herbert (1976), 'Communication and Cultural Domination', *International Journal of Politics*, 5:5, pp. 1–127.

Schwartz, Vanessa R. (2007), *It's So French!: Hollywood, Paris and the Making of a Cosmopolitan Film Culture*, Chicago: University of Chicago Press.

Stringer, Julian (2003), 'Introduction', in Julian Stringer (ed.), *Movie Blockbusters*, New York: Routledge, pp. 1–15.

Shaw, Deborah (2013), 'Deconstructing and Reconstructing "Transnational Cinema"', in Stephanie Dennison (ed.), *Contemporary Hispanic Cinema: Interrogating Transnationalism in Spanish and Latin American Film*, Woodbridge: Tamesis, pp. 47–66.

Shaw, Deborah (2017), 'Transnational Cinema: Mapping a Field of Study', in Rob Stone, Paul Cooke, Stephanie Dennison and Alex Marlowe-Mann (eds), *The Routledge Companion to World Cinema*, London: Routledge, pp. 290–298.

Shaw, Deborah (2015), *The Three Amigos: The Transnational Filmmaking of Guillermo Del Toro, Alejandro González Iñárritu, and Alfonso Cuarón*, Manchester: Manchester University Press.

Tomlinson, John (1999), *Globalization and Culture*, Chicago: University of Chicago Press.

Vanderschelden, Isabelle (2007), 'Strategies for a Trans-national / French Popular Cinema', *Modern & Contemporary France*, 38, pp. 37–50.

Vanderschelden, Isabelle and Darren Waldren (eds) (2007), *France at the Flicks: Trends in Contemporary French Popular Cinema*, Cambridge: Cambridge Scholars Publishing.

Vincendeau, Ginette and Richard Dyer (1992), 'Introduction', in Ginette Vincendeau and Richard Dyer (eds), *Popular European Cinema*, New York: Routledge, pp. 1–15.

Vincendeau, Ginette (1996), *The Companion to French Cinema*, London: Cassell.

Vincendeau, Ginette (2000a), 'Issues in European Cinema', in John Hill and Pamela Church Gibson (eds.), *World Cinema: Critical Approaches*, Oxford: Oxford University Press, pp. 56–65.

Vincendeau, Ginette (2000b), *Stars and Stardom in French Cinema*, London: Continuum.

Vincendeau, Ginette (2003), *Jean-Pierre Melville: An American in Paris*, London: Bloomsbury.

Vincendeau, Ginette (2014), *Brigitte Bardot: The Life, the Legend, the Movies*, London: Carlton Books.

Wallerstein, Immauel (1983), *Historical Capitalism*, London: Verso Editions.

Wayne, Michael (2002), *The Politics of Contemporary European Cinema: Histories, Borders, Diaspora*, London: Intellect Press.

Wyatt, Justin (1994), *High Concept: Movies and Marketing in Hollywood*, Austin: University of Texas Press.

Yudice, George (2004), *The Expediency of Culture: Uses of Culture in a Global Era*. Durham, NC: Duke University Press.

World Film Market Trends (2000–2018), Brussels: European Audiovisual Observatory.

1. THE LANG PLAN AND ITS AFTERMATH

This chapter offers a brief history of the political-economic conditions that made way for the current dynamics of film production culture in France. The account begins with a set of wide-ranging audiovisual reforms in the 1980s – themselves the results of political upheaval. While the election of Socialist president François Mitterrand in 1981 first seemed to repudiate the liberalised economic approach of his conservative predecessor, Valérie Giscard d'Estaing, the ensuing economic downturn of 1982 forced the new administration to roll back plans to re-nationalise commerce and industry. Today, most historians view this abrupt 'U-turn' in 1983 as a decisive moment in the shift to market liberalism in Europe – and a central paradox of Mitterrand's presidency. It also signalled the arrival of economic globalisation across the continent, spurring greater cooperation among European countries during the following decade.

French cultural politics of the 1980s and 1990s mirror the larger ambivalence of how one nation-state sought to channel the energies of a changing market economy to support its media industries. Amidst all of this reform, the single most important figure to emerge was Mitterrand's charismatic Minister of Culture, Jack Lang. While many of his directives sought to stimulate the development of a sort of commercial entertainment that could compete in new ways, Lang's policies also actively counteracted the economic concentration that was the most likely outgrowth of that same strategy. Recent accounts of these events propose different vantage points on this history of policy initiatives, as well as their long-term consequences. Among them, a number of French economic historians and social scientists have shed welcome light on the film industry since then, including Laurent Creton (Creton 2000; Creton 2002; Creton 2003; Creton 2008; Creton, Dehèe, Layerle and Moine 2011; Creton 2016), René Bonnell (Bonnell 2006), Claude Forest (Forest 2001; Forest 2013), Joëlle Farchy (Farchy 1994; Farchy 1999; Farchy 2011), François Benhamou (Benhamou 2017) and Frédéric Gimello-Mesplomb (Gimello-Mesplomb 2000). Meanwhile, in English, a series of recent essays by Isabelle Vanderschelden offer targeted inquiries into important debates (Vanderschelden 2009; Vanderschelden 2016), complementing the valuable earlier work by Anne Jäckel (Jäckel 2003) and Martine Danan (Danan 1996; Danan 2000; Danan 2002; Danan 2006).

In terms of the political-economic reforms most in question in this chapter, two particularly authoritative accounts of Lang's policy changes have emerged in just the past several years to complement earlier inquiries into Lang's cultural agenda like David L. Looseley's *The Politics of Fun* (Looseley 1995). Jonathan Buchsbaum's *Exception Taken* overviews the entire period traced in this chapter from a political-economic perspective, highlighting how French audiovisual policy found new ways to defy Hollywood dominance during the period (Buchsbaum 2016). Meanwhile, Olivier Alexandre's *La règle de l'exception* offers a detailed map of what he calls the 'ecology' of the contemporary French industry, unveiling the sociological functioning that has helped it to survive the past three decades (Alexandre 2015). The aim here is to complement these broad-based accounts by teasing out a specific thread of the industry's production strategies over the past thirty years – the creation of a new class of putative 'French blockbusters'. Since the 1980s in particular, the intermittent success of 'big' French films has become both a symbol of Lang's tenure and an enduring source of controversy.

THE SEEDS OF REFORM

A number of factors made the 1980s ripe for policy reform in French cinema. As theatrical attendance waned during the 1970s, the government gradually liberalised its approach to television, and a rising class of corporate-minded executives looked for novel ways to combine the financial prospects of the two industries. Mitterrand's decisive victory in 1981 offered them a chance to act. Most industry leaders initially viewed television as a complication rather than a solution to their problems. As in other European countries, the small screen was initially government-run in France, and until 1963 there was only one national channel. Even with the addition of two more public channels in 1964 (Antenne 2) and 1973 (France 3), television long remained an unchallenged public enterprise. Centre-right administrations of the 1970s made incremental steps towards decentralisation. Giscard dismantled the

Office de Radiodiffusion Télévision Française (ORTF) in 1974, replacing it with an 'internal market' centred on three nationalised stations, with the initial one to be renamed Télévision Française 1 (TF1). Despite the expanded capacity, all programming still came from one source – the *Societé Française de Production* (the SFP) – that could not satisfy increased demand (Forbes 1995: 234). Instead, the three channels ended up importing American productions on the cheap – the same 'unintended consequence' (*effet pervers*) that plagued movie theatres several decades earlier. In 1979, Giscard relented, allowing the channels to produce their own programming.

Meanwhile, the film industry braced for a new source of competition. With cinema exhibition as its primary source of revenue, the role of the Centre National de la Cinématographie (CNC) had been comparatively straightforward. By using a box office tax to fund automatic and selective subsidy programmes for the cinema, public funding provided welcome stability for a fragmented film production sector, which otherwise depended on distribution companies to provide funding on a case-by-case contractual basis. As attendance figures waned during the 1970s, these *à valoir* engagements with distributors grew scarce as the entire system became more averse to risk – uncertainty that also meant the rapid consolidation of chains. Most notable of these was the Pathé-Gaumont Group, which merged the country's two largest chains in 1968 and owned over 600 locations in Paris alone. As film funding began to orbit around this more concentrated exhibition sector, analysts warned that Pathé-Gaumont could begin to dictate the terms of which films got made and when.

Several other factors shook the status quo as the 1980s approached. The most pressing of these was the advent of other new media platforms. Cable and satellite television had emerged in America in the late 1970s, beginning with Home Box Office (HBO) in 1975 (Grantham 2000: 80). Meanwhile, the format war between Beta and VHS was in the process of determining which type of format would become the standard bearer for recorded video playback. Traditional state-centric methods of film policy were ill suited to counteract the impending shift to new technologies. For France, neighbouring Italy repre-sented a cautionary tale, as government instability and indecision had allowed entrepreneur Silvio Berlusconi to buy up television stations. By the early 1980s, Berlusconi made overtures towards the French market as well.

Amidst the uncertainty about these older modes of operating, the leaders of a future reform movement emerged. In November 1976, a graduate student named René Bonnell defended an economics dissertation before a committee including Lang, then a professor of international law (Bonnell 1986: 14). The thesis, enititled 'Cultural Initiative in a Market Economy: The Example of French Cinema Since 1945,' argued that the French film industry was growing out of touch with economic reality, and that the present attendance crisis derived from its obsolete interventionist methods. The dissertation was soon revised and published as *Le cinéma exploité* (1978), a playful title referencing both the literal function of movie venues ('exhibited') and the economic imbalance towards larger cinema chains ('exploited'). Bonnell's main suggestion was that the support system be revised by incorporating ancillary markets (mainly television) into the CNC's redistributive mechanisms. The book struck a chord in the industry, articulating the frustrations of producers and distributors and appealing to a rising class of corporate-minded intellectuals. One of these was the young executive Daniel Toscan du Plantier, named head of production at Gaumont in 1975.

Trained in marketing and advertising, Toscan thought that French cinema should capitalise on the marketability of national culture as a buttress against Hollywood universalism. As Jean-Michel Frodon writes, Toscan aimed for a 'guiding principle beyond the clivage [between art and commerce], almost a nostalgic one in its larger sense: culture' (Frodon 1995: 528). He envisioned cultural products that could travel between media forms, much like the model he saw in Hollywood practices of the day. The key to this strategy was the acquisition of intellectual property, and Toscan engineered Gaumont's purchase of several publishing houses in 1981 (Editions Ramsay and Gallimard) and a recording company in 1983 (Erato), with the goal of making 'opera films' that could link the marketing of soundtracks with box office sales (Frodon 1995: 528). During his time in command, Toscan also sought to acquire the rights to marketable auteur films from around Europe. His commercial bent would make Gaumont both the ally and the adversary of government operatives over the next several decades.

Along with the Socialist victory of 1981 came a window for this generation of reformers. In 1979, Bonnell was named head of distribution at Gaumont. Just two years later, Lang was named Minister of Culture, and called on the young economist to help guide a structural revision of the *fond du soutien*. Meanwhile, Toscan's strategies at Gaumont offered a nascent model for how French studios could envision big budget, commercial films that would also be culturally specific. In the years that followed, Lang, Bonnell and Toscan played crucial roles in redefining the cultural politics of an emerging audiovisual market – one they agreed could profit from an ambitious renewal of the capacities of film production.

THE LANG PLAN – TAKE ONE

Though his influence on French cinema is often called the 'Lang Plan', the new Minister of Culture enacted a variety of reforms during separate terms over a twelve-year period (1981–1986 and 1988–1993). Lang's remit for leading a sweeping agenda called *Le Tout Culturel* extended to other creative industries, but the cinema became in many ways his most symbolic concern.

Despite making early headlines with anti-American, anti-imperialist rhetoric, Lang's legacy remains notable today for the ways his administration injected free-market principles into France's 'mixed-economy' approach to the cinema support system. As he put it in a memorable early speech at UNESCO in Mexico in 1982: 'Art and commerce are the same battle!' (Frodon 1995: 561).

To begin his mandate for the cinema, Lang commissioned a wide-ranging analysis of the industry from his friend and colleague, lawyer Jean-Denis Bredin (Eling 1999: 117) (father to current CNC president Frédérique, who was herself Lang's personal cinema advisor at the time). Published in November 1981, the Bredin report laid groundwork for the reforms of the next five years and beyond. Its preface warned of a 'triple threat' facing French cinema: the seduction of Hollywood blockbusters, the need to address television, and the arrival of other new technologies. For Bredin, these could tempt the industry to pursue the wrong sort of solutions to its problems. He warned: 'In France we always dream of combating the empire, of forming French majors with prestigious films that can win both the Oscars and mass audiences [. . .] [but] French cinema will only continue to be a true alternative to Hollywood if it continues to be itself' (Bredin 1981: 6). Since Bredin, innumerable reports from the CNC and the Ministry of Culture have confronted a similar dilemma. A primary difficulty has been the industry's ongoing indecision about what 'continuing to be itself' actually means.

For Lang and his cohort, a significant part of that answer involved finding ways to fund new types of films that could circulate beyond the big screen. Released on 1 April 1982 as 'the most important reform for the cinema since the Liberation' (Weitzman 1991: 24) the first Lang plan sought to 'reconquer popular audiences' by stimulating aid for film production through new sources of investment (Maurin 1982: 2). Per Bredin's recommendations, the plan intro-duced two new methods to encourage investment in domestic filmmaking – a risk guarantee programme for banks called *Institut pour le Financement du Cinéma et des Industries Culturelles* (IFCIC) and tax shelters for compa-nies called *Sociétés pour le financement de l'industrie cinématographique et audiovisuelle* (SOFICA). Meanwhile, to counteract the potential for too much economic concentration around more expensive productions, the plan also split up the Pathé and Gaumont exhibition chain; created a Commission for Fair Competition called the *Commission Nationale de la Concurrence Loyale* (CNCL); appointed an ombudsman to handle future distribution disputes; and founded an aid programme for regional distribution to encourage print circulation outside Paris.

The most consequential part of the reform, however, would be a 'fourth television channel' to which Bredin had referred only elliptically. A variant on HBO and a throwback to the French 'national champions' of *les trentes glo-rieuses*, Canal Plus entered the market in 1984. Though it quickly became the anchor of a new audiovisual landscape, uncertainty revolved initially around how Canal fit into the 'media chronology' for film releases (Looseley 1995: 201). By 1985, Canal founder André Rousselet and the conjoined cinema lobby, the *Bureau de liason des industries cinématographiques* (BLIC) agreed that an annual slate of 400 films would go to Canal, each of them available twelve months after theatrical release but six months prior to public television broadcast.[1] In exchange for its prioritised position in this framework, Canal agreed to invest 20% of its profits in film production (9% of it would go to French films and 11% to European films). The other channels would invest 5.5% for a smaller lot of 120 titles per year. The 1986 Audiovisual Law enacted this pecking order and added two generalist channels (M6 and La Cinq) to the previous three (TF1, Antenne 2, France 3)[2] and by the mid 1990s, this group of six channels broadcast upwards of 1000 different films per annum, with Canal alone responsible for 40% of them (Bonnell 2006: 490).

The largest single contributor to the new system, Canal's influence as the unofficial 'second *agrément*' to the CNC was soon apparent to all. Compounding the uncertainty about this new state of affairs, the Socialist losses in the 1986 parliamentary elections meant Lang's policies would mature on the watch of his centre-right successor. Yet despite his aggressive rhetoric, François Léotard's two-year tenure as minister of culture led to just one deci-sive change – the privatisation of TF1. As David Looseley suggests, that may have been because Lang's course was already sufficiently liberalised (Looseley 1995:197–212). Moreover, all sides of the political spectrum were concerned about the unprecedented consolidation of their main competition, as President Reagan's lenient Federal Communications Commission (FCC) regulations had given way to a series of mergers between 1986 and 1989 that dominated the headlines (News Corporation/Fox, Sony/Columbia, Disney/Touchstone, Time/ Warner) (Bonnell 2006: 212).

Amidst the ascendance of these multimedia conglomerates, the erstwhile French majors also moved to re-consolidate their power. Pathé stirred legal conflict in 1989 with its acquisition of several companies owned by Italian entrepreneur Giancarlo Paretti, including the US firm Cannon Entertainment, the French energy company Suez and the French bank Rivaud. In the aftermath of that controversy, the French energy giant Chargeurs bought controlling inter-est in Pathé, announcing subsequent plans to enter film production. Meanwhile, the third major cinema operator, *Union Générale Cinématographique* (UGC), was acquired by the French water giant (*Compagnie Générale des Eaux* (CGE) in 1988 and Gaumont re-emerged as a leader of domestic produc-tion (Bonnell 2006: 243). Though Toscan's reign ended in 1984 when his expansion plans led to huge losses, the new team under Nicolas Seydoux and Patrice Ledoux continued his push to acquire intellectual property (Bonnell 2006: 232). Taking advantage of Lang's new funding opportunities, Gaumont garnered a series of co-production deals with television companies, signed agreements with Hollywood's growing distribution affiliates in Europe, and offered exclusive contracts to producer-directors Luc Besson (*Les Films du Loup*) and Claude Berri (*Renn Films*). By the end of the decade, Gaumont had become the primary source of big-budget, French-language filmmaking, most notably with the success of Berri's *Jean de Florette* and *Manon des Sources* (both 1986), Besson's *Le Grand Bleu* (1988) and *Nikita* (1990), and Yves Robert's *Le Gloire de mon père* and *Le Château de ma mère* (both 1990). Yet this success did not mean overall health for the market. French films remained strong until 1982, when they commanded 53.4% of attendance despite the arrival of Stephen Spielberg's *E.T.*, but by 1986 that number fell to just 43.7% (against 43.4% for US films) (Forest 2001: 35). Three years later Hollywood commanded 55.5% behind franchises like *Batman*, *Lethal Weapon*, *Indiana Jones and the Last Crusade*, *Ghostbusters 2* and *Back to the Future 2* (Simsi 2001: 75–80). To make matters worse, a global drop in attendance numbers that year did not seem to affect Hollywood's fortunes; the losses were exclusively French (Frodon 1995: 185). Never before had a small number of huge American films been quite so destructive.

By the time the Socialists returned to office in 1988, consensus was building in the industry about the need for more audacious films that could compete with Hollywood. An open letter published in *Le Film Français* by the producers union *Fédération National des Cinéastes Français* (FNCF) pleaded with Lang for 'concrete actions' that could 'win back film attendance and conquer French audiences' (Douget 1988: 10). The exact role of public funding in that endeavour remained disputed. Some argued that making bigger films could never be a direct result of state intervention. Producer Gérard Ducaux-Rupp put it succinctly in a 1986 interview with *Le Film Français*: 'What we need is not more film policy but a willingness to finally let cinema determine its own politics more freely.' ('Production' 1986: 6). Others argued that government support for bigger films should be a major part of the strategy moving forward. A 1987 study by an audiovisual think tank, *Centre d'Etudes et de Recherche du Cinéma et de l'Audiovisuel* (CERCA), rehearsed much the same argument that would be used thirty years later to explain the revisions to the *crédit d'impôt* – making more big films would 'help to finance the more 'difficult' films so dear to artists and their public' ('Une enquête du CERCA' 1988: 8–9).

THE LANG PLAN – TAKE TWO

During its two-year exile, the Left formulated an aggressive response to the widespread calls for action. Socialist press secretary Jean-Jack Queyrenne telegraphed the eventual plan in an interview with *Le Film Français* in 1987: 'We should be fighting! [. . .] we should be gathering the resources necessary for developing the production of very big budget films that can draw large audiences in a time of crisis – like *Jean de Florette* or *The Name of the Rose*' (Rival 1987a: 4). Leadership was still cautious about encouraging the wrong kinds of economic concentration around the bigger films. An article printed alongside Queyrenne's interview stressed the need to mitigate the involvement of television (especially TF1) in determining the characteristics of the new productions (Rival 1987b: 4). In 1989, the industry would stage a two-week strike to make that point even more forcefully for Lang and his cohort.

Canal Plus would be pivotal to any new strategy. Two years after the BLIC agreement, Bonnell estimated his office received close to 500 funding requests per calendar year – out of which it was able to offer financing to 150 (Rival 1988: 65). Nearly everyone wondered whether the omnipresence of the station would make it a de facto 'second *agrément*' – behind the CNC in theory, but often overruling its authority in practice. Bonnell bristled at the suggestion, defending his autonomy of taste ('I choose the best screenplays') and asserting that any cinema 'that doesn't have to answer to market demand' would 'always be a cinema without any true appeal' (Rival 1988: 65). What the industry needed, he claimed, was internal focus on productions that could attract multiple viewings at cinemas and draw big audiences on television. French producers, he argued, should address 'banks and big financial groups' and 'sell the kind of projects that might actually have value to them'. He reassured colleagues that this did not mean abandoning independent production. Rather, French cinema could play the blockbuster game on its own terms:

> All we need to get back those 20 to 30 million in attendance is a dozen or so films per year that do only half as well as *Le Grand Bleu* or *The Last Emperor*. In no way does this need to ever stop us from continuing our dedication to the type of smaller productions that have always allowed us to discover new talent every year. (Rival 1988: 65)

With leadership from Bonnell at Canal and the ongoing domination of Hollywood blockbusters, the political climate was primed for change.

On 7 February 1989, Lang announced a second major agenda for the cinema, this time to pursue a class of prestigious, culturally-oriented blockbusters. The goal was to generate a more competitive and, in some sense, more 'democratic' French culture, capable of appealing to both mass audiences and to elites. As Kim Eling points out, the challenge of passing the second plan involved two main obstacles (Eling 199: 123–125). First, supporting big films required a recalibration of the automatic funding available from the *fond du soutien*, which since the 1960s had been geared to favour independents (with no links to major companies). Until Lang, any film with receipts between 18 and 50 million francs was given a reimbursement of 85% of its budget while films larger than 50 million francs were given 40% and all other films 120%. The new plan proposed levelling all categories at 120%, hence supporting big budgets more than its predecessor. Lang admitted that his negotiations with different unions became a question of linguistic nuance:

> I tried to accomplish a kind of semantic feat, so that our support for one category did not look like a withdrawal of support for others [. . .] I did not say 'supporting' big budget films, I said 'not penalizing' big budget films. 'Not penalizing' big budget films did not give the impression that we were supporting them. [. . .] So it was aimed at the two points of view, it allowed us to avoid a direct affront to the independent experimental directors, the independent producers. (Eling 1999: 124)

Defining 'independence' had become a careful rhetorical balancing act.

The second component of Lang's plan set up support mechanisms for larger films. Unlike Gaumont's films, the productions financed by the second Lang Plan would seek to operate as 'independent' entities. Their backbone would be financial programmes implemented during Lang's first term – the IFCIC and the SOFICAs. To the former, Lang added two new elements – apparently proposed to him by Toscan, then still the chair of Erato and a key union spokesperson (Eling 1999: 125). The first was a loan guarantee programme geared towards banks taking risks on financing bigger budgets (*fond de garantie*) and the second was a 'Club of Investors' (*Club des Investisseurs*), a group of successful industry operatives who would be hand picked by the Minister and overseen by the IFCIC. Presided over by Georges Prost, this 'pool' of investors included representatives from five national banks.[3] The films he proposed would be large budget epics that would also be formally separated from the interests of big television companies. As productions drawn up not in the board rooms of Gaumont, Canal Plus or TF1, but around the table of a government-run 'panel of experts' focused on the matter of competing with Hollywood, their theatrical profits would be (after the parts for exhibition and distribution) the exclusive property of their 'independent' producers, and not of any large company.

The second plan was put in motion quickly. By summer 1989, there were six boards accepting applications for the new strategy, and by November eight projects had been announced – each pre-financed by banks, guaranteed by the IFCIC to return 70% of attendance (Dacbert 1989: 6). The hope was that block-busters *à la française* could be a fast acting salve, launching a class of movies that would stimulate the economy, bring audiences back to cinemas, and generate funds for other films. As Sophie Dacbert wrote for *Le Film Français*, 'According to the 'Club of Investors,' after they fill these locomotives of French production with coal for next year, the only thing they will need to do is win their bet: that the French public will start coming to cinemas again (Dacbert 1989: 6). Shortly after proposing his plan, Lang worked to assuage related worries about the emerging relationship between broadcasters and producers. He commissioned another report, this one from IFCIC director Georges Prost, to detail how banks would relate to the Investors Club. While he emphasised the need for bigger films, Prost advocated creative 'independence' for producers, proposing that television channels be prohibited from being majority contributors to any one production, and that the proceeds from commercialisation should return to the film producer and not its financial partners in television. Prost's suggestions were taken up in a 1990 decree (later modified in 2001) that stipulated the proper relationships between film production and television funding. To avoid the growth of horizontally integrated multimedia companies, French television could finance films only via co-production agreements delegated by separate production affiliates, and were barred from being the majority producer of any production – whether made in France or abroad (Bonnell 2006: 75).

Despite consensus about the need for aggressive strategies, responses to the second reform were not uniformly enthusiastic. Some representatives of the production sector, like Christian Oddos of *Union de Producteurs des Films* (UPF), lauded the plan's 'ability to reinvigorate and protect French cultural identity' while 'maintaining both its artisanal character' and 'cultivating a real, competitive market that has adapted products and methods of financing' (Oddos 1989: 4–5). Pascal Rogard, head of the *Chambre Syndicale*, supported the plan, but expressed dismay at what he saw as an unsustainable double standard: 'pluralism and transparency in the private sector; concentration and opacity in the public– or semi-public–sector' (Rogard 1989: 4). One of the most critical voices was Bonnell, who approved of easing the penalties on commercial films, but accused Prost of ignoring the international dynamics that caused the crisis, and placing limits on television which 'pretended that all competition takes place in a perfect Hexagon' while the real antagonists were multi-national groups 'chopping down the door with an axe' (like Jack Nicholson in *The Shining*) (Rival 1989: 3). Moreover, Prost's plan to 'ensure risk' ignored the role that television revenues would also play in calculating any film's economic performance. If they had no say in the types of productions that would fill their airtime, television executives would be disinclined to prioritise French products at the outset, hence perpetuating the appeal of American programming, and reinforcing the strength of the 'speculative model' that the plan initially meant to counteract (Rival 1989: 3).

Both Rogard and Bonnell would prove prophetic in their misgivings and Lang's most caricatured 'mixed-economy' programme would be short-lived. The Club's first film, *Cyrano de Bergerac* (Rappeneau 1989), was an enormous success, but the twelve films that followed between 1990 and 1992 failed miserably – most of them mediocre, big-budget, costume dramas reminiscent of the 'Tradition of Quality' of the 1950s. Prost admitted later that *Cyrano*'s popularity and the influx of funding led to a lack of rigour on the part of the selection committee – 'Don't ask me about how we chose the films – we accepted everything!' (Weitzmann 1991: 25).

The folly of the Investors Club exposed the challenges facing any attempt to generate 'independent' blockbuster films that did not have connections to integrated companies. *Cyrano* actually accounted well for itself, drawing 4,590,000 attendees – which covered 77% of its 90 million franc production budget on the national market alone. However, nearly all of the Club's other entries performed badly, which was a particularly embarrassing result compared to the films they were supposed to rival.[4] Rather than any fanfare for the Langian productions, 1990 was most remarkable for the success of the three aforementioned Gaumont films (the Robert diptych and *Nikita*) which all drew over four million viewers and made their money back on box office receipts alone. Moreover, since the producers of the Lang blockbusters were 'independent', they did not ensure their own risks with foreign sales or television rights, banking on cinema attendance for a return on their big investments. In early 1991, the front cover of *Le Film Français* reported that Lang's Investors Club would soon end for primarily this reason ('Le club des investisseurs en question' 1991: 1). Lang concurred in a 1991 radio interview, suggesting that the programme was always meant more as a symbolic call-to-arms than a sustainable strategy:

> This strategy came about two years ago during a period when we all desperately needed a change of pace. We were in the midst of the attendance crisis, and my message had to be clear and loud – 'Don't give up! Be audacious!' Maybe some people heard me a little too clearly. In any case, I think the program has played its role by now, and we won't be continuing the Investors Club. (Heyman and Frodon 1991)

Much like the dismantling of the Pathé-Gaumont chains ten years before, the Investors Club now ranks as a symbol of Lang's persona as a statesman. A state-centric gesture at 'independent' blockbusters, the second reform failed to wrestle big budget French filmmaking away from its newest financial mainstays in the private sector. Interpretations of its legacy, of course, vary depending on how the speaker sits vis à vis the dueling economic philosophies at the core of the industry's strategy since Mitterrand. For some, the failed attempt at founding a state-run brand of blockbuster cinema offered decisive proof that the French government should roll back its involvement in the commercial sector once and for all. One journalist opined on the general sentiment around the industry: 'Unfortunately, the majority of these people did not quite understand how to take advantage of the aid they were offered or how to use it to develop a full-fledged image industry' (Weitzmann 1991: 25). On the flipside, many supporters of the programme's essential state-centric philosophy have since gained resolve against the commercial influence of the television sector that provides most of their revenue. In this way, the Investors Club has to be viewed as a turning point, when the state dispensed with any pretence at maintaining a commercial production culture free from the interests of television. An 'upper' tier of productions does persist as part of France's overall strategy, but there is no longer such a coordinated attempt to make top-down 'cultural' alternatives to Hollywood.

STUDIOCANAL AND THE POST-LANG LANDSCAPE

The summer of 1993 offered an illustration of why the aesthetic priorities of any future plan had to remain flexible.[5] Just as calls for a European 'cultural exception' to Hollywood resounded from the GATT negotiations in Uruguay, Gaumont's *Germinal* (Berri 1993) looked poised to challenge the attendance figures of *Jurassic Park* earlier that summer. Though not technically a product of the Investors Club (Berri opted out at the last minute) *Germinal* embraced its emblematic cultural vision – a Zola adaptation starring Gérard Depardieu, fresh off worldwide accolades for *Cyrano*. But the competition between these two blockbusters soon lost box office headlines to the surprising run of *Les Visiteurs* (Poiré 1993), a comedy starring Jean Reno and Christian Clavier as medieval time travellers, which outdrew both of them for the year (Simsi 2001: 98).

Whatever their stylistic features, the element that *Germinal* and *Les Visiteurs* shared – large budgets relative to the prior French norms – would eventually become more important politically than anything separating them. Costume dramas and comedies would both become fixtures on the post-Lang landscape of French production, as television investment resurrected the industry from its slumber with a new set of funding norms, which would be typified by the campaign around Berri's subsequent film, *La Reine Margot* (1994) ('Le pouvoir mediatique' 1994). Moving forward, Canal and its partners became a sort of tacit 'Investors Club', and by the time of Lang's departure, the industry had embraced a new rhetoric – that any mixed-economy system with a hope to maintain its share of attendance would have to embrace a *cinéma à deux vitesses* committed to supporting both commercial films and lower-budget auteurist ventures. Lang's conservative successor, Jacques Toubon, dispensed with most all of his predecessor's pretence about 'high culture', instead prais-ing the dual strategy:

> We need a varied menu these days if we want to survive. To keep its audi-ence, a national cinema must also produce big budget films with special

effects or a prestigious cast – I'm thinking here, of course, of *Germinal* or *Les Visiteurs*. These films, far from threatening art films [...] help keep audiences attached to the domestic product in all its variety. ('GATT Reaction' 1993: 6)

Despite Toubon's resolve, many industry insiders wondered whether such an economic strategy would be financially sound. A 1994 issue of *Le Film Français* devoted a special issue to the funding and marketing of big films, noting that 'the conditions necessary for conceiving and producing these big films have thus far done nothing to reassure those who are nervous about such a dangerous level of investment' but also that 'these productions are more necessary than ever to maintain market share against Hollywood' (Boudier 1994: 8–9).

Canal and the generalist channels found themselves at the paradoxical heart of the ambivalence about the new audiovisual funding system (Fansten 2003: 51). Although the staggered release windows of the 'media chronology' could determine who had access to what and when, it did little to assuage fears about what the economics of television might mean for the long-term qualities of French filmmaking. The 1986 Audiovisual Law, reinforced by the decree of 1989, limited the channel's engagement with film content, prohibiting production affiliates from contributing more than half of the budget to any one film, and hence disqualifying them from CNC support as *producteurs délégués* (Bonnell 2006: 254). Limiting the channels' access to automatic subsidies was increasingly irrelevant though, especially by the time Canal and TF1 added their own production affiliates (Studio Canal Plus and Ciby 2000, respectively) (Bonnell 2006: 250–254). These new companies viewed their funding obligations as a 'sort of tax' for acquiring the films they knew had a reliable audience on television (Fansten 2003: 52). By 1992 though, they also realised that there was another opportunity waiting to be seized. The 1986 Audiovisual Law placed restrictions on pre-production investment, but did not stop companies from paying in advance for broadcast rights, which meant they would control a product after its run in cinemas. Pre-sales henceforth became a primary loophole for finessing the requirements of the regulatory system. Large companies used these agreements as a way to influence the sorts of programming they wanted. Michael Fansten, head of TF1 during that period, put it trenchantly:

> TF1 rapidly re-oriented all of its choices of projects to films that could be both successful in cinemas and a draw for audiences on television later on. This meant films like *The Closet* or *Crimson Rivers* – comedies and action films – were now much more desired than *auteur* cinema. (Fansten 2003: 52)

The shift to presales in turn drove up the price for 'predictable commodities' (*valeurs surs*) like stars, name directors or big budgets, which could ensure larger television viewership.

Amidst the shift, Canal went from a 'national champion' of the television industry to the epicentre of troubling new trends. Founded in 1990, Studio Canal Plus (reorganised and renamed StudioCanal in 2000) expanded the ambitions of its parent company, backing an aggressive stance beyond French borders that could 'take a bite out of the American market' once and for all (Boudier 1993: 6). The plan was to invest in US blockbusters from the ground-up, reaping more revenue from the titles that would eventually grace both French marquees and its own programming. The studio announced it would purchase a stake in Carolco, an independent US production company that became known for hits like *Terminator 2* (Cameron 1992). It also backed the sci-fi epic *Stargate* (1994) starring James Spader, which it could fund 100% since it was an international production (Rival 1990: 1–2). Meanwhile, under intense pressure from TF1 mogul Francis Bouygues and Rousselet, the government passed the Carignon Law of 1994, which among other things changed the production investment cap for private channels from 25% to 49% (Lescure 2014: 269). Later that year, the Studio acquired a majority share of *Les Films Alain Sarde*, signed an agreement with the American company Regency to orchestrate co-productions, and sought similar co-production agreements in Italy, Spain and Germany (Paris 2002: 94). As the director of the studio, Bonnell assured readership of *Le Film Français* that the Studio's production influence would always remain modest on the national level, whatever its overseas activities (Rival 1990: 1–2).

The ambivalent mandate of the Investors Club had not gone away as much as been displaced by private studios. Despite its legal constraints as a funding partner, it was clear that the Studio would be expected to provide coverage for the endangered 'independents' of the system, while pursuing its own commercial goals. In 1992, the Studio added Canal Plus Ecriture, a screenwriting wing headed by Alain De Greef and tasked with masterminding a new sort of genre cinema. Bonnell voiced a familiar refrain about French cinema's 'audacity' in 1994, though now he seemed to be repeating marching orders:

> At the request of government authorities, I'm enlarging the station's range of contributions to films with more marketable value for the screen. This means that I won't hesitate to spend 20 million Francs for the pre-purchase of very large films. The archetype here is again *Germinal*: we're looking for ten or so films like that, because if they each draw half of what that film did, we'd already have our 30 million in attendance. (Boudier 1994: 8–9)

Bonnell had advocated such a policy before Lang, but seemed more reticent after GATT – perhaps because Canal played a far different role in the mid 1990s, funding 80% of all French productions. In the process, an enormous amount of jealousy built up against those 'independent' producers perceived to have an unfair advantage because of their links to the Studio. Lescure bristled at the suggestion: 'Alain Sarde has no editorial clout at Studio Canal Plus. He gives his opinions about certain decisions but he has no executive functions other than to direct Les Films Alain Sarde' (Boudier and Villeret 1994b: 9). But the lines were fuzzy about just how 'involved' an affiliated studio could be in a project. Earlier that month, an ambitious young executive, Olivier Granier, was fired for violations of the station's pledged neutrality. Bonnell explained his decision, as if scripted by the *Loi Audiovisuel*: 'As a company, the Studio does not produce itself; it accompanies other producers' films. This policy thus does not permit a high-level executive to spend all of his time guiding production crews. In a certain way, for real professionals, it can be very frustrating'. (Boudier and Villeret 1994a).

In a broader sense, the upheavals at the Studio were symptoms of the disorienting financing process that emerged in the space of a few years. What remained constant between the two systems was that large numbers of films were still being made in France with little to no regard for the market for them. Bonnell did not hide his antagonism:

> One of the many perversities of this system we have here is that there are so many different funding windows, all of them with very different goals. The thing that keeps happening lately is that no sooner is a film is refused by Canal+ that the producers return with, say, the *avance sur recettes* and *Arte* in hand, demanding that we reconsider our initial judgment, usually pressuring us by saying 'it isn't fair for you to stop this film from existing!' (Boudier 1993: 6)

Exasperated, Bonnell began to call (as he had with *Le cinéma exploité* years earlier) for the deregulation of the relationship between film and television. This time, however, his target was not exhibition but production: 'The market should be able to sort out which of our films are for the cinema and which of them are for television', he argued, 'GATT should have inspired us to seriously rethink the *fond du soutien*, where the arbitrary lines between film and television are starting to make our disagreements sound like fights between pastry chefs and bakers about who owns the legal rights to puff pastry' (Boudier 1993: 6). Bonnell's own workplace would soon be rocked by an even bigger scandal related to who his boss would be going forward. For Canal Plus had just been drafted into France's own burgeoning multinational business endeavour – a new consortium of the Générale des Eaux, Havas and Société Générale. Just while his station was reportedly in talks about a merger with the German giant Bertelsman, Rousselet was abruptly removed from his presidency after making derisive comments about the Balladur government's forced merger between France Télécom and Havas. Replaced by Lescure, the original Canal Plus headman was unabashed about blaming the government's neoliberal agenda for his sacking, and his incendiary op ed in *Le Monde* – 'Edouard killed me!'/'Edouard m'a tué!' – remains emblematic as a sort of turning point in the cultural politics of the French audiovisual sector. The aftershock of Rousselet's departure was felt widely. With many mergers imminent, two authors in *Le Film Français* wondered: 'What will this many-headed monster accomplish?' (Boudier 1994: 8).

By the time Bonnell left the Studio in 1996, it was mutating into a far different arrangement. Endowed with a catalogue of over 5,500 films and 6,000 hours of programming from a slew of acquisitions, then united with UGC via its Vivendi parentage, it became 100% the property of Canal Plus and the Vivendi group (Bonnell 2006: 251). It was, all of a sudden, poised to become a force in film production, distribution and exhibition. The former champion of 'independent' cinema was now aiming to become a European major. Just a few years after Lescure replaced Rousselet at Canal Plus, the 'many-headed monster' that owned the company would get another name. Buying up audiovisual rights with gusto under an ambitious executive named Jean-Marie Messier, Vivendi announced that it would merge with Universal Studios, and the company was renamed Vivendi-Universal in 1999. A year later, Studio Canal Plus officially changed its name to 'StudioCanal,' marking the occasion of its first entrance on the stock exchange (Bonnell 2006: 252). As Brahim Chioua, studio director at the time, recalled, 'There certainly was a drive to try to better respond to the needs of the public. [. . .] instead of sprinkling our obligations into a lot of different places, we can concentrate on bigger projects, from time to time even initiating them' (Paris 2002: 94). Just fifteen years after it first appeared, Canal Plus (via its production wing StudioCanal) had become a vertically integrated giant in its own right.

THE 'DEATH' OF THE CULTURAL EXCEPTION

In the context of global trade, Lang's conjoined ethos of state-based economic support and alternative aesthetic practices is often referred to as either the French exception (*l'exception française*) or the 'cultural exception' (*l'exception culturelle*). These two terms invoke a history of state subvention of culture and the arts dating as far back as Louis XIV (Regourd), but both expressions began to enter more common parlance in the late 1980s – and specifically with the publication of *La République du centre: La fin de l'exception française?* (1988), a collection of essays about the centrist politics of 1986–88, when politicians on both the left and right responded to Mitterrand's failed nation-alisation efforts with a bipartisan move to deregulate the economy (Collard 2004: 19). The modifier 'French' was first replaced with 'cultural' in cinema-specific speeches by Lang, and decisively entered mainstream vernacular during the 1993 GATT negotiations in Uruguay, when a European bargaining team fresh off the Maastricht Treaty (1992) argued that EU audiovisual media should be left out of North American free trade agreements. As star-studded protests took place on the Champs Elysées, Lang, Mitterrand, and European Commission president Jacques Delors all articulated a similar slogan – that audiovisual media 'should not be considered a piece of merchandise like any other'. Today, this negative assertion remains the closest approximation of a definition for the term (Regourd 2002: 3–4).

The publicised diplomatic drama around GATT also tends to mask ways in which the French film industry had already been positioning itself to profit from a new state of affairs. In a memorable turn of events in 2001, Messier fired Lescure after publicly proclaiming his support for the Canal Plus headman just a few weeks prior. Although his ensuing proclamation to the press – 'the *exception culturelle* is dead' – became his most infamously tone-deaf moment, it was not without some basis in reality. Under Lescure's uncertain leadership, StudioCanal had been haemorrhaging funds for several years, primarily as a result of its investment in Carolco, which went bankrupt shortly thereafter. Moreover, as Christopher Meir has shown, leadership upheaval has been the norm at StudioCanal ever since, as its Vivendi ownership vacillates between national and international investment priorities, and as different leadership teams respond to these mandates from varying angles (Meir 2019). In a recent memoir, Lescure himself admitted that Messier's main error was the use of a rhetoric that his colleagues were not quite ready to hear (Lescure 2014). This was understandable for an executive turned towards larger goals – many of them in line with France's ambitions to organise a more competitive regional alternative to Hollywood.

Moreover, while the GATT 'victory' of 1993 may have seemed like a turning point, its rhetoric proved of limited use for organising European countries around a common cause. Throughout the 1990s, the widespread adoption of liberal trade practices across Europe made France increasingly isolated in attempts to establish common interventionist methods in practice across borders. Beginning in 1989, the *Télévision sans frontières* initiative proposed a system of basic quotas and programming windows (*chronologie des médias*) for television that could be common to all EU members. A few years later, it was obvious that enforcement would be difficult, and the first version of the accord in 1995 included a 'whenever possible' clause – allowing countries to opt out of the rules as they saw fit (Bonnell 2006: 322). The *Plan Média* initiative of 1991 tried to extend the principles of the *fond du soutien* to a EU level by establishing a pool of funding for European projects and adding an automatic aid for pan-European distribution. This was followed by *Média II* (1995) and *Média Plus* (2001, extended in 2004) and supplemented by *Eurimages*, a support fund established by the European Council for cinematic projects that did not otherwise qualify for support in the thirty participant nations (Bonnell 2006: 312–319). Although this programme has provided substantial aid to production, distribution and exhibition across the continent, it has largely failed to establish a cohesive response to the hegemony of North American media – likely due to the specificities of how each nation-state responds to accelerating market competition. For Bonnell, this means that a true European 'space' for the exchange of audiovisual media 'does not exist' – at least not so far (Bonnell 2006: 325).

These misadventures in uniting Europe against Hollywood contributed to the official abandonment of the 'exceptional' vocabulary in the late 1990s. At a UNESCO meeting in November 1999, Minister of Culture, Catherine Trautman, announced that the 'cultural exception' would soon be replaced by a new term – 'cultural diversity.' (Regourd 2002: 111). Since 2005, the new term has been UNESCO's official rubric for supporting European cinema as a state-based initiative. In theory, the term expresses a united support for regulated audiovisual markets and the promotion of alternatives to Hollywood; in practice, it brims with the contradictory rhetorical positions of different countries and interest groups. As Buchsbaum puts it, '"cultural diversity" is now "the most ubiquitous if elusive term, permeating virtually all of the diagnostics of the European film industry"'. (Buchsbaum 2005: 47). As we have seen, the term's malleability is also a consequence of several decades of French-led efforts to establish a combined new sort of audiovisual policy – anchored in the renewed economic strength of French-based companies. In other words, for the case of French cinema at least, the more flexible language of 'cultural diversity' arrived just in time to appease the vastly different strategic dispositions that had emerged within the domestic industry itself.

A New Oligopoly

At least since Bredin, the French industry had been seeking to establish a new base of vertically integrated companies capable of better holding the line against global Hollywood. By the late 1990s, that vision had been at least partially realised, as all sectors of the French industry were concentrated around a new (or at least re-invigorated and re-specialised) centre of commercial film production. The members of that group operate from different strategic vantage points on the market, and by recent count number three more-or-less vertically integrated production companies (Pathé, Gaumont, EuropaCorp); production affiliates of private television stations (StudioCanal, TF1 Productions;

THE LANG PLAN AND ITS AFTERMATH

M6 Films) and the largest telecom company (Studio Orange); an integrated exhibition-distribution chain (UGC); and a distributor of independent films (Wild Bunch). Other entities, including the production affiliates of the generalist channels (France 2; France 3; France 5) and smaller production companies orbit around this loose grouping, usually unable to mount films – or at least visible ones – without substantial help from the centre.

Critics of the current system argue that the vertical integration Bredin and Lang permitted to flourish thirty years prior has now run its course, giving way to a de facto horizontal integration among the powerful companies wrought by their reforms. The maturation of the SOFICAs offers a case in point. Since its inception in 1985, the tax shelter system has been revised repeatedly in order to make it more than a glorified loophole for big groups. Meanwhile, films that get mass distribution to cinemas increasingly follow the money. That is, the best distributed films are also those backed by the finite number of production companies that can now benefit not once but twice from the current state of affairs – first, from their positions of economic power, and second, from their ability to access the same system of support as smaller companies (Lévy-Hartmann & Lalévée 2007). Though the largest affiliates still do not legally have the right to produce films alone, they continue to oversee large swaths of pre-financing for their affiliated television stations. In the case of Pathé-Gaumont, leverage derives from a vertically-integrated business plan and the increased strength of a 2003 merging of catalogues, which gave it the audiovisual rights to hundreds of the most programmed national films on French television. For Luc Besson's EuropaCorp, it comes from a 'go-it-alone' business model, aimed at gaining complete financial sovereignty by negotiating European distribution deals directly with American companies.[6] In any case, all of the members of this unofficial group are ideally placed to both incur profits from film distribution and to reap the benefits of the system's innumerable incentives wherever possible.

The sorts of economic concentration that Socialist reformers lost sleep over in the early 1980s pales in comparison to what has occurred little more than a decade later. Much as Bonnell had predicted in his initial response to the Prost Report, the competition from large multinational corporations (and the lure of joining them) has been too much to resist. In a 1994 declaration to the trade press, then-BLIC president, Alain Terzian, illustrated the mainstreaming of a new sort of conviction, calling for an immediate agenda to promote 'triangular concentration' so that French companies could establish a presence abroad, much like Canal Plus and Arte already had. In so doing, he rejected out-of-hand the objections he anticipated from some of his colleagues, who he claimed did not want to face the practical necessity of 'better adapt[ing] our product to a market that is now made up mostly of 15 to 25 year-olds' ('BLIC' 1994: 4). Indeed, in the years since GATT, the two other branches of the French film industry have standardised their practices to fit a model more closely resembling Hollywood's methods – a process that requires more prints, shorter runs, saturation booking and a much larger overall investment in marketing and advertising.

Along with the ballooning of production budgets, the rapid rise of French multiplexes is perhaps the most conspicuous recent change on the French film-going landscape. France was the last country in Western Europe to build even one of the American-style venues that had spread across the US in the 1980s. However, by the mid-1990s, French-owned multiplexes – often referred to derisively by intellectuals as the cinematic equivalent of McDonald's or 'aircraft carriers' for blockbusters –outnumbered those in all neighbouring countries (Hayes 2005: 17). By 1992, Lang's Pathé-Gaumont decision looked like a mere slap on the wrist, and the two venerable majors were once again in cahoots. Their exchange of a handful of cinemas (Pathé swapped a portion of its presence in Paris for a share of Gaumont's provincial coverage) was a prelude to the first two Pathé multiplexes, opened in 1993 (Delon 2000: 10). Similar establishments cropped up across the country over the next decade, climbing from a total number of 22 in 1995 to a whopping 140 in 2005 (Bonnell 2006: 137). In the process, nearly 1,000 screens and almost 150,000 seats were added to the national market and big theatres dramatically increased their share of attendance figures from 11% of attendance in 1995 to 50% just ten years later (Bonnell 2006:137).

Historically speaking, distribution has long been the weakest link in the French protectorate. By the early 1970s, the American majors had agreed to form two combined sources for distributing their films, which the largest French firms in turn had to depend on to stay afloat (Bonnell 2006: 105). The attendance crisis of the mid 1980s once again marked a turning point, as the top French independent distributors of the period also began to disappear, a trend that was punctuated by the 1987 buyout of L'Agence méditerranée de location des films (AMLF) by Chargeurs, which had recently bought Pathé's chain of cinemas and would thereby change the firm's name to Pathé Distribution (Bonnell 2006: 105). In the 1990s, the rapid appearance of multiscreen venues paved the way for even more consolidation, as French companies sought financial backing needed to compete with the American films that were shown there (Bonnell 2006: 105, 243). By 2005, although there were still some 400 authorised distributors in France, over half of them handled only one film per year, and the top ten were responsible for 40% of film releases and 78% of profits (Bonnell 2006: 243). The biggest hits of the last decade – films like Les Ch'tis, Intouchables and Qu'est-ce qu'on a fait au bon dieu? – show the extent to which one title can determine the fortunes the entire market. Behind Boon's Ch'tis, the top ten distributors raked in three quarters of the profits in 2008, with the biggest single winner – Pathé Distribution – garnering 21%

by itself, thanks in large part to the unprecedented run of the *Ch'tis*, but also to three of its other productions – *Astérix aux Jeux Olympiques* (Forrestier and Langmann) and the two-part franchise, *Mesrine* (Richet 2008) (CNC 2009: 101).[7] Hand-in-hand with all of this, of course, came an explosion of promotional, marketing and print costs – all necessities for commercial French films hoping to compete. In 2008, the CNC reported that American films, all told, received some 225 million Euros worth of advertising and marketing (compared to 55 million Euros in 1999), whereas their French competitors only got 128 million Euros (compared to 27 million Euros in 1999) (CNC *Bilan* 2009: 101).

From the perspective of the industry's other branches, the blockbuster-friendly strategies employed since GATT have been a mixed bag. Two CNC reports find that, despite their best efforts, French productions are still having a hard time keeping up with the Spielbergs – and in trying to do so, they are actually taking resources away from other films that might help the cause. The Goudineau Report, compiled in 2000, reaffirms the difficult transition that occurred as the industry shifted to distribution techniques that were more in-line with the Hollywood majors. Though the scope of his study was limited to three years, the report's findings sought reasons for why 'there has been no clear link between the number of French films distributed and the overall attendance figure' since 1986 (Goudineau 2000: 6). During the sample period studied, he found that Hollywood films had an advantage of nearly two to one in the first week of film distribution in France (Goudineau 2000: 15). Likewise, those same US films spent an average of 50% of their total budget on marketing and publicity while the typical French film spent only 6%, with even the absolute biggest productions between 8% and 10% (Goudineau 2000: 16). Worst of all, the category with by far the biggest disparity, Goudineau emphasises, is not the biggest titles, but the mid-tier French ones – those that received 100- to 400-print distribution on the first weekend. Yet it was not clear that this increased commitment to larger films was helping to close the gap. Although the majority of films that got high attendance marks in France could be considered 'big budget' projects (over 40 million francs), the inverse was not true. That is, the majority of big budget films during that three-year span did not achieve the one-million-ticket mark (only 27 out of 79 did). Goudineau claims, therefore, that there is no quantifiable correlation between the marketing of big films and their box office success (Goudineau 2000: 23). Instead, he blames the rise of locally produced blockbusters for the conspicuous lack of mid-range genre films, which he claims is the real place where French cinema is losing out (Goudineau 2000: 28). Without rethinking its commitment to big budgets and their marketing, he opines, the industry will be doomed to produce both big and medium-sized films that continue to struggle (Goudineau 2000: 28). In a CNC-commissioned report on the same subject in 2006, Jean-Pierre Leclerc concurs with most of Goudineau's findings, reflecting that French cinema has now decisively entered an era of 'big distribution' where films are given the shortest release windows and consumed in the largest sheer quantity possible (Leclerc 2006: 6). He concludes his study with a familiar, tentative, 'mixed-economy' plea:

> Faced with the sheer extent of these changes, the inclination of many people is to call the entire system of regulations into question and to reform them in their entirety [. . .] Others would prefer to leave the whole thing in the hands of the free market. The view of the present report is, as mentioned, more restrained. (Leclerc 2006: 67)

The Leclerc report's 'restraint' is perhaps its most defining feature (along with its length). Moreover, its inventory of small-scale changes – a 'consideration' of caps on the numbers of films and prints, a 'reflection' on potential changes to the release calendar and the media chronology and a 'possible revision' to the aid system for exhibition, among others – are typical hesitations of a regulatory apparatus that continues to face numerous internal obstacles to true reform.

Like the rise in film production costs, the consequences of the concentration of exhibition and distribution in France remain open for debate. On one hand, as Lang himself had hoped, there is now a more equitable geographical distribution of screens across France. Multiplexes have increased that number by over 1,000 since the early 1990s. Compared with the mid-to-late 1980s, when widespread closings left many small and medium-sized French towns without theatres, it is safe to say that the cinema – and French-made films – are now more widely available. On this view, French-owned multiplex chains play a crucial role in the rejuvenation of attendance levels and, thereby, a welcome expansion of the industrial base in the battle against the pressures of globalisation. But the building of multiplexes and circulation of prints has now accelerated to such a degree that the distance – both economic and cultural – between commercial cinema and art houses has never been greater. While *Art et essai* films now represent some 60% of the films made in France every year, they get only 30% of the distribution and 25% of the attendance (Leclerc 2006: 25). It is not clear how long such disequilibrium can last, especially given the overwrought presence of television, which has caused many critics to call for reform – though not for the same reasons that their predecessors did a decade ago.

New Challenges

In many ways, the reforms of the mid-1980s now look like a first step in a longer transition from a heavily regulated post-WWII television economy to a full-fledged media industry. Lang's overall success at domesticating cable television via Canal Plus has been a main axis of this chapter, but his administration was not as successful with video, which arrived in France shortly after cable, but was initially barred from the national market entirely. Though the government revamped that approach in 1994 by administering a 2% tax on video (and later DVD) sales, the damage had been done, and the movie rental market – by then a boon to the Hollywood majors – never really benefited French companies as it could have. Legislators today often cite this past precedent as a cautionary tale when they speak about how to address the current challenges posed by streaming services and file-sharing websites. Abetted by the market disruption of handheld media over the past decade, new media forms threaten to render the time-tested strategies of Malraux (box office taxes) and Lang (television funding) obsolete. Not surprisingly, considerable current research energy at the CNC and Ministry of Culture focuses on finding ways to update the system's philosophical approach to an expanding audiovisual market where new routes of content circulation continue to evade the oversight of state regulation. It remains to be seen how – and how quickly – the vaunted 'mixed economy' approach behind the 'cultural diversity' of the French system will be able to respond to such a moving target.

One axis of recent debates involves the ongoing clash between online file sharing and intellectual property laws. The first coordinated government response to the new state of affairs occurred under conservative president Nicolas Sarkozy, whose administration established *Haute autorité pour la diffusion et la protection des droits sur internet* (HADOPI) in December 2009. A centralised organisation with some fifty employees dedicated to surveying IP addresses across the Hexagon for illegal downloading activity, the programme featured a widely criticised 'graduated punishment' policy, which used a 'three-strike' method for sanctioning users guilty of illegal file sharing (first an email, then an official letter, and finally a trial with the potential for fines or even temporary loss of internet access). After a Socialist wave election pushed Sarkozy from office in 2012, president-elect François Hollande proposed revisiting the policy and tasked his new Minister of Culture Aurélie Filippetti with finding a more democratic replacement. The new administration drew on the resonance of Lang's tenure by recruiting Lescure to lead a so-called 'Second Act' of the *exception culturelle* for the era of online digital culture. The former head of Canal and his team convened over a year's worth of research, conducting interviews with representatives from across the media industries, from Google Europe to a crowd-sourcing startup KissKissBankBank (now a major player) and from the iconoclastic activist *Parti pirate français* to media scholars Françoise Benhamou and Jean-Pierre Benghozi. In May 2013, the *Mission Lescure* produced a 700-page document, but before the majority of its proposals had been fully discussed, Filippetti and her staff were engulfed in the Hollande administration's larger political failures. She ultimately resigned amidst upheaval in the cabinet in August 2014, leaving the legacy of *Acte 2* to her successors (Leussier). As a result, Lescure's report now seems consigned to enacting cosmetic changes at the most – with HADOPI's administrators simply moving offices and losing their ability to prosecute violators of the 'third strike' policy.

When a disgraced Hollande retired from political life in 2016, the foremost debates about cultural policy had already shifted to other pressing problems. At the time of Lescure's report, the delay between a film's cinema run and its appearance online was mandated at 36 months, putting online providers at the end of the media chronology – like DVD and video – after Canal, the other cable channels and the public TV networks. As the report rightly indicated, the main consequence of this was to make the most recent (hence most desirable) content unavailable in France by legal means online. Canal's grand bargain in 1986, of course, had hinged on the leverage of film release points, with the new pay-per-view channel gaining access to films six months prior to all other channels. Built in to that strategy was a basic philosophical hierarchy between art forms, as Lang's plans placed theatrical distribution ahead of all others and then used consumer demand for other formats to mandate the support of film content made-in-France. Yet while in the past the distinction between cinematic and televisual content was buttressed by the different distribution platforms for the two media, the digital revolution of the 2000s – whereby content circulates in manifold new ways beyond the control of the industry – has made those distinctions increasingly difficult to conceptualise for policymakers. Letting go of the precepts of a system that previously served the industry so well as a stimulant for an entire industry has been slow and difficult.

As this account is written, the growing popularity of long-form television series has emerged as a new frontier for unregulated Anglo-American dominance. HBO is credited with pioneering the 'Original Content' revolution in North American television of the 2000s, a trend that Canal Plus (*Les Revenants*; *Engrenages*) and EuropaCorp (*The Transporter*) moved quickly to imitate, as did concurrent reforms at the CNC, which created a separate revenue stream from the *fond du soutien* to benefit television production. Yet the more recent transformation of online streaming providers into content creators has made serial television and 'binge-watching' the contemporary equivalents of what blockbusters and saturation distribution were in the mid-1980s. The epicentre of these issues of late has been Netflix. Born in 1996 as an online DVD rental-and-delivery service, Reed Hastings's company shifted primarily to streaming in 2008 and began producing its own content in 2013 with the Kevin Spacey political drama *House of Cards*. Given its flexible format and growing market influence, Netflix initially refused to establish operations in France due to the 2% video tax, instead setting up an office in Luxembourg to circumvent the rule via geographic proximity. Filippetti agreed to rescind the tax in 2014, and two years later Netflix introduced its real market gambit – original French-language content in the police procedural *Marseille*, starring Gérard Depardieu and Benoît Magimel. Adding insult to injury, Netflix seemed to mock the entire concept of the media chronology itself when it made two original feature films – *The Meyerowitz Stories* (Baumbauch 2017) and *Okja* (Bong Joon-Ho 2017) – available to streaming simultaneously with their premiere screenings at Cannes (Tiffany 2017). Just a few months later, Amazon Video, Netflix's main US competitor, acquired the rights to stream France 2's popular series *Zone Blanche* in other European countries. Largely in response to these aggressive manoeuvres for the French-language market, the newly elected Macron administration reinstituted the 2% video tax in November 2017. Meanwhile, citing these new dynamics in the industry, the leadership teams at Canal Plus and other channels continue to advocate for a change in their funding obligations for cinema, which they claim both exacerbate their declining profit margins and hamper their ability to address the fluidity of a market now dominated by cable stations and streaming providers who produce their own original content, regardless of screen. Under the guidance of aggressive new CEO Maxim Saada, Canal is reportedly quite likely to buck its financial obligations soon unless they can be realigned to its new agenda of producing original content. Despite an impressive history of adapting to change over the past three decades, it remains to be seen how the resources of French cultural policy will manage to keep pace this time around.

Conclusion

This chapter has sought to demonstrate the political economic origins of a set of ideological fissures that continue to lie beneath the status quo of contemporary French filmmaking. From the beginning, the Lang agenda was tasked with potentially conflicting goals. On one hand, it aimed to equip a national cinema to combat a newly global Hollywood cinema. On the other hand, it aimed to curtail the economic (and hence cultural) power of the very companies it created to lead the charge. One would be remiss not to acknowledge the many successes of this approach. In large part due to the new incentive system provided by adding Canal Plus to the media chronology, French television grew in twenty years from a modest public sector medium to the anchor of a leading European media industry. In many respects, the same basic architecture of Lang's reforms remains today, ensuring the industry's survival, providing funding for its cultural aims, and offering some basic principles for how policymakers might address further challenges.

Most recent accounts agree that the time for reform has arrived once more. Lang's legacy is now cited most often for a combination of good intentions and the 'unintended consequences' (*effets pervers*) that tend to come along with state-based regulations when they are left to flounder in a sea of capitalist expansion. As Susan Hayward suggests in her early review of Lang's mandate, the moral of this lengthy back-story may ultimately be a familiar one about the limits of state regulation in an era of accelerated global flows (Hayward 1993: 391). Yet the founding of Canal Plus and the connections it forged between television and cinema have also had long-lasting positive effects on French film production, supporting independent artisanship while encouraging ambitious commercial productions that compete for local market share. Though the Socialist ambitions of the 1980s arguably ceded ground to the types of concentrated power they most hoped to avoid, the emergence of a new production centre in French cinema has also allowed the industry to thrive during a period when many of its neighbours floundered. Moreover, the reforms of the 1980s set in place many of the concrete political-economic conditions on which current actors in the system depend to ply their trade (Canal Plus; television funding; the media chronology; IFCIC; SOFICAs).

Keeping this longer history in mind, the remaining chapters of this book seek to highlight some of its less quantifiable outcomes in the cultural realm – most notably how knowledge and disagreement about the tensions traced here also have regular impact not only on how films are made, but also on the attitudes that filmmakers and critics adopt about the nature of the challenges they face. Most agree that the policies of the Lang years did find a way to preserve the French film industry through the upheaval brought about by Hollywood blockbuster franchises, but that they also intensified a bifurcated approach to cinema policy that has become increasingly at odds with itself. And amidst all of the political-economic change of the past thirty years, the aesthetic qualities of incipient 'globalised' French forms of cinema have become a persistent concern for French film culture at large. With that in mind, the next chapter outlines how the stylistic features of recent French commercial films have entered political discourse – often becoming a hinge point for debates about the status of contemporary French filmmaking, its cultural role in France, and its mission in the world.

NOTES

1. Presently the BLIC includes *L'Association des Producteurs Independents* (API), the *Féderation Nationale des Cinémas Français* (FNCF), the *Féderation Nationale des Distributeurs de Films* (FNDF), the *Féderation Nationale des Industries Techniques* (Fitcom) and the *Syndicat de l'Edition Vidéo Numérique* (SEVN).
2. France 5 would go bankrupt a few years later and then become part of a joint Franco-German venture called Arte, which continues to this day.
3. These included Crédit Lyonnais, la Caisse de dépots et de consignation, Crédit Agricole, Crédit nationale and OBC.
4. The percentages given after each of the following titles represent how much of the

total reported production budget was reached via the producer's share of the box office profits. In 1989, the Club's releases performed quite poorly: *Jeanne Putain du Roi* – 166,000 for its 100 million francs (9%); *Jean Galmot Aventurier* – 401,000 for its 70 million francs (9%); *Vanille Fraise* –789,000 for its 50 million francs (23%). The next year it was more of the same with *Le Braisier* – 386,000 on 90 million francs (8%) – and *Lacenaire* – 290,000 francs for 60 million francs (7%). And although they did draw substantially more viewers and were more memorable in quality, the final four films to go through the programme also failed to approach a profitable margin when they were released in 1992: *Madame Bovary* (Chabrol) – 1,290,000 viewers from 51 million francs (38%); *Van Gogh* (Pialat) – 1,300,000 viewers from 66 million francs (30%); *Indochine* (Wargnier) – 3,100,000 viewers from 120 million francs (39%); *Dien Bien Phu* (Schoendorffer) – 914,000 viewers from 78 million francs (18%). By comparison, *La Gloire de mon père* drew 6,246,000 on 42 million francs (208%), *Le Château de ma mère* got 4,267,000 viewers (142%) and *Nikita* drew 3,776,000 on 42 million francs (130%). 'Les films poids lourds: succès brillants et 'fours' retentissants.' *Le Film Français* 2499 (24 March 1994) 8.

5. I owe the larger analysis of the connection between these films and GATT to Graeme Hayes and Martin O'Shaughnessy, who make similar comparisons among them in the introduction of their special issues of *French Politics, Culture and Society* (Hayes and O'Shaughnessy 2005: 1–2).

6. For an account of the rise of EuropaCorp in this context, see Chapter 4 of this book.

7. The results were as follows: Pathé Distribution 21%, Paramount Pictures France 10%, Warner Brothers France 7.1%, Buena Vista International 7.0%, Twentieth Century Fox 6.5%, StudioCanal 5.8%, Sony Pictures Releasing 5.6%, Metropolitan Film Export 4.8%, SND 4.1%, EuropaCorp 2.9%. (CNC 2009: 101).

Works Cited

Alexandre, Olivier (2015), *La règle de l'exception: Ecologie du cinéma français*, Paris: Editions EHESS.

Benhamou, Françoise (2017), *L'économie de la culture*, Paris: La Découverte.

'BLIC: les six propositions d'Alain Terzian (1994), *Le Film Français*, 2488: 1 July, p. 4.

Bonnell, René (1978), *Le cinéma exploité*, Paris: Editions de Seuil.

Bonnell, René (2006), *La vingt-cinquième image: Une économie de l'audiovisuel*, 4th edn, Paris: Gallimard.

Boudier, Christian (1993), 'Canal+ veut d'autres 'Germinal', *Le Film Français*, 2484: 10 December, pp. 6–7.

Boudier, Christian (1994), 'Que les gros budgets lèvent le doigt', *Le Film Français*, 2499: 25 March, pp. 8–9.

Boudier, Christian and Carole Villeret (1994a), 'Canal Blues', *Le Film Français*, 2494: 18 February, pp. 4–5.

Boudier, Christian and Carole Villeret (1994a),'Pierre Lescure: Pas de star-system au Studio Canal+', *Le Film Français*, 2494: 18 February, p. 6.

Buchsbaum, Jonathan (2005), 'After GATT: Has the Revival of French Cinema Ended?' *French Politics, Culture & Society*, 23:3, pp. 34–54.

Buchsbaum, Jonathan (2016), *Exception Taken: How France has Defied Hollywood's New World Order*, New York: Columbia University Press.

Bredin, Jean-Denis (1981), *Mission de réflexion et de propositions sur le cinéma*, Paris: Ministère de la Culture.

'Le club des investisseurs en question' (1991), *Le Film Français*, 2344: 5 April, p. 1.

CNC (1996–2016), *Bilans*, Paris: Editions CNC.

Collard, Sue (2004), 'The French Exception: Rise and Fall of a Saint-Simonian Discourse', in Emmanuel Godin and Tony Shafer (eds), *The End of the French Exception? Decline and Revival of the 'French Model'*, London: Palgrave Macmillan, pp. 17–35.

Creton, Laurent (2003), *Cinéma et (in)dependence. Une économie politique*, Paris: Théorème, Presses Sorbonne Nouvelle.

Creton, Laurent (ed.) (2000), *Le cinéma et l'argent*, Paris: Nathan.

Creton, Laurent (ed.) (2002), *Le cinéma à l'épreuve du système televisuel*, Paris: CNRS Editions.

Creton, Laurent (2016), *L'Economie du cinéma*, 2nd edn, Paris: Armand Colin.

Creton, Laurent (2008), *Cinéma et stratégies. Economie des interdépendences*, Paris: Théorème, Presses Sorbonne Nouvelle.

Creton, Laurent, Yannick Dehée, Sébastien Layerle and Caroline Moine (2011), *Les producteurs. Enjeux créatifs, enjeux financiers*, Paris: Broché.

Dacbert, Sophie (1989), 'Le "club des investisseurs" parie sur huit films français', *Le Film Français*, 2270: 3 November, p. 6.

Danan, Martine (1996), 'From a "Prenational" to a "Postnational" French Cinema', *Film History*, 8:1, pp. 72–84.

Danan, Martine (2000), 'French Cinema in the Era of Media Capitalism', *Media, Culture and Society* 22: pp. 355–364.

Danan, Martine (2006), 'National and Post-National French Cinema', in Paul Willeman and Valentina Vitali (eds), *Theorising Transnational Cinema*, New York: Routledge.

Delon, François (2000), *Les Multiplexes*, Paris: CNC.

'Entretien Pascal Rogard' (1989), *Le Film Français*, 2237: 17 March, p. 4.

Douguet, G. (1988), 'La FNCF insiste: 200 millions pour passer l'été', *Le Film Français*, 2198: 17 June, pp. 10–11.

Eling, Kim (1999), *The Politics of Cultural Policy in France*, London: Palgrave Macmillan.

Fansten, Michel (2003), 'La place de la télévision dans l'économie de la production et son evolution actuelle', in Jean Cluzel (ed.), *La télévision a-t-elle tué le cinéma?*, Paris: Cahiers des sciences morales et politiques.

Farchy, Joëlle (1999), *La fin de l'exception culturelle française?*, Paris: CNRS Editions.

Farchy, Joëlle (2011), *Et pourtant ils tournent . . .: Economie du cinéma à l'ère numérique*, Paris: INAthèque.

Farchy, Joëlle and Dominique Sagot-Duvauroux (1994), *Economie des politiques culturelles*, Paris: Broché.

Forbes, Jill (1995), 'The Rise of Audiovisual Culture', in Jill Forbes and Michael Kelly (eds), *French Cultural Studies: An Introduction*, Oxford: Oxford University Press, pp. 232–246.

Forest, Claude (2001), *Economies contemporaines du cinéma en Europe. L'improbable industrie*, Paris: CNRS Editions.

Forest, Claude (2013), *L'industrie du cinéma en France. De la pellicule au pixel*, Paris: La Documentation Française.

Frodon, Jean-Michel (1995), *L'âge moderne du cinéma français: De la nouvelle vague à nos jours*, Paris: Flammarion.

'GATT Reaction: Interview: Jacques Toubon' (1993), *Le Film Français, 2477*: 22 October, p. 6.

Gimello-Mesplomb, Frédéric (2000), 'Enjeux et stratégies de la politique de soutien au cinéma français: un exemple: la nouvelle vague: économie politique et symboles'. Thèse de doctorat, Université Toulouse le Mirail.

Goudineau, Daniel (2000), *La distribution des films en salles*, Rapport au ministère de la culture et de la communication, Paris: CNRS Editions.

Grantham, Bill (2000), *Some Big Bourgeois Brothel: Contexts for France's Culture Wars with Hollywood*, Luton: University of Luton Press.

Hayes, Graeme (2005), 'Regulating Multiplexes: The French State between Corporatism and Globalization', *French Politics, Culture and Society*, 23:3, pp. 14–33.

Hayes, Graeme and Martin O'Shaugnessy (2005), 'Introduction', *French Politics, Culture and Society,* 23:3, pp. 1–13.

Hayward, Susan (1993), 'State, Culture and the Cinema: Jack Lang's strategies for the French film industry, 1981–1993' *Screen*, 34:4, pp. 380–391.

Heyman, Danièle and Jean-Michel Frodon (1991), 'Entretien avec Jack Lang', *Le Monde*, 4 March 1991.

Jäckel, Anne (2003), *European Film Industries*, London: British Film Institute.

Leclerc, Jean-Pierre (2006), *Mission de médiation et d'expertise relative aux conditions actuelles des sorties des films en salle*, Paris: CNC Editions.

Lévy-Hartmann, Florence and Fabrice Lalevée (2007), *Le soutien à la production cinématographique française: à qui profite l'exception culturelle?* Paris: Groupe d'Economie Mondiale.

Lescure, Pierre (2014), *In the baba*, Paris: Grasset.

Looseley, David (1995), *The Politics of Fun: Cultural Policy and Debate in Contemporary France*, Oxford: Berg Publishers.

Maurin, François (1982), 'Un plan pour le cinéma français: Jack Lang l'a presenté hier', *Humanité*, 2 April, p. 2.

Meir, Christopher (2019), *Mass Producing European Cinema: Studio Canal and its Works*, London: Bloomsbury.

Oddos, Christian (1989), 'Une approche positive quant aux principes, mais quelques lacunes et des insuffisances inquiétantes', *Le Film Français*, 2237, 17 March, pp. 4–5.

Paris, Thomas (2002), 'Studio européen d'une major américano-européenne: Studio Canal: Entretien avec Brahim Chioua', in Guy Hennebelle (ed.), *Quelle diversité face à Hollywood?*, Paris: Corlet-Télérama.

'Le pouvoir médiatique de *La reine Margot*' (1994). *Le Film Français*, 2499: 25 March.

'Production: Les humeurs de Gérard Ducaux-Rupp' (1986), *Le Film Français*, 2121:16 December, p. 6.

Regourd, Serge (2002)., *L'exception culturelle*, Paris: Presses universitaires de France.

Rival, Pierre (1990), 'Création du Studio Canal Plus', *Le Film Français,* 2328: 14 December, pp. 1–2.

Rival, Pierre (1988), 'René Bonnell: Les équilibres dans le secteur ne sont pas sains' *Le Film Français*, 2216: 21 October, p. 65.

Rival, Pierre (1987a), 'Jean-Jack Queyrenne plaide pour une mobilisation générale', *Le Film Français*, 2127: 6 February, p. 4.

Rival, Pierre (1987b), 'Chaine privées: Les producteurs s'inquiètent des risques de concentration verticale', *Le Film Français*, 2127: 6 February, p. 4.

Rival, Pierre (1989), 'Le débat de l'ACECCA sur le Rapport Prost', *Le Film Français*, 2243: 28 April, p. 3.

Rogard, Pascal (1989), 'La concurrence à deux vitesses' *Le Film Français* 2237, 17 March, p. 4.

Simsi, Simon (2001), *Ciné-Passions*, Paris: CNC Editions Dixit.

Tiffany, Kaitlyn (2017), 'Netflix booed at Okja's Cannes premiere', *The Verge*, 19 May, <https://www.theverge.com/2017/5/19/15662542/netflix-cannes-film-festival-booed-okja-premiere> (last accessed 31 January 2019).

'Une enquete du CERCA sur le marketing cinématographique aux Etats-Unis' (1988), *Le Film Français*, 2198: 17 June, pp. 8–9.

Vanderschelden, Isabelle (2009), 'The *Cinéma du milieu* is falling down: New challenges for Auteur and Independent French Cinema in the 2000s', *Studies in French Cinema*, 9:3, pp. 243–257.

Vanderschelden, Isabelle (2016), 'The French Film Industry: Funding, Policies, Debates', *Studies in French Cinema*, 16:2, pp. 89–94.

Weitzman, Marc (1991), 'Dix années de cinéma: le bilang', *7 à Paris*, 8–14 May, p. 25.

2. POPULAR FRENCH CINEMA AND 'CULTURAL DIVERSITY'

Beginning with the 'Lang Plan' of the 1980s and early 1990s, the French film industry embraced a number of new strategies for surviving the challenges of multi-media capitalism. Among the most visible of these has been the arrival of a new class of big-budget, French-made movies – more conspicuously linked to television funding and more openly primed to compete for popular audiences than ever before. While their full back-story rarely gets enumerated as it did in Chapter 1, these films are the inveterate offspring of more than three decades of fraught, strategic compromise. Small wonder, then, that the most successful or ambitious among them often serve as fodder for the resurgence of fiery philosophical differences in the industry and critical establishment.[1] To distant observers in North America and elsewhere, skirmishes of this sort – which range from detail-oriented critiques of film policy to sweeping broadsides on the 'state' of French film aesthetics – often get written off as the petty infighting of an industry rather too fond of 'eating its own'. What this dismissive gesture willfully misses, however, is that these discussions, if endowed with historical perspective, betray the revealing structural animosities in a media industry comprised of passionate individuals who continue to actively search for new forms of cultural relevance in a multi-platform, multi-media era. In order to grant a shade more historical and critical nuance to these matters, this chapter proposes a way to map some of their more common rhetorical forms.

Recent debates about the artistic quality and commercial ambitions of popular French filmmaking often hinge on a term that is widely bandied about, yet varies widely in its concrete invocations: 'cultural diversity'. Methodologically speaking, unearthing the underpinnings of collective language usage in this way has been the goal of a growing body of research on French cinema, as well as more broadly among humanities disciplines focused on the cultural effects of globalisation.[2] This chapter contributes to that literature by outlining three prominent 'framing' tendencies that circulate in recent discussions of the 'cultural diversity' of contemporary French cinema, especially in regards to its most commercialised practices. For heuristic purposes, we term these three formations the *exceptionalist*, *professionalist* and *pragmatist* discourses.

While a tri-partite model like this one does not exhaust the expressive possibilities on such a topic, it captures a set of collective concerns and oppositional energies that cut across the discursive practices and interpretive frameworks that together comprise the dynamics of a vibrant contemporary culture industry. By bringing disparate voices together – from bureaucrats to filmmakers, producers to critics, and executives to film scholars – we can better weigh how the very act of interpreting the most popular or ambitiously commercial French-produced films also echoes much longer-term conflicts about the implications of 'global' film style, some of them dating back to post-war French debates about 'quality cinema' (Burnett 2013: 140–148). In a socio-critical sense, outlining these three distinct takes on a common term helps to show how the features of the films themselves tend to become specimens of a deep-seated ambivalence about the ongoing challenges of cultural globalisation.

Exceptionalism

The first framing of Jack Lang's legacy for French cinema takes an exceptionalist slant, retaining vocabulary that the Socialist minister used in his fiery early speeches rallying the French industry against free trade proposals during the General Agreement on Tariffs and Trade (GATT) negotiations of 1993. As a rhetorical tendency, exceptionalist rhetoric places a premium on finding ways to extend the separation between 'art' and 'industry' formally overseen by the Centre National de la Cinématographie (CNC) since World War II, and preserving a place for cinematic creativity free of concerns about appealing to the audience. These views thus marry a broadly Keynesian view of how to manage global economic flows with a wariness about the aesthetic costs of making concessions to market demand. On this view, 'big' French commercial interests of any sort already have the cards stacked against them, as they are deemed to represent – sometimes explicitly, and almost always implicitly – the imminent decline of artistic quality that accompanies the rise of commercial ambitions.

This argument is, of course, not new. In many ways, it has become the dominant intellectual refrain used in current debates about the fortunes of mainstream French filmmaking, and remains fundamental to conceptions of what makes it distinct from Hollywood commercialism. Echoes of Truffaut's famous treatise 'A Certain Tendency of the French Cinema' ring loudly here, as do numerous academic accounts of French film history, pitting narratives of individual artistic agency (the auteur) against a rising tide of corporatism. In his synoptic view of French cinema at the end of the Giscard years, for instance, historian Jean-Pierre Jeancolas telegraphs the fundamentals of this stance, analysing how mainstream filmmaking of the late 1970s has become a place 'where savage commercial ambitions coexist with a few enclaves for true artists to survive' (Jeancolas 1979: 290). Though Jeancolas could not quite have foreseen what was to come in the following decade, his words anticipate an argument that has taken on far more urgency of late. More recent polemics continue in this vein by calling into question the 'objective' statistical measures of the CNC and other government agencies, which they hold are compromised by the drive for a more universalist sort of cinema since Lang. Many commentators warn that the success of just one film (*Les Visiteurs* in 1993 or *Intouchables* in 2011) skews the box office record so much that the market share of French cinema becomes misleadingly hopeful – and naively grateful to the success of a very few. Moreover, the overall concentration of resources around event films – whether from Hollywood, France or elsewhere – renders older methods of measuring French success obsolete, since neutral statistical accounts about market share and audience totals often serve to veil a behind-the-scenes fragility of both the industry and of French film culture. Even worse, there is now, more than ever, a blatant disconnect between the CNC's own methods of categorising 'French' films (according to a point system of content, thematic characteristics and personnel) and the national sources of financing. Hence the concern in 2004 about Jean-Pierre Jeunet's *A Very Long Engagement*, produced by a 'Trojan horse' company for Warner Brothers that directed most of the film's ancillary profits back to Hollywood coffers. In a multimedia era with daily monetary exchanges, traditional statistical measures are unable to paint a clear picture – much less to stop – the dimensions of a corporate invasion of French cinema's culture from the inside.

For critics predisposed to think in this manner, the vagueness of a term like 'cultural diversity' serves as a thinly veiled excuse to ignore the ongoing subterfuge of late capitalism. When the term was introduced, it was met with immediate objections along these lines. Senator Jack Ralité, a prominent voice in the GATT demonstrations, likened the new term to 'Esperanto', even drawing parallels with the consensual rhetoric of French sympathisers of the Vichy government (Regourd 2004: 74). Producer René Cleitman argued that 'there [had] been a thievery of terms' for 'while the "exception" contradicts and works against the principle of a generalisation of liberal commerce, "diversity" is actually a very "correct" concept, very in style, and to be frank ... very liberal' (Regourd 2004: 73–74). The most prestigious critical enclaves in France tend to share this view as well. In a show of general support for the backlash to 'cultural diversity', Jean-Michel Frodon – then head cinema editor for *Le Monde* – convened a group of journalists, directors, and producers into a group called *L'Exception* with the express intent of preserving the philosophical bent of the older language of exceptionalism and of producing publications that could thoughtfully counter the dominant, consensual discourses propounded by UNESCO and the CNC (Frodon 2004; Frodon 2006). Over the past decade, this view has only gathered strength as an organised counter-movement within the industry. It gained a united purpose in 2007 on the occasion of director Pascale Ferran's acceptance speech for her film *Lady Chatterley* at the César Awards. Citing Truffaut, Ferran's speech takes aim at the intractability of a production sector that she sees as increasingly split between two types of film and two types of filmmaking communities:

> In tracking poor films toward artistic goals and rich films toward entertainment, reinforcing the barriers between the two categories, and making it next to impossible for a director to cross between them, the current system betrays our heritage and the practices of our greatest directors, whose goal was to never dissociate their personal views from a cinema that could reach the most people possible. In doing so, the system is destroying the taste of its audience – and that's a shame, since for decades the French public was considered the most curious, principled and cinéphilic audience in the world. Here as elsewhere, the violent strength of the world economy has managed to dumb down our popular taste and then to pit us against one another. It won't be long now. The two systems of solidarity – between the films themselves and those who make them – are about to be torn completely apart. So maybe its time that we wake up! Maybe its time for us to say that our individual love for cinema, strong as it may be, is not quite strong enough. Maybe it is time to fight again, very methodically, to reform our broken system and to restore healthy conditions of production and distribution for a sort of cinema that, in showing the world in all its complexity, can be both artistically creative and spectacular at the same time. (Ferran 2007: 191)

Inspired by these words, a group of thirteen insiders from different sectors of the industry joined Ferran in her cause, meeting regularly at the CNC to study the sources of the new 'crisis' (the opening pages of the report are explicit that the group was not funded by the CNC, although they also express their gratitude to CNC president Véronique Cayla for providing them with space and sandwiches for meetings). About a year later, in May of 2008, they published their findings in a volume that was circulated widely in the industry (Ferran *et al.* 2008). During the months before its release, the 'Ferran Report' gained high profile endorsements from hundreds of figures in the industry (Claude Chabrol blithely called it a great chance to 'wake up the idiots' / '*détourner les cons*').

Although its generic status remains a bit ambiguous (the media called it both a 'manifesto' and a 'report') the Ferran group's contribution makes clear the main concerns of their 'Club of Thirteen' – to diagnose the multiple reasons behind the 'declining quality' of French filmmaking. Rejecting the more targeted, statistical methods of typical CNC reports on individual sectors and issues, the sprawling 200-page document was released to some fanfare in April 2008, and its collective perspective leant a new sense of urgency to longstanding worries about the consequences of budget polarisation. As the authors put it, the goal of the document is to conduct a rare 'transversal study' (*étude transversale*) that could combine first-person testimony from a diversity of different sectors of the industry in order to 'better understand the current difficulties in producing and showing a certain type of French cinema, and to offer suggestions for how to address the problems' (Ferran *et al.* 2008: 2). Most notable of these, from their perspective, is the disappearance of the 'mid-range productions' (*films du milieu*) that used to provide the most reliable artistic and economic category for French cinema at home and abroad.

In straightforward, passionate prose, the authors describe a myriad of behind-the-scenes changes in the practice of French filmmaking. The initial functioning of the Lang reforms, they claim, is compromised by the escalating power of television stations and the growth of multiplexes in France. In terms of production, they argue most pointedly about the *Fond du soutien*, which they claim has become an accomplice to the market-driven agenda of television groups, whose sole aim is to fill prime-time programming slots and fill video distribution coffers. Although they continue their contractual obligations to the film industry, these groups have no lasting regard for the cultural quality of their output – and indeed cannot, given their commercial obligations. The result, the authors argue, is a production gap between 'haves' (defined as over €10 million) and 'have-nots' (under €1 million). The former, comfortably supported by television pre-financing and co-production deals, receives wide distribution and fosters a new focus on highly paid stars and visual effects. The latter, forced to cobble modest funds from multiple government funding coffers, stands little chance of public visibility. Meanwhile, the ground in between these two categories – the 'middle range' of productions they deem so historically noteworthy in France – suffers most. Their framing of these matters emerges best when quoted at some length:

> Although it should correct the laws of the market, to keep control of it most harmful artistic effects, the current system of regulation does little but accompany it. The redistributive mechanisms – most notably

the *fond de soutiens automatiques* for production and distribution – no longer play the regulatory role they once did. Rather, they have been progressively led astray from their primary objectives, and now dispro-portionately favor the profit of television chains and large conglomerates. Their main function today is to accentuate the rapidly growing concen-tration of resources and power. We must level the playing field. We must rethink everything. (Ferran *et al.* 2008: 8)

The report follows up these sweeping claims by offering four lengthy individual chapters, each analysing one branch of the industry in depth (production, distribution, exhibition and export).

For the Club of Thirteen, the main culprit in the 'crisis' of French film content is the 'commercial logic' of television. While they rehearse common arguments in many CNC reports of the previous decade, the authors also provide a somewhat rarer qualitative account of how new commercial ele-ments result in a culture of standardisation [*formatage*]:

In a certain sense, the stations don't even need to intervene at the level of the screenplay in order to determine their content. [. . .] These require-ments are actually connected to the [the television] medium itself. A film has to be able to draw the largest audience possible in prime time, preferably as part of a pre-planned, predictable broadcast schedule. It has to be mainstream, to avoid subject matter that is too personal, and to be entertaining. It should therefore be a simple story, usually a linear one, easy to 'pitch' and, if possible, feature a happy ending. (Ferran *et al.* 2008: 35)

Meanwhile, the bipolarisation of budgets ensures that those filmmakers who choose to resist against these unspoken norms find themselves restricted to a smaller range of budgets (from €500,000 to €2 million). From this perspec-tive, the push for bigger films becomes an unintended symptom of a protec-tive system that no longer effectively deters the effects of multimedia capital (Ferran *et al.* 2008: 4–8).

A television-influenced push for more dependable returns makes it more diffi-cult for individual agents (producers, directors and actors) to navigate between a lower class of art cinema and an upper class of 'televisual' films that enjoy guaranteed nourishment from the system. Unlike in years past, when directors like Truffaut and Malle could move comfortably between art and popular cinema, the industry culture itself revolves increasingly around two economic poles with very little communication between them. Moreover, the biggest films – whatever their characteristics – are little more than the instruments of a powerful, commercial class (big television companies and exhibitioin chains) that is increasingly in control of both the funding of French productions and their aesthetic qualities. In their conclusion, the authors suggest twelve specific revisions for the subsidy system aimed at correcting the savage inequalities that they see resulting from the 'unnatural' and 'forced marriage' that Lang and his cohort established between television and the cinema some two decades years earlier. The majority of these suggestions focus on the *Fond du soutien* – to give it additional tax revenue from 5.5% of other multiplex profits (concessions, pre-screening advertisements, etc.); to make co-producers (mostly television affiliates) explicitly ineligible for profit from the *avance sur recettes*; to roll back the favouring of 'big films' first implemented by the second Lang Plan in 1989 (Ferran *et al.* 2008: 38).

Though they are quick to indicate where the problems lie, the Club of Thirteen is less clear about where an improved quality of French filmmaking will come from. Their condemnation of the funding system and its standardisation of film content is quite thorough, but the authors stop short of castigating the entire industry. Rather, they acknowledge that the system still has room for creative inspiration at all ends of the spectrum. However, for small films, reaching an audience involves miraculous luck since they are 'excluded from the system throughout the entire process' of production and distribution. Meanwhile, the larger ones still have a chance to obtain authentic creative heights – a 'true liberty of tone and spirit' – when the 'artistic standards of the actor, producer and director' are given preference, as they are in Jean Dujardin's collaboration with producer Eric Altmayer and director Michel Haznavicius on the *OSS 117* films or in Jamel Debbouze's work with producer Jean Brehat and director Rachid Bouchareb on *Indigènes* (2008) (Ferran *et al.* 2008: 38). Moreover, they also admit that certain individual directors have succeeded in circumventing the system, producing their films in a personal manner that runs against the grain of the larger shift towards corporatism.

As internal exceptions to the argument mount within the report's examples, one might begin to question the connections between the Club of Thirteen's political-economic analyses and their larger claims about aesthetic standardisation. Despite their demonstration of the systemic weaknesses in the funding patterns of French cinema, it remains less clear how more regulation of television stations might solve these problems. For critics of the report, the core of the issue lies in the evasive definition of the 'middle-range film' (*film du milieu*) which associates 'liberated' aesthetic approaches with a nostalgic view of a budget category rather than looking at the reality of how films are made. Frodon actually makes this point trenchantly in a response in *Cahiers du cinéma*, charging that the term was 'less a concept than a utopia in the guise of a critical term' (Frodon 2008). Moreover, as Buchsbaum points out, there was nothing particularly novel about their point-of-view, which had already been spelled out – albeit in a more piecemeal fashion – in

CNC research documents and trade press articles over the previous decade (Buchsbaum 2016: 183–185).

While the proposals of the Club of Thirteen pose difficult questions about exactly how they will be operationalised, there seems no question about the significance of the arguments advanced by Ferran and her colleagues. A 'bottom-up' call-to-arms for French film artisans, the report gives collective, qualitative clout to a type of polemic long relegated to CNC reports, scathing opinion editorials, and debates in hallways. Cast in this light, it is likely to remain a signal document for charting a certain view of the widespread localised effects of globalisation on a national culture industry. By pinpointing the ways in which France's 'cultural exception' to free market philosophies now often serves as an accomplice to the larger trends of the French market economy, the Ferran report thus outlines the first major current slant on how France's ascendant, business culture of efficiency militates against its cinema's traditional strength of creativity – the localised solidarity between Franco-European artisans of many different sorts.

Aesthetic Exceptionalism

In recent years, backhanded references to the aesthetics of mainstream French cinema have become a corollary to exceptionalist arguments about the decay of French film financing – and of most calls for reform. In these accounts, the main antagonist is no longer Hollywood cinema, but rather a 'global cinema' (*cinéma-monde*) or what Frodon terms the 'program' (*le programme*) (Frodon 1999: 692), which he defines as 'the dominant state of representation as it becomes more and more unified and powerful' (Daly 2005), and of which Anglo-American films unfortunately remain the dominant de facto representative. Turning other national markets to its cause while using its neo-liberal marketing tentacles and feel-good 'politically correct' messages, this is a view of globalised cinema as a nefarious, imperialist force – massaging conformity into communities that otherwise contain far greater potential for specificity and creativity. From this vantage point, controversies like the one around *A Very Long Engagement* in 2004 point not only to the essential manipulability of global film economics, but to the potential paradoxes of trying to develop anything like a rational system for measuring cultural value. Indeed, in the eyes of many such advocates, the very quest for a more marketable, 'universalist' type of product bears with it incalculable risks for the cause of a meaningful cultural politics. Therefore, any useful programme for 'cultural diversity' should concern itself with supporting the weakest and most susceptible arteries of artistic research. In aesthetic terms, these are those 'independent' projects that offer a demonstrably different approach to filmmaking than mainstream productions – whether from Hollywood, France or elsewhere.

In academic terms, the critical cause of what we might call 'aesthetic exceptionalism' follows the argument modelled by essays like John Hill's often cited response to Andrew Higson's 'Concepts of National Cinema', which reclaims the term 'national cinema' as a political choice that preserves certain types of alternative, artisanal practices (Hill 1992). Such a view recoils on principle from engaging in the value of economic considerations and questions of popular culture, which it views as too subjected to the dominant (and thereby abusive) tendency of the global market. As Dudley Andrew puts it, 'from the standpoint of economics, there is one national cinema – Hollywood – and the rest of the world is its nation' (Andrew 1995: 54). The proper rejoinder for academic film scholars, for Andrew at least, would be one that emphasises aesthetic singularities that otherwise will not be brought out by the caprice of supply and demand. In a passionate call for renewed attention to the artisanal aesthetics and cultural specificities of French cinema, Andrew writes:

> In the shadow of the juggernaut, under the sheer weight of Hollywood's technology and capital, and in the anxiety brought on by brand new systems of distribution, national cinemas must find themselves intimidated; evidently, scholars are intimidated, too, intimidated or excited by the stakes involved, for film journals speak increasingly of markets and blockbusters. Yet from another point of view, socioeconomics tells us first and primarily about the conditions of possibility under which any cinema operates. 'Value' is a term thicker than the ticket stub it has come to be identified with. Value applies to culture, too. (Andrew 1995: 55–56)

Spelled out more thoroughly in his later manifesto called *What Cinema Is!*, Andrew's view tends to shrug its shoulders at commercialised forms of film-making, which from his perspective present at best a co-opted imitation of the 'global' success that the art form reached by 1960, well prior to the digital era, at the crest of the New Wave (Andrew 2010). More strident renditions of a similar argument tend to issue from within French scholarship and criticism, which has recently become a veritable cottage industry for broad-scale attacks on the aesthetics of 'corporatist' filmmaking. Take, for instance, the cynical warnings of Benoît Delmas and Eric Mahé, who opine in their book *Western Mediathèque* that multinational conglomeration will lead to 'a pasteurization of culture, supported by the desire to sanitize our souls'. (Delmas and Mahé 2001: 101). They continue:

> Multinational corporations see culture as a homogenized product that should please the largest number of people possible. The planetary

village, currently shared by AOL-Time Warner, Vivendi-Universal and Murdoch & Co., will soon own a myriad of multiplexes offering a handful of bloated American machines (*Pearl Harbor 2*, *The Mummy Wishes You Well 5*, *Jurassic Park 7*), a bookstore of pre-packaged novels (John Grisham, Danielle Steel, Mary Higgins Clark), paintings that you can buy for 40 Euros – complete with the frame, like at Ikea – and music that you download at your leisure . . . (Delmas and Mahé 2001: 101)

For those who share these sentiments, the quest for a globalised popular French cinema is not only a very bad idea – it may actually portend the imminent end of French film culture itself.

Most recent accounts of the problem are not nearly this hyperbolic, yet some form of this argument continues to circulate as the strongest warrant for upholding the global cause of French art house cinema against the other important changes that have occurred in commercial filmmaking. By this rationale, any focus on the dynamics or strategies behind economic success simply redoubles the agenda of late capitalism and – some might claim – makes scholars into mouthpieces for the mainstream chatter about box office revenues. The standard version of the 'national' that emerges from this perspective, then, counters the sheer economic dominance of commercial films by upholding a tradition of great directors as rebels who practise a more introspective, contingent sensibility, amenable to the cultural traditions and artistic categories of European modernism and high art.

An exceptionalist view of the state of French cinema has also frequently been the ideological dominant in scholarly camps – especially where aesthetic analysis is concerned. If the political-economic focus of the first sections of this book ring hollow to some readers, that is likely because they are wary of the incipient connections between French cinema and big business, aesthetic excess and commercial success – all of which run against the grain of received versions of national film history. In traditional terms, this is also a view that places France and Hollywood on opposite sides of a chasm in transatlantic modes of film production – the former specialising in state-subsidised auteur cinema and the latter in big screen, studio entertainment. What results is an assumption about French cinema's current role as both an indispensible part of and a leading advocate for the best interests of global cinema's oppressed peripheries.

It is rather hard to exaggerate the influence of the exceptionalist discourse on aesthetic accounts of French – and even world – film history. Most obviously, that is because politico-economic approaches to French film history have long been subordinate to just the type of aesthetic evaluation Andrew and so many others proffer – one that abstracts stylistic endeavours from their economic moorings in the name of pursuing a form of 'cultural' value that cannot be reduced to audience or market concerns. As Ginette Vincendeau and Richard Dyer point out, many scholars continue to preach and practise a historiography that valorises – without examining – the consequences of a caricatured difference between national modes of filmmaking (Vincendeau and Dyer 1992: 1–13). In these accounts, French film culture emerges as the leader of a resistance movement based on thoughtful, low-budget differentiation from more 'global' cinematic forms and economic competition. While present in earlier avant-garde movements in France, this philosophy took on a more institutional bent with Malraux's reforms in the late 1950s, and an aesthetic one when a generation of talented young filmmakers followed by cultivating an approach to film technique that molded creative virtues out of modest local resources and their cinéphilic knowledge of popular 'global' forms.

On this view, French cinema is not only one national cinema – it is, in many ways, *the* global counter-example of what cinema should look like in the West. The force of this notion of a French national cinema qua global alternative continues today, and with it a sense of the 'cultural exception', together evoking how a romantic sense of artistic sensibility goes hand-in-hand with a politico-economic counter-strategy, drawing on a tradition of planned irregularity that shuns the hallmarks of contemporary Hollywood's 'commercial aesthetic' that amps up an 'excessively obvious' formal and industrial tradition (Bordwell 1985) with marketing strategies and high-tech special effects that can maximise potential audience identification (Maltby 2003: 5–31) and 'high concept' marketing capability (Wyatt 1994). Over the years, then, a production mentality has become both a durable strategy for product differentiation and a marketable method for cultural (and critical) resistance, aligning art film directors with the protective mission of the CNC and giving them a more loosely-defined aesthetic tradition of their own. This sensibility also became the progenitor for a slew of other national film movements in Europe and elsewhere, as well as within the academic and critical discourses of film studies, resulting in a collective disciplinary bent that looks askance at the types of filmmaking that might qualify as 'French blockbusters', most often brushing them aside as the uncomplicated symptoms of an ongoing march towards homogenisation.

At its core, the aesthetic exceptionalist argument goes something like this: if Hollywood is already winning the battle for mainstream audiences, then the goal of national cinema (and the film scholarship tracking it) should be to uphold a plurality of alternatives to the dominant mode. Given the hegemony of Hollywood products abroad, this slant on recent commercial filmmaking stands on firm ground. Rooted in a *volontariste* political culture and emanating primarily from a small group of academics, auteurist critics and independent producers, it sets its sights on globalised cinema as the apotheosis of a new conventional wisdom in film culture – one it sees as far too commercial and banal. At the same time, while this view of contemporary French film practice often figures itself as disempowered, defending authentic cinematic forms that toil 'in the shadow of a juggernaut', it is frequently a rhetorical position that asserts its own form of intellectual dogma, pushing other views to the periphery with an insistence on privileging perspectives on media forms that it wrests 'free' or 'independent' from market concerns. These judgments then trickle down to even the most passing academic assessments of the films that Andrew pejoratively terms the 'New HollyWave' where 'remakes, cosmopolitan styles, repression of the home language and so on' mitigate the resources of a creativity that must always lie beyond the bottom line (Andrew 1995: 54). Yet in the process of carving out its space, this position also operates from a rather self-determined, narrow vantage point – one that discourages the possibility of serious engagement with a whole class of recent French-made films that embrace (rather than reject) the challenges of adapting to the competitive frontiers that previous generations most feared.

Professionalism

After Jean-Marie Messier's infamous proclamation about the 'death' of the Franco-French cultural exception in 2001, the brazen Vivendi CEO did not back down, instead spelling out his views at more length in an article for *Le Monde*. In an appeal to colleagues fearing cultural standardisation, his words remain one of the more straightforward examples of the second major rhetorical tendency for framing 'cultural diversity':

> This fearmongering about a growing 'homogenization' of our culture, to me, shows a rather superficial understanding of the situation, and it runs contrary to fact. I do understand that behind this fear there are other real concerns: that despite our good intentions, the economic logic of globalization [*la mondialisation*] will end by causing a narrowing of our cultural choice, and that it will transform all of our cultural products into mere commercial ones. There too, I think we need to carefully look at the facts. What narrowing of cultural choices? I would actually say that, quite to the contrary, our choices have never been so broad or so diverse! (. . .) Culture is a living, breathing thing. It needs to have strong economic support and an effective distribution network. It also needs a way to find new talents, and to give them the resources they need to express themselves. But for future generations, I don't think culture will be about American hyper-domination or the French cultural exception, but about how cultural differences are accepted and respected. 'Culture-exception?' No, because an exception excludes, and exclusion is incompatible with culture. 'Cultural domination?' No, because culture

does not like uniformity either, and it cannot really be controlled anyway. (Regourd 2004: 75–76)

Published while Messier was still at the wheel of a sputtering Vivendi-Universal, these words only exacerbated the image problem (and the financial woes) that eventually led to his downfall in France. By the same token, his overall line of argumentation still resonates today – different only to a degree from the prevailing wisdom among many corporate elites in the film industry.

This second major discourse on a globalised cinema from France places ambitious film budgets at the centre of a more aggressive role in the international movie game. So the argument goes, French firms must appeal to larger audiences if they are to have any hope of remaining players on a national (or global) stage. Quite similar to their predecessors, many of whom were behind the second Lang plan, the purveyors of this argument insist that audacious films must play a role in the calculation, the economic standard-bearers for maintaining the global viability of French culture. Not surprisingly, they do not share the exceptionalist alarmism about the role that budget inflation might play in the quality of Gallic production across the board. On its own terms, this second framing of popular French filmmaking often strong-arms its detractors by claiming more 'realistic' grounds for combating Hollywood. For unsympathetic critics, its transparent concern with profit margins makes it complicit with any number of derogatory adjectives – 'imperialist', 'neo-liberalist' or 'corporatist' – associated with long-time Motion Picture Association of America chief Jack Valenti, the Hollywood majors and widely-read American thinkers like Thomas Friedman (Friedman 2000) or Tyler Cowen (Cowen 2004).

Yet it is also useful to wrestle this rhetoric away from both the bombast of figures like Messier and the most neo-liberal of public American commentary on culture. If we do, a word like 'professionalist' also serves to clarify a rhetorical purpose and attitude that pervades today, distinct from but overlapping with more exceptionalist accounts of the same subject matter. And what unifies this second argument as a whole is a vision of filmmaking as a craft that must operate amidst the de facto conditions of a global industry driven by rapid economic innovation and mutating distribution platforms. Many French executives today continue to argue, much as Messier did in 2001, that France can still become a leader in the global film industry, but only if it adopts a sleeker, more contemporary form of business practice that works to keep its audiences (both global and national) in mind. This view of 'cultural diversity' sheds quite another light on globalisation and *cinéma-monde* than does its exceptionalist counterpart, arguing for aggressive French-based initiatives and economic opportunities, and seeking to make films that can attract larger audiences. When we use this lens, Lang's legacy appears rather differently, most notable for the ways in which it set the agenda for a vital new form of entrepreneurial possibility. Likewise, television companies and commercial culture figure not only as vital parts of the industry's continued survival, but as the production centres most adapted to the task of maintaining the cause of 'diversity' itself. The take on film aesthetics, from this perspective, is one that simply aims to maintain the status quo – trumpeting the virtues of films when they do succeed, and using market share figures as the main indicator for their success or failure.

Not surprisingly, the liberalised cultural approach of the Sarkozy administration fomented more support for this line of argument. A strong advocate for deregulating the audiovisual market and a friend of TF1 since his time as Chirac's finance minister, candidate Sarkozy was viewed as an ally of cable and satellite television and a supporter of new technologies. One of the four main authors of the Club of Thirteen, prominent exporter François Yon, even claimed that the timing and 'transversal' nature of the Ferran report were specifically aimed to appeal to the administration's penchant for efficiently run programmes (Yon 2008). Rhetoric notwithstanding, these hopes proved unrealistic given the wide gulf between the Club of Thirteen and the views of the administration, which got clear-throated advocacy in the 2008 Perrot-Leclerc report to the Ministry of Culture. Rather than corralling the economic concentration around television companies, the conservative authors suggest that the French system would do well to further adapt its approaches to economic models that can promote greater competition. In so doing, they question the long-held assumptions about the relationship between the size of a company and the quality of its creative output:

> In the film sector, independent or small-sized actors are generally considered the main route to cultural diversity, since concentrated companies are judged less apt to take on innovative or ambitious cultural projects. It would be interesting to actually test this widely held opinion in a quantitative manner since the relation between concentration and uniformity of products is not upheld by economic theory. To the contrary, there is often a positive link between the number and variety of products and the size of an enterprise. (Perrot and Leclerc 2008: 15)

Furthermore, as the authors of the report claim, the health of the industry actually depends on the big, successful films to be the engines of the system, hence calling for a diversity of budgets and market approaches. Citing the success of the comedies *Camping* and *Les Bronzés 3* in the summer of 2006, the authors conclude that 'it would be paradoxical to impose a limitation that would penalize successful films' and that 'it also seems preferable to retain incentives for films that actually produce better box office results' (Perrot and Leclerc 2008: 55).

Largely due to the intervening financial crisis in 2008, the Sarkozy government neglected to institute any major changes for audiovisual policy. However, by suggesting that the debate be re-focused on statistical modelling and empirical analysis, the Perrot-Leclerc report highlights the resilience of a new (if measured) French antipathy for exceptionalist arguments like those pronounced by the Club of Thirteen, which fly on the assumption that preserving an economic 'space' for artistic inspiration is directly tied to a fragmented production sector littered with small firms. By the same token, the view I term as a 'professionalist' account of commercial French film-making also turns a blind eye to the majority of other recent, market-based accounts of the topic, which offer another view entirely. Rather than blaming the corrosive cultural force of television funding for the problems with film quality, many other economic accounts interrogate the complicated interface between global flows of commerce and the current 'mixed-economy' system, asking anew whether the current industrial practices actually work to promote the interests of a 'diversity'. The majority of these accounts cite the same disequilibria between *Art et essai* and blockbuster films as do Ferran and her colleagues, but also adopt the view that the real problem is a redistributive system that unintentionally discourages its own firms from seeking to promote different types of products. In perhaps the largest extant body of recent work on the topic, Laurent Creton argues consistently that French cinema should seek new strategic avenues for resisting Hollywood – and that the current system no longer works as it should. One of the concepts Creton sees as most destructive to the French cause is its unexamined adherence to an ideology of 'independence'– which he sees as a shifting term with waning practical application in an era of media conglomeration (Creton 1997). At the same time, Creton tempers his economic views with concerns quite similar to his counterparts in aesthetic camps, warning readers about the implications of embracing what he and other French scholars call the style of a *cinéma-monde* ('global cinema'). Noted political economist Patrick Messerlin argues in a similar vein that the crop of recent Hollywood inspired blockbusters from France are the results of systemic dysfunction in the French model of film funding:

> By nature, protection induces domestic producers to take the place of foreign producers, and it protects some domestic producers to the detriment of others. Films do not escape these two laws. French filmmakers, protected from American movies, have tried to produce films that are 'clones' of American movies – in particular after the 1989 Plan Lang [. . .] focusing on films with 'large' budgets (large in the French definition meaning budgets roughly equivalent to the average size of the advertising budget alone of American movies with 'large' budgets). In sum, public

> funding incentivizes 'Americanized' new French talents and erodes the 'French difference' at a stronger and faster pace. (Messerlin 2001: 329)

On this view, Messerlin argues, most current blockbusters made in France stand scant chance of making back their investments unless they ferret out specific market niches either at home or abroad. The result is two main trends that attract investment – big budget films that imitate Hollywood and big budget films that focus on attracting a maximum audience in France and, occasionally, Europe. In either case, Messerlin argues, these strategies are the result of misguided practices that result not from the pressure of a corporatist invasion from abroad, but from overwrought dependence on a system of subvention that effectively pays for its risk-taking in advance – hence discouraging genuine risk-taking. The problem is hence not the 'commercial logic' of television funding per se, but rather the profusion of indirect subsidies, which underwrite most French productions prior to their actual contact with the market (Messerlin 2001: 329).

Although they share some of the exceptionalist antipathy for the current redistributive system, these more market-driven economic accounts differ in the types of solutions they propose. Short an endless supply of money to pump back into the system, analysts like Bonnell hazard that a stronger game plan moving forward will be to further liberalise the industry, allowing for a smoother movement of products between film and other platforms rather than reinforcing the barriers between them. Although the initial result might be a painful plummet in market share, these economists argue that such a move will eventually free up local producers to pursue projects on a more healthy economy of scale – dispensing with the artificially ballooned Langian strategy for good. So while they frequently converge with exceptionalists in their dislike of recent films, professionalists are similarly sparing in their proposals for how to improve it. And, as Buchsbaum notes, most of the extant economic accounts are long on complaints and rather short on practical solutions (Buchsbaum 2005: 42).

In 2008, the Ministry of Culture's immediate response to the Ferran report illustrated the growing chasm between what I am calling here the exceptionalist and professionalist discourses. Days after the Ferran document was made public, the office of the Minister of Culture, Christine Albanel, responded with a polite press release, citing the general 'importance' of the Club's arguments and their findings while implying they would soon be taken into account. The problem with her comments was not their content but their timing – they were published several days before the report had so much as crossed her desk (Yon 2008). In a transparent effort to placate the authors before reading their words, Albanel showed, perhaps better than anything in the actual report, the disconnect between those positioned to dictate policy changes and the most vocal elements of the cinema lobby. The Club's adamant argument for supporting 'independent' and 'creative' producers, of course, is largely out of step with almost all more recent government legislation. While giving lip service to the importance of resistance, Albanel's actions as Minister consistently sided with the Sarkozy agenda of streamlining and productivity, as have those of her successors under François Hollande and Emmanuel Macron. Indeed, given the political agendas that followed his downfall, Messier's incendiary remarks about the 'death' of the cultural exception look rather quaint nearly two decades later.

AESTHETIC PROFESSIONALISM

Unlike exceptionalism, the discourse I am calling professionalist is not a particularly self-reflective one in terms of film aesthetics. As rhetoric most associated with executives and their day-to-day logistics, it does not spend undue time debating conceptions of 'culture' or the political bent of film style. Even so, it might be said that the 'voice' of professionalist imperatives resonates the most powerfully of the three discourses in contemporary film style itself. This occurs most often not through any statement by a filmmaker or critic, but via the hegemonic influence of the powerful new (and newly-powerful old) production companies that have arrived since Lang, and that continue to distribute a more commercialised sort of product across the country's multiplexes. This aesthetic thus might be said to find its most influential 'arguments' in the reality of concrete, physical and geographical change. Since the late 1980s, these include both broad-based alterations to industry infrastructure (the construction of multiplexes, the concentration of distribution and the production of bigger budget films) and the commercialised practices that follow them closely in other media (glossy magazines like *Première* and *Studio*; press coverage of box office results; satellite and cable television 'infotainment' shows focused on star gossip and glamour; an increased number of posters and prints focused on each new release by a major studio). Indeed, the professionalist argument about 'cultural diversity' might be seen to make its aesthetic case simply through its overwrought presence in the everyday status quo of film going in France. On these terms, the content of the films themselves becomes secondary to the sheer force of an invigorated commitment to the marketing of popular forms.

Therefore, although this second discourse plainly does extend to film content, most of its attitude towards a 'cultural diversity' of film aesthetics can be said to derive from a professed deference to the 'market appropriateness' of film products. In this formulation, then, the cause of aesthetic pluralism in French cinema should not be only a defense of underrepresented or endangered techniques, but a measured appreciation of all types of cinematic production – and realism about the range of films necessary for appealing to audiences in

France and beyond. In a recent 'how-to' guide published by Editions Dixit for use by young French producers, Jean-François Camilleri offers a representative claim of this sort:

> We all know that the cinema is a market of supply and demand. If the films are there, the public comes to see them. People only ask to be seduced. If there is nothing to see, they will spend their time doing other things. (Camilleri 2007: 199)

Likely in response to continued attacks by critics, the professionalist argument also asserts a second, related claim rooted in the arguments initially made by the reforms of the second Lang plan – that blockbuster films are a necessary concession to the realistic conditions of economic survival, and hence should be allowed to remain impervious to the aesthetic considerations of auteur cinema. Camilleri continues:

> The 'crises' that are constantly brought up by the most pessimistic folks are often due more to the scheduling of big films [. . .] or to a weak crop of films. But let us not lose sight of the fact that the big investments in exhibition of the past ten years require at least 200 million spectators per year. (Camilleri 2007: 199)

Therefore, constant complaints about the artistic quality of big films are not based on a realistic view of how the system actually works – using profits from the biggest films to recycle funds back to those that need it most. As the Perrot-Leclerc report puts it:

> [. . .] whatever our judgment of [blockbusters], they contribute to the overall balance of the sector, through its intermediary the *compte du soutien*, by giving direct resources to distributors and exhibitors. They therefore support other films and also attract less frequent spectators back to the cinema. (Perrot and Leclerc 2008: 15)

In other words, for this view, French cinema is at its most 'diverse' when it embraces a form of filmmaking that follows new forms of consumption and deregulated commerce. For seething exceptionalists, the 'national' and the 'cultural' in this context become little more than a function of generic branding, one that seeks to keep all audiences (or at the very least French-speaking ones) interested in French-produced content on both big and small screens.

Given the blunt verbiage of many executives and bureaucrats, it may be difficult to find this view sympathetic. There is, however, a way in which a professionalist aesthetic can fashion itself as driven more by economic survival and populist taste than by some philistine disregard for quality. Not coincidentally, when the contours of this view do appear in the press, they are often in response to the most exacting of exceptionalist critiques. A famous recent instance of this point-counterpoint occurred in the spirited 2001 debate about Jean-Pierre Jeunet's *Amélie* (analysed at some length in Chapter 3), but animosities of this type were also predated by a rather mean-spirited exchange between director Patrice Leconte and the critical establishment in late October 1999. As Martin O'Shaugnessy points out, although such spats have been a recurrent theme throughout the history of French cinema, the 'Leconte affair' was signal not just for who was arguing (filmmakers versus critics), but for how it became ensconced within the larger French conversation about the role of aesthetic judgement in the emergence of an 'all-conquering capitalist global order' during the late 1990s (O'Shaugnessy 2001: 65). The conflict began when Leconte, a noted director of crowd-pleasers across mainstream genres, wrote a complaint to his union, the *Association des Réalisateurs et des Producteurs* (ARP) urging colleagues to express their consternation about the critical reception of popular French films. Angered by what he deemed to be unduly harsh reviews, particularly by the most respected left-of-centre critical publications (O'Shaugnessy cites *Le Monde*, *Les Inrockuptibles*, *Libération*, *Télérama* and *Cahiers du cinéma*), he accused the critical establishment of unfair attacks against their own cinema (O'Shaugnessy 2001: 67). Moreover, he claimed that this bias was especially unfortunate given the recent precipitous fall in market share for French films – and since he claimed not to see equal critical contempt for American films. Leconte had actually telegraphed this same position in an interview with *Le Film Français* the previous May: 'Since the New Wave, you are only considered a *cinéaste* if you are an *auteur*. One of my goals in my work has been to disprove that notion. The majority of great American filmmakers were never considered *auteurs*' (Arbaudie 1999: 15) He was particularly critical of Frodon, whom he claimed of course had 'the right not to like a film', but 'not the right to attack its director in the manner he does' nor to express such 'contempt' and 'a deliberate will to do it damage' (Arbaudie 1999: 15). Taken at face value, Leconte's argument about limiting film criticism might verge on the absurd, but his intervention also brought to the surface the tendentious role of aesthetic taste in a developing transnational discourse in French cinema.

To no one's surprise, Leconte's letter spurred a series of barbed editorials and statements by other filmmakers and critics, all expressing their individual takes on how aesthetic evaluation should function in the context of a marketplace increasingly susceptible to the pull of corporatism both from without and within its borders. Frodon was particularly incensed by Leconte's audacity, calling him a 'spoiled brat with a fragile ego' who was pretending that French criticism should have double standards, between an 'auteur cinema that is criticized and a popular cinema that is not' (Pliskin 1999). For the critical establishment, among the most unsavoury of Leconte's rhetorical moves was his invocation of Luc Besson's claim that his films, because of their overt lack of political ambition, should be received as 'innocent objects' rather than as purposeful statements or serious ideological arguments (O'Shaughnessy 2001: 68).

For our purposes here, Besson's 'innocent objects' refrain actually constitutes the closest approximation of a professionalist aesthetic in the 'cultural diversity' debate. For as O'Shaugnessy suggests, the phrase itself actually only really makes sense within the push and pull of rhetoric about how to interpret the look of recent commercialised French film culture. Indeed, a few days after the letter, ARP responded to Leconte's plea by authoring a manifesto entitled 'Nous cinéastes . . .', which was quickly republished in *Libération* with a rather more provocative headline: 'The Angry Directors' ('Les cinéastes en colère'). The prose of the manifesto backed up Leconte's words in more nuanced terms, citing a series of specifically 'unfair' accusations by critics, and arguing for a more globally-conscious ethics of film criticism that could be sensitive to their challenges in a transnational context:

> We must remember that [without our cooperation as a community] the logic of the global economy would probably silence our voices altogether – condemning our directors to unemployment and their works to relative obscurity. A reading of this text as the complaints of a group of spoiled filmmakers against hard-working journalists would probably making it seem like the worst kind of pamphlet. [. . .] But our profession, whether supported by the market or film critics [. . .] is always subject to extreme financial unpredictability. That is why we are angry – not because we want our films to receive unquestioned support, but because we want to ensure that they are debated and discussed with the objectivity, humility and clarity that we all know are the marks of intelligence. Hoping that we have been heard, if even for an instant, we will now go back to making films ('Le manifeste des cinéastes en colère' 1999)

Indeed, because it included the most concerted professionalist call for sympathy in recent years, the fireworks of the 'Leconte affair' remain symptomatic of the larger rifts between so-called 'intellectual' critics and popular directors, which have lately become so regularised that it is not uncommon for certain publications to be barred from major sneak previews and promotional events.[3]

As should be clear, a defining characteristic of what we have termed a professionalist rhetoric of globalised French cinema – and one of its biggest critiques – has to do with aesthetics. Yet although the professionalist repertoire on these films often gains a surly edge from the no-nonsense executives who measure the aesthetic value of films primarily according to economic viability, it has also taken on a more plaintive, reasoned slant, which tends to come from directors and producers. It is also important to remember, though, that none of this language would have been necessary in quite the same way a few decades previously, when France's largest national firms mostly lacked the resources – and socio-economic wherewithal – for mounting their 'own' rendition of blockbuster cinema.

Pragmatism

Somewhere between these first two tendencies we see a nascent third framing, one that takes a pragmatic slant on how to mediate the current situation. This third rhetoric offers an ostensibly more 'even-handed' account of how a healthy French film industry should involve both auteur films and a dynamic, popular genre cinema. It is frequently found, for instance, in the always diplomatic and non-committal language of the CNC and other government bodies, bearing equal influence from a Malrauvian and a Langian rhetoric of cultural policy reform. It therefore seeks a middle ground, arguing for the continued relevance of the 'mixed-economy' policies of Lang, both by tweaking older subsidy programmes and ensuring investment opportunities for new, commercial projects. It does this all the while keeping in mind the vastly different economic and aesthetic goals of other arguments – and, in many cases, preferring incrementalism to sweeping change. In embracing this middle ground, however, pragmatist arguments run the risk of standing equally accused by both ideological extremes. That is, while the most militant of exceptionalists accuse its diplomatic stances of doing too little to curb the onslaught of deregulated capitalism, the most militant of professionalists complain about its inability to capitalise on the most recent innovations and trends in the market.

Of course, the pragmatist discourse gains its power from the de facto functioning of a slew of different interest groups. It embraces, via this mediating, consensual stance, the very ambivalence of French cultural policy as it applies to the problem of supporting audiovisual media in the 21st century. And while the terms of that relativism may be marginalised in both the language of business (which calls it too 'sclerotic') and academic film criticism (which calls it too 'corporatist'), the pragmatist path is arguably the one most endorsed by the regulatory system as a whole – and the central dynamic of what Tim Palmer has called the contemporary French film 'ecosystem' (Palmer 2011: 1–13). The stand-off between 'artistic research' and market competition thus produces a fraught middle ground – one that stands as the most plausible single explanation for why the French film industry currently uses its (comparatively) generous financial resources to produce both more films (approximately 150 fully-financed projects per year) and more big films (approximately 20 or more above €10 million annually) than ever before. The cluster of arguments that I am calling the pragmatist discourse of transnationalism in French cinema thus dovetails quite closely with most of the recent institutional attempts to preside over a mixed-economy approach to film financing that has become, in recent years, increasingly split between exceptionalist and professionalist points of view.

What emerges here is a holistic view of 'cultural diversity'– one that affirms both the new corporatist prospects of the industry and its legacy of support for artisanal independence. With these two perspectives tugging in quite opposite directions, the CNC and other government bodies often find themselves in the rather tumultuous concessions inherent to a 'mixed-economy' system. Annual publications, for instance, often present just this sort of compromise, suggesting that the most effective path for the industry might lie in a middle ground – one that encapsulates both versions of the 'diversity' argument. Minister of Culture Catherine Trautmann's speech that first introduced 'cultural diversity' to UNESCO in 2001 offers a case in point:

> [cultural diversity] is not a semantic slippage hiding some occult reality, nor is it an *a fortiori* abandonment of [the cultural exception]. Put simply, the two notions are not on the same plane. 'Cultural diversity' refers explicitly to the goal of our negotiations. The 'cultural exception,' on the other hand, refers to the juridical means, in my eyes non-negotiable, of attaining that goal of cultural diversity. [...] This is a new, positive notion, which expresses a will to preserve all cultures of the world, and not only our own culture, against the risk of uniformity. It is no doubt not a perfect term, but it has the merit of escaping the expression of an 'exception,' which, by itself, is only a means and not an end. (Trautmann 1999: 73)

Trautmann mediates here between two viewpoints. On one hand, she implies, this new direction aims to move beyond manichaean views of the conflict between the 'global' and the 'national.' On the other, she clearly aims to assuage those listeners who still believe in some 'occult reality' of global imperialism that threatens French culture. She references this view only to mark her rhetorical distance, suggesting it has been debilitating to pan-European initiatives, and seeking a flexible agenda that embraces logistical differences between European attitudes about how to address capitalism.

Perhaps the most consistent voice in this regard throughout the period in question has been the late Toscan, who time and again proclaimed his prevailing wisdom to the trade press and to international forums throughout the 1980s and 1990s (before his tragic death in 2003). It is a strategy that continues to be true of French cinema's path today – one that extols a 'two tier' cinema as the best possible solution to the problem of maintaining a culture industry in an era of global flows. As Toscan put it in a 1994 interview with *Le Film Français*:

> I am actually for the *cinéma à deux vitesses*. Mind you, that doesn't mean I'm for a completely separate double sector where public-financed products are out of luck and where the market is run by the big groups who can keep pace. [. . .] No, we need to protect this unique blend that we have here in France. Sure, there are some slight changes we can make – probably to be more efficient and less narcissistic. But above all what we need is to protect the specificity of our approach to the problem, which is totally original. (Rival 1995)

No surprise, perhaps, that Toscan became the president of Unifrance one year later in 1995 – and that his views spearheaded the larger goals for publicity and export that the non-profit organisation (founded in 1989) would pursue going forward.

AESTHETIC PRAGMATISM

In critical and scholarly camps, we can also see the emergence of a similar third perspective. This approach advocates a type of research that considers not what French cinema *should* be but what it *can* be, given the changing circumstances of Hollywood's domination and the shifting dynamics of the global audiovisual economy. While the CNC's ongoing promotion of both auteur films and commercial cinema comes close to this type of position, it rarely accompanies that view with an aesthetic argument. In academic circles in France, this position is still a minority one, usually lost between the militant views of the exceptionalist camp and economic analyses that suspend aesthetic judgements. What this third discourse does, then, is to ask the questions differently – from a perspective cognisant of economic challenges but also open to the ways in which different types of filmmaking can contribute to the vitality of an industry.

The most concerted academic statement on this third framing comes from a collected volume edited by sociologist Thomas Paris and entitled *Quelle Diversité Face à Hollywood? (What Diversity Against Hollywood?)*. Bringing together voices from across media and scholarship, Paris proposes a revised philosophical approach to the strategic problems faced by the industry. He spells out his stance at some length in the introduction:

> [. . .] our only ideological viewpoint is pragmatism. It means letting go of a manichean discourse and approaching the question analytically. That

is, in the current relations between Hollywood and other cinemas, what is the situation, what are the problems, and what can be done to remedy them? The problem is actually simple: there is a real demand for films that don't always have the chance to be made. From this perspective, it isn't a question of denouncing the behavior of certain agents in the process, but to start with the idea that this is not a question of good and evil, and to accept the idea that all strategies can be legitimate. (Paris 2002: 24)

Even for a pragmatic approach, commercialised aesthetics remain a difficult topic to broach directly. By far the most well-trodden academic route for highlighting the stylistic contributions of popular French cinema today continues to re-route questions of its overt market goals back through an auteur-based mode of analysis. By pitting the agency of individual visionaries and great artists against a rising tide of business culture in France, this approach provides a convenient ideological escape hatch for academics, for while it duly acknowledges the contributions of new aesthetic trends borrowed from advertising and television, it also allows critics to address the 'post-modern' or 'late capitalist' tendencies in French filmmaking without necessarily condoning their corporate influences.

In the critical literature around French cinema, the most common point of reference for the emergence of such arguments is the so-called *cinéma du look* of the 1980s. Although the term was initially intended as a pejorative way to describe the advertising influences on three emergent filmmakers (Besson, Jean-Jacques Beineix and Léos Carax), it is now most commonly cited in the literature in terms of the effective (and quite necessary) backlash to that argument – a move that still retains many of the essential responses to a purely exceptionalist aesthetic argument about French cinema more generally. While many critics assailed the 'BBC boys' for their rapid cutting and fascination with the 'beautiful image', they were later embraced as 'post-modern' by such luminaries as Pauline Kael and (most famously) Fredric Jameson in his case for Beineix's *Diva* as a post-modernist film (Jameson 1982; Jameson 1992). However, the basic lines of this counter-argument were modelled earlier on by French critic Raphael Bassan, whose defense of Besson, Beineix and Carax as 'neo-baroque' filmmakers (Bassan 1989) anticipates many of the arguments later levied by Vincendeau and Dyer (Vincendeau and Dyer 1992). In an approach later expanded in different ways by Laurent Jullier (Jullier 1997) and Marie-Thérèse Journot (Journot 2005), Bassan's article offers a rare, spirited defense of directors frequently dismissed for their blatant 'aestheticisation' of the image. Rejecting this approach as oversimplified, he instead argues that the three directors in question should be appreciated for their ability to engage in an aesthetics of pastiche and self-parody, hence using strategies that broadly call into question the increased commercialism of French image culture taking place more generally around them.

Many recent scholarly publications take to heart the pleas of Vincendeau and Dyer about the need for engagement with popular trends, arguing for an even-handed approach to French film production that treats all cinematic objects as worthy of study. The most prolific of these arrive from a growing cadre of Anglophone historians – many based in the UK or otherwise affiliated with the journal *Studies in French Cinema*, founded in 1999 by Susan Hayward. Clearly influenced by the methodologies propagated Raymond Williams, Stuart Hall and others from the Birmingham School of Cultural Studies, the journal frequently takes up the cause of commercial French film-makers rarely touched on by scholarly discourse in France or the US until quite recently. Book-length avatars of this intellectual trend date to the late 1980s and early 1990s. As mentioned in Chapter 2, Hayward's *French National Cinema* broke new ground in the direction of theorising such an approach in general terms, most specifically in her insistence that the 'national' of French cinema should be approached as a bundle of necessarily contradictory and competing discourses – many of them popular ones (Hayward 1993). It is also in this vein that several early monographs on the so-called *look* directors first emerged. In the first book-length treatment of Besson's work, for instance, Hayward argues that the director's significance for the state of the industry lies in the way he has crafted a strain of big budget cinema that competes actively with Hollywood while also retaining intermittent traces of cultural specificity (Hayward 1998). In a similar vein, Phil Powrie's *Jean-Jacques Beineix* suggests that the director's work, while often categorised under the misleading rubric of the *cinéma du look*, actually operates to dismantle many of the fundamental presuppositions of an 'aesthetics of advertising' via an engagement with psychoanalytic approaches (Powrie 2001). In the past few years, a series of other director-based books have continued to take up these issues in intermittent ways, most often addressing them in terms of individual directors (Downing 2004; Higbee 2006; Ezra 2008). Not surprisingly, many of these studies open with a caveat about how their subject matter has thus far been treated only sparingly in the academic literature – likely because of the perception that the films in question are too overtly commercial for serious academic exegesis.

There remain comparatively few accounts of post-Lang trends that attempt to span the changes in corporate and commercial French cinema as a whole. An exception is a 2005 update of Hayward's book, which features a rewritten final chapter by Will Higbee that devotes several pages to what he calls 'spectacular genre films'. Like Hayward before him, Higbee summarises big-budget trends in the industry, citing Besson's *The Fifth Element* as a model for pointing to the strategic, small nuances that mark popular French films with difference even when they work within a transnational idiom (he points to the use of historical settings, French-designer costumes and generic twists on Hollywood conventions). Still, Higbee's consideration of these issues remains brief, and his only real analytical statement is displaced and indirect, as he mentions that many such films remain 'open to accusations of vacuity and surface seduction of the image from high-brow critics', and that, despite occasional, small moments of innovation, the use of a 'US-influenced blockbuster formula' precludes most French culture in the name of making films that are 'equipped to compete with Hollywood in the global market-place' (Higbee 2005: 298–299).

Rather than problematising – or at least acknowledging – the place for other perspectives in a larger debate about the emergence of global forms of film-making in France, most recent research proceeds along these lines, acknowledging the intellectual case against commercial French films without endorsing it or engaging it. Yet one also has to wonder whether traditional modes of auteurism remain the most revealing optic for discussing the particularities of the films in question. Simply reporting that such films have been 'open to accusations by highbrow critics' is to tacitly allow such claims to carry the day. And so, while recent English-language criticism has made numerous inroads towards an often neglected body of films, it also sidesteps some of the most pressing issues they raise – namely, whether or not the ideological critiques that caused their initial oversight continue to have merit across the board. Another route, less explored, might be to find a language that can account for the plurality of ways in which the French film industry and, ultimately, French films themselves, negotiate competing discourses about the 'global' and the 'national'. It is challenging to find models for this approach that do not fall back on auteurism as a methodological cover for the questionable motivations behind commercial forms of entertainment.

One notable exception to these trends is a series of essays by Martine Danan on the the emergence of a 'post-national' French cinema (Danan 1996; Danan 2000; Danan 2002; Danan 2006). To categorise recent French attempts to compete directly with Hollywood, she proposes that the French film industry might now be thought of as promoting two distinctly different modes of filmmaking – one 'national' and one 'post-national'. The latter, she argues, works explicitly against the aesthetic and cultural differentiation that usually characterise the former:

> Above all, by focusing on excess spectacle, the 'postnational' mode of production erases most of the distinctive elements which have tradition-ally helped to define the (maybe) imaginary coherence of a national cinema against other cinematographic traditions or against Hollywood at a given point in time: for example, an explicit or implicit world view, the construction of national character or subjectivity, certain narrative discourses and modes of address, or intertextual references. Instead, these 'New Holly-Wave' films attempt to downplay their 'Frenchness' as they depart from Hollywood production only through the presence

of iconic French elements or the choice of subject matter. (Danan 2006: 177)

After establishing her two master categories, Danan claims that they are both part of an important dynamic in contemporary French cinema, wherein the 'homogenization of cultural representation fostered by postnational cinema and more generally by global mass culture becomes part of a complex dialectic between national identity and globalization' (Danan 2006: 182). She advances this model further by citing Stuart Hall's influential essay on the cultural logic of globalisation as an uneven process (Hall 1991), one that can only 'rule through other capitals, rule alongside and in partnership with other economic and political elites' and cannot 'attempt to obliterate them' but rather 'operates through them' (Danan 2006: 182). Like other theories of the interaction between the 'global' and the 'local' mentioned in Chapter 1, Danan's work carves a new theoretical place for the diversity of contemporary French cinema as it navigates the competing pressures of a globalised economy. Yet while her engagement with the interactions between aesthetics and cultural politics are welcome, Danan's approach stops short of capturing the sometimes quite complicated textual elements of the films themselves, not to mention the responses to them.

If cultural homogenisation is no more simply 'Hollywoodian' than cultural specificity is 'French', then we need a nuanced model, sensitive to the competing discourses within the purview of French cinema itself. Indeed, if theorising the national dimensions of commercial French cinema is a difficult job these days, this is because it involves dealing simultaneously with Hollywood's considerable influence, with expanding definitions of Europe, and with the imprecise ways in which critical tastes and individual films fit into that equation. In their current form, American films and corporate influence are more than just a brand name or an invasive species; they are both the over-determined 'other' for film industries around the world and a given characteristic of their daily functions; they are a challenge to their economic livelihoods and an influence on their aesthetic approaches. For this reason, there is a generous amount of critical and scholarly precedent against the wisdom of studying films that operate too clearly within a model perceived as 'American' or 'universal'. As the self-anointed leader of the European movement towards protecting national cinemas (the weak) against Hollywood products (the strong), French cinema has often brought with it a form of scholarship and criticism that makes this project particularly difficult – and pressing.

Danan is doubtless correct that the 'global' and 'local' elements of French filmmaking often engage in dialectics, but separating these energies between two dominant 'modes' of filmmaking runs the risk of oversimplifying the textual and cultural effects that often occur in the French production sector, where artisans have been travelling back and forth to Hollywood (and elsewhere) for decades. For when conceived as two broad categories of filmmaking, her 'national' and 'post-national' labels also imply dominant readings for individual texts – profiled as either immersed in French cultural specificity or complicit with its uncertain (therefore ideologically suspect) beyond. Even from a more heuristic point of view, putting films squarely on one side or the other of a dividing line does little for our understanding of the ways that recent films both encounter and exemplify the 'disjunctures' (Appadurai 1990) or the 'complex connectivity' (Tomlinson 1999) brought about by the different economic, political and cultural pressures endemic to how any one national formation responds to the multi-faceted phenomenon we call globalisation. To the contrary, I would argue, as have many film historians, that the very concept of a 'national' cinema brings with it concomitant terms of the 'global' and the 'local', which often surface – or are brought to the surface – by the conflicts between competing taste communities, institutional prerogatives and commercial goals (Choi 2005) and by the film practitioners who 'make do' in that layered ecosystem by producing aesthetic objects that combine 'pop' and 'art' influences in vibrant ways (Palmer 2011: 95–150). Arbitrarily separating films along national / post-national lines therefore also obscures the fascinating ways in which 'art' and 'commerce' actually collide in the cultural machinations of contemporary France and in the particular textual dynamics of its idiosyncratic body of recent films.

CONCLUSION

Since the official adoption of 'cultural diversity' by UNESCO in 2005, the term has held pride of place in government documents and official discussions about French and European cinema's resistance to Hollywood. However, within the emerging literature on the topic, there exist several overlapping interpretations of what the term actually means. In a discursive sense, these might be delineated according to the three mutually interposed frames of reference proposed in this chapter – exceptionalism, professionalism and pragmatism. Each of this trio of viewpoints mobilises a separable view of the politico-economic challenges facing French cinema and often uses that view, in a more elliptical manner, to underwrite how it approaches the aesthetic qualities of cinema itself. In my view, if we are to properly contexualise recent French-produced films as 'transnational', 'global' or 'national', these constitutive interpretive differences need to be acknowledged and engaged in a relational manner that investigates how film production and reception also frequently become enmeshed in preconceptions about their enduring value and legitimacy in the cultural sphere.

France's particular formation of national cinema is a notoriously moving target, composed of competing discourses and rhetorical positions. To root out the varying and contingent senses of 'Frenchness' in cinema is to immerse oneself in the bundle of theoretical insights first initiated for film studies by Higson and others some two decades ago (Higson 1989). At the same time, it is to draw on their subtext in the broader, sociological literature around cultural globalisation, one that posits symbolic practices as an 'uneven' process, rife with the consequences of how capital ebbs and flows in the auspices of formerly-contained 'national' or 'regional' entities. Among the most controversial of these for recent French cinema has been the tantalising possibility – for some a strategic necessity – of making films that might more readily compete with Hollywood and, in some way, help French cinema not only to survive but to profit from the onset of a more concentrated, global media industry.

Though the strategic and thematic roots of these three basic arguments about 'cultural diversity' date back to Lang and well before him, they form a distinct tributary to the conversations about French cinema that took place at the most recent turn of the century. In an industry often caught between competing perspectives on how to best proceed in an era of global flows, this tripartite schema offers options for mapping the complex and often contradictory ways in which individual films and filmmakers have been brought to align with rather different causes of the transnational. In other words, the act of separating these three tendencies, while artificial to some extent, offers a way to navigate the sheer variety of polemics that tend to crop up around French filmmaking in its most commercially successful modes. By proposing them, the present account seeks an alternative to other recent approaches to commercial French filmmaking, many of which figure different strategies of the industry on either side of a bipartisan divide between a 'national' and a 'post-national', 'trans-national' or 'global' cinema, 'art' or 'industry'. Instead, we suggest here that there are (at least) three overlapping interpretive frameworks at play in French cinema today, and that each of them gives way to a different slant on the same set of interlocked dilemmas facing the industry. This approach thus offers a way to view contemporary commercial French films not merely as the homogenised products of a top-down Hexagonal rush towards digital platforms and global capitalism, but rather as the complex productive consequences of a culture industry submerged in the throes of adapting to new paradigms. What remains now is to look at how these matters have actually played out with respect to the films themselves.

NOTES

1. These include public debates about the ethical role of critics in supporting popular cinema ('l'affire Leconte' in 1996); the 'whitewashed' depiction of multi-ethnic Paris in a popular film (the '*Amélie* effect' of 2001); the Hollywood resources behind a transnational production (the Warners France case around *Un long dimanche de fiançailles* in 2004); the disappearance of 'middlebrow' filmmaking (the 'Club des

13' manifesto in 2008); the 'racist' qualities of a popular comedy (the '*Intouchables* effect' of 2011); the elevated compensation of French stars ('L'affaire Maraval' in 2012); and, most recently, the corrosive influence of Netflix on art film exhibition and the Cannes film festival (still raging loudly as this account is written).

2. Since the early 1990s the social sciences have been concerned with finding ways to articulate how global flows affect the realm of cultural production within and without the arbitrary 'container' of the nation state. While approaches like these relate more naturally to the traditions of British cultural studies, they are also gaining momentum in recent French scholarship on the cinema, often in the work of scholars interested in gauging the different ideological influences at play in popular films – whether couched in terms of genre (Moine 2002; Moine 2015; Gimello-Mesplomb 2013), taste (Jullier 1997; Jullier 2012) or more broadly in terms of socio-economics (Gimello-Mesplomb 2006a; Gimello-Mesplomb 2006b; Depétris 2008; Escande-Gacquié 2012; Alexandre 2015). Sociological work often accomplishes this by showing how the contributors to a given field of discourse adopt different 'framing' devices in order to 'make sense' of the effects of globalisation on different levels of culture (see Fiss and Hirsch 2005; Fairclough 2006).

3. Isabelle Vanderschelden notes that Jean-Pierre Jeunet began this practice after the brouhaha around *Amélie*, banning critics of *Les Inrockuptibles* from the major events around the release of *A Very Long Engagement* (Vanderschelden 2007: 85).

WORKS CITED

Alexandre, Olivier (2015), *La règle de l'exception: écologie du cinéma français*, Paris: Editions EHESS.

Appadurai, Arjun (1990), 'Disjuncture and Difference in the Global Cultural Economy', *Theory, Culture & Society*, 7: pp. 295–310.

Arbaudie, Marie-Claude (1999), 'Entretien: Patrice Leconte', *Le Film Français*, 21 April, p. 15.

Andrew, Dudley (1995), 'Appraising French images', *Wide Angle*, 16:3, pp. 53–65.

Andrew, Dudley (2010), *What Cinema Is!*, London: Wiley-Blackwell.

Bassan, Raphael (1989), 'Trois néo-baroques français: Besson, Beineix, Carax.' *Révue du cinema*, 449, pp. 45–53.

Bordwell, David (1985), 'An Excessively Obvious Cinema', in David Bordwell, Kristin Thompson and Janet Staiger (eds), *The Classical Hollywood Cinema: Film Style and Mode of Production to 1960*, London: Routledge, pp. 3–12.

Buchsbaum, Jonathan (2005), 'After GATT: Has the Revival of French Cinema Ended?', *French Politics, Culture & Society*, 23:3, pp. 34–54.

Buchsbaum, Jonathan (2016), *Exception Taken: How France has Defied Hollywood's New World Order*, New York: Columbia University Press.

Burnett, Colin (2013), 'Cinema(s) of Quality' in Tim Palmer and Charlie Michael (eds), *Directory of World Cinema: France*, London: Intellect, pp. 140–148.

Camilleri, Jean-François (2007), *Le marketing du cinéma*, Paris: Editions Dixit.

Choi, Jinhee (2005), 'National Cinema, the Very Idea', in Noël Carroll and Jinhee Choi (eds), *Philosophy of Film and Motion Pictures*, pp. 310–319.

Cowen, Tyler (2004), *Creative Destruction: How Globalization is Changing the World's Cultures*, Princeton: Princeton University Press.

Creton, Laurent (1997), *Cinéma et marché*, Paris: Armand Colin.

Daly, Fergus (2005), 'The Critical Exception: An Interview with Jean-Michel Frodon', *L'Exception: Groupe de réflexion sur le cinéma*, <http://lexception.rezo.net/article36. html> (last accessed 6 February 2019).

Danan, Martine (1996), 'From a "Prenational" to a "Postnational" French cinema', *Film History*, 8:1, pp. 72–84.

Danan, Martine (2000), 'French cinema in the era of media capitalism,' *Media, Culture & Society* 22, London: Sage Publications, pp. 255–364.

Danan, Martine (2006), 'National and Postnational French Cinema', in Paul Willeman and Valentina Vitali (eds), *Theorising National Cinema*, London: British Film Institute, pp. 172–186.

Delmas, Benoît and Eric Mahé (2001), *Western médiathèque ou les mésaventures du cinéma français au pays de Vivendi*, Paris: Mille et une nuits.

Depétris, Frederic (2008), *L'Etat et le cinéma en France*, Paris: L'Harmattan.

Downing, Lisa (2004), *Patrice Leconte*, Manchester: Manchester University Press.

Escande-Gacquié, Pascale (2012), *Pour en finir avec la crise du cinéma français. Le cinéma français crève l'écran*, Paris: Broché.

Ezra, Elizabeth (2008), *Jean-Pierre Jeunet*, Bloomington: Indiana University Press.

Fairclough, Norman (2006), *Language and Globalization*, New York: Routledge.

Ferran, Pascale (2007), 'Texte prononcé par Pascale Ferran aux Césars 2007', Annexe 1, *Le milieu n'est pas un pont mais une faille*, p. 191.

Ferran, Pascale *et al.* (2008), *Le milieu n'est plus un pont mais une faille: Rapport de synthèse*, Paris: Stock

Fiss, Peer C. and Paul C. Hirsch (2005), 'The Discourse of Globalization: Framing and Sensemaking of an Emerging Concept', *American Sociological Review*, 70, London: Sage Publishing, pp. 29–52.

Friedman, Thomas (2000), *The Lexus and the Olive Tree: Understanding Globalization*, New York: Picador.

Frodon, Jean-Michel (1999), *L'âge moderne du cinéma français: De la nouvelle vague à nos jours*, Paris: Broché.

Frodon, Jean-Michel (ed) (2004), *Le cinéma sans la télévision: Le Banquet imaginaire/2*, Paris: Gallimard.

Frodon, Jean-Michel (2006), *Horizon Cinéma: L'art du cinéma dans le monde contemporain à l'âge du numérique et de la mondialisation*, Paris: Cahiers du cinéma.

Frodon, Jean-Michel (2008), 'Situation du cinéma français selon le Club des 13', *Cahiers du cinéma* 633, 1 April 2008.

Gimello-Mesplomb, Frédéric (2013), *L'invention d'un genre: le cinéma fantastique français: Ou les constructions sociales d'un objet de la cinéphilie ordinaire*, Paris: L'Harmattan.

Gimello-Mesplomb, Frédéric (2006a), 'La politique publique du cinéma en Franc', in Philippe Poirrier (ed.), *Art et pouvoir de 1848 à nos jours*, Paris: Canopé-CNDP (Centre national de documentation pédagogique), pp. 60–63.

Gimello-Mesplomb, Frédéric (2006b), 'The economy of 1950s popular French cinem', *Studies in French Cinema*, 6:2, pp. 141–150.

Hall, Stuart (1991), 'The Local and the Global: Globalization and Ethnicity', in Anthony D. King (ed.), *Culture, Globalization and the World System*, Minneapolis: University of Minnesota Press, pp. 19–39.

Hayward, Susan (1993), *French National Cinema*, London: Routledge.

Hayward, Susan (1998), *Luc Besson*, London: British Film Institute.

Higbee, Will (2005), 'Towards a Multiplicity of Voices: The Age of the Postmodern, Part II – 1992–2004', *French National Cinema*, 2nd edn, New York and London: Routledge, pp. 293–328.

Higbee, Will (2006), *Mathieu Kassovitz*, Manchester: Manchester University Press.

Higson, Andrew (1989), 'The Concept of National Cinema', *Screen*, 30:3, pp. 36–47.

Hill, John (1992), 'The Issue of National Cinema and British Film Production', in

Duncan Petrie (ed), *New Questions of British Cinema*, London: British Film Institute, pp. 10–21.

Jameson, Fredric (1982), 'On Diva', *Social Text*, 6, pp. 114–119.

Jameson, Fredric (1992), 'Diva and French Socialism', *Signatures of the Visible*, London: Verso, pp. 75–85

Jeancolas, Jean-Pierre (1979), *Le cinéma des Français: La Vème République 1958–1978*, Paris: Stock.

Journot, Marie-Thérèse (2005), *Le Courant de l'aesthetique publicitaire dans le cinéma français des années 80: La modernité en crise*, Paris: Editions l'Harmattan.

Jullier, Laurent (1997), *L'Ecran post-moderne*, Paris: Harmattan.

Jullier, Laurent (2012), *Qu'est-ce qu'un bon film?*, Paris: Broché.

'Le manifeste des cinéastes en colère. Texte integrale'Nous cinéastes . . .', (1999) *Libération*, 25 November, <http://www.liberation.fr/culture/0101297690-le-manifeste-des-realisateurs-en-colere-texte-integral-nous-cineastes> (last accessed 1 February 2019).

Maltby, Richard (2003), *Hollywood Cinema*, 2nd edn, London: Blackwell.

Messerlin, Patrick (2001), *Measuring the Costs of Protection in Europe: European Commercial Policy in the 2000s*, Washington, DC: Institute for International Economics.

Moine, Raphaëlle (2015), *Les genres du cinéma*, 2nd edn, Paris: Broché.

Moine, Raphaëlle (2002), 'Vieux genres? Nouveaux genres?: Le fabuleux destin de quelques films français', *Cinéma contemporain, état des lieux: actes du colloque de Lyon*, pp. 151–167.

O'Shaugnessy, Martin (2001), 'Republic of Cinema or Fragmented Public Sphere: The Debate Between Film-makers and Critics', in John Marks and Enda McCaffrey, (eds), *French Cultural Debates*, Melbourne: Monash University Press.

Palmer, Tim (2011), *Brutal Intimacy: Analyzing Contemporary French Cinema*, Middletown: Wesleyan University Press.

Paris, Thomas (2002), 'Introduction', *CinémAction: Quelle diversité face à Hollywood?*, Paris: Corlet, pp. 23–26.

Pliskin, Fabrice (1999), 'Les 'Fossoyeurs' se Rebiffent', *Le Nouvel Observateur*, 1828, November 19.

Perrot, Anne and Jean-Pierre Leclerc (2008), *Cinéma et Concurrence*, Paris: Ministre de la culture et de la communication.

Powrie, Phil (2001), *Jean-Jacques Beineix*, Manchester: Manchester University Press.

Regourd, Serge (ed.) (2004), 'De l'exception à la diversité culturelle', *Problèmes politiques et sociaux*, Paris: CNRS Editions.

Rival, Rival (1995), 'Entretien: Daniel Toscan du Plantier', *Le Film Français*, 2556, 28 April.

Tomlinson, John (1999), *Globlization and Culture*, Chicago: University of Chicago Press.

Trautmann, Catherine (1999), 'L'exception culturelle: un moyen juridique d'assurer la diversité culturelle', in Serge Regourd (ed.), *Problèmes politiques et sociaux*, Paris: CNRS Editions, p. 73.

Vanderschelden, Isabelle (2007), *Amélie*, London: I. B. Tauris.

Vincendeau, Ginette and Richard Dyer (eds) (1992), *Popular European Cinema*, London: Routledge.

Yon, François (2008), Exporter at *Films Distribution*, Personal Interview with the author, 18 June.

3. THE DEBATABLE DESTINY OF
AMELIE POULAIN

In recent years, Jean-Pierre Jeunet's name has become almost synonymous with the paradoxes of making French culture in and for a global market. None of his films has been more emblematic of this topic than his fourth feature – and first without former partner Marc Caro – *Le Fabuleux déstin d'Amélie Poulain* (2001). Although *Amélie* (as it is known in English) appears in many ways an intimate project, consistent with its director's personal preoccupations, the film's production history also offers a mixture of marketing practices largely absent from Jeunet's earlier projects. These incorporated an extended pre-planning stage and special effects post-production techniques that marked a shift in the strategies of French filmmaking circa 2001 (Austin 2004). The film's lavish publicity campaign included teasers, test screenings, radio and television spots, posters featuring star Andrey Tatou's smiling face all around Paris, and even the temporary renaming of the Abbesses metro station as 'Station Amélie' (Vanderschelden and Waskewicz 2002: 151–155). A reported budget of just over 11 million Euros (adjusted from the original amount in francs) meant that it was more modest than the year's other ambitious commercial releases but not impoverished by any means. At the same time, almost no one could have predicted the sheer volume of the film's popularity – or the extent of its cultural impact. Jeunet, despite his cachet as the co-director of *Delicatessen* (1991) and *The City of Lost Children* (1995), had been forced to shop the project for months just to get the necessary funding, finally negotiating a last-minute co-production agreement with a German company to foot the production costs

(Vanderschelden 2007: 19). And, when audiences responded en masse during the film's first week, TF1 distribution responded to the demand by pumping 110 more prints into circulation.[1] This was, then, a well-funded film that also had the full extent of its blockbuster-ness 'thrust upon it' (Stringer 2003: 10) first by throngs of adoring French audiences and, later, by foreign ones in unprecedented measure.

Acknowledging the nuances of *Amélie*'s economic upbringing is just the first step in accounting for its relevance to any discussion of French cinema's recent efforts to mount new forms of popular entertainment. In the context of a larger discussion about transnationalism, *Amélie*'s popularity is notable for how it ignited vigorous debates about just what contemporary popular French cinema should look like. The so-called '*Amélie* effect' (Bonnard 2001) – and the ensuing polemics about the film itself – spurred a resurgence of longer-term questions. Could a French movie made to appeal to commercial sensibilities be at once local and universal, national and global, moral and appealing? Indeed, could such a film manage to be both authentically French and a successful blockbuster at the same time? While some of the responses to these questions were of a familiar, kneejerk variety – as if 'too much interest in pretty visuals is somehow, in and of itself, suspicious.' (Austin 2004: 293) – their sheer volume and variety makes the reception of the film an exemplary case study. The film did not seem to fit pre-existent formulas, nor to assert its politics in any obvious way. Most voices actually trumpeted its virtues in this regard, but their consensus on such matters soon induced a backlash from others, who charged Jeunet with mortgaging authentic creativity at the door of his universalist goals. If *Amélie* offered a product that was 'French', they claimed, then this was only in the marketable image of the broad stereotypes of yesteryear. The most polemical of these critiques was Serge Kaganski's furious *Libération* op-ed 'Amélie pas jolie', which actually generated a media event of its own by claiming that Jeunet's vision was not only stereotypical but downright racist or even fascist. This in turn spurred other critics to retort, with equally nationalist anger of a different sort, that 'elitest' critics like Kaganski and his peers were clearly out-of-touch with the tastes of everyday French citizens – with whom French cinema should, they claimed, at long last really be concerned.

In nearly two decades since these weighty initial responses, commentary on *Amélie* has continued to serve as a sort of canvas for the expression of sentiments about the past, present and future of French-language filmmaking in a global context. Most any analysis of the film seems to entail larger pronouncements about cultural politics and their relevance to the state of French cinema as an art and an industry. In a perceptive early analysis of the film's reception in France, Raphaëlle Moine teases out three subtly different ways in which *Amélie* was read as a 'popular' text, ultimately highlighting how some critics (led by Kaganski) reframed its features by moving them 'from a globalised perspective to one of national identity' (Moine 2007: 49). Likewise, in her monograph on the film, Isabelle Vanderschelden cuts across the literature circa 2007, suggesting that the film and the cultural phenomenon it generated 'reposition[ed] the future of French cinema in the debate of globalised cinema versus cultural diversity' (Vanderschelden 2007: 96). An apt summary, this account nevertheless simplifies the highly ambivalent and politicised nature of the term 'cultural diversity' in terms of the history traced in the present book. Indeed, by the time of *Amélie*'s release, there had already been at least two decades of strategic preparation and philosophical discussion about how to cultivate and integrate a new sort of popular-yet-also-national filmmaking into the newfound 'openness' of the post-Mitterrand marketplace. On this view, 'cultural diversity' was never purely opposed to globalised concerns, but rather a catchall term that allowed adequate cover for vigorous and ongoing debates about how French cinema could best adapt to new challenges. In this sense, in retrospect, the success of *Amélie* as an uncharacteristic blockbuster became less about a 'repositioning' of 'cultural diversity' than a moment when strategic and aesthetic fault lines within it could be seen vibrating in the radically different interpretations of a text that audiences shared. Released just a few months after the Messier scandal and barely a year into UNESCO's first official consideration of a new 'diversity' rhetoric, here was a clever movie that seemed to embody both the hopes and contradictions at the core of any commercial drive for a newly-globalised cinema in France.

STYLISTIC DEPARTURES

If Jeunet's recent work has often come to symbolise French cinema's conflicted relationship with the global market, that is because his signature style continues to be at once commercially appealing and nationally identifiable. All of Jeunet's French-language films (the English-language *Alien Resurrection* is the notable exception) fairly pulse with playful references to French iconography and cinematic heritage. At the same time, his work employs a sleek aesthetic that both draws on and appeals to trends in global filmmaking practice, including state-of-the-art special effects and rapid editing techniques more often associated with Hollywood. Throughout his career, these features have inspired some critics to embrace Jeunet as a populist, crossover auteur – and others reject him as an all-too willing instrument of corporate profiteering and 'advertising aesthetics'. Though *Delicatessen* (Jeunet and Caro) did not actually appear on the scene until several years after the debate about the *cinéma du look*, many of the same sorts of misgivings circulated around its glossy, carefully-planned visual style. Chief among critical concerns was Jeunet's perfectionist mise-en-scène, which often places his films at odds with narrative development – making them more about surface-level 'inventions' and gags than dramatic investment.

In early interviews, Jeunet often reports feeling stifled by his country's almost total lack of interest in producing the fantastic genres he was interested in exploring. This complaint is common to many of his generation of popular French directors, most of whom who cut their teeth in the midst of the 1980s shift to a deregulated audiovisual sector. In the shadow of Lang's reforms, these were years punctuated by the rapid rise of television funding, the emergence of new media platforms, the arrival of Hollywood blockbusters, and the uncertain place of cinematic 'Frenchness' within all of these changes. Eager to incorporate the visual sensibilities they saw pouring in from Hollywood and elsewhere, many directors of this period experienced split affiliations – appreciative of the opportunities afforded by French cinematic culture and its institutions, yet frustrated by the limitations of all of those same frameworks.

At the outset, authorial claims about Jeunet's career are further complicated by his nearly two-decade collaboration with Marc Caro. Together, the two young artists would create an aesthetic inspired by the look of graphic novels, invested in a certain macabre, grimy artifice, and inscribed in ahistorical story space, tinged with a retro feel yet difficult to situate in any particular period. They first met at an animation film festival in Annecy in the late 1970s, and Jeunet soon made several short films including *Le Manège* (1980), which starred marionnettes designed by Caro and won a César for best short film. The duo's first official shared endeavour, *Le Bunker de la dernière rafale*, came one year later in 1981, earning further recognition on the festival circuit. Yet another co-directed short – *Foutaises* (1991) – gave Jeunet his first chance to explore character development through the catalogic listing of 'likes' and 'dislikes' that would eventually play a crucial role in the opening scenes of *Amélie*. Festival laurels in hand, Jeunet and Caro began to write screenplays together, hoping to parlay their success into a feature-length production. Unfortunately, they would not get a chance to do so until almost a decade later, as both French studios and the *avance sur recettes* were reticent to invest in their ideas, which sounded much too grandiose to reasonably finance (Parra 1991: 30–32). In the meantime, the duo continued to produce shorter-format projects – festival films, but also music videos and commercials for television. These experiences would allow Jeunet to make connections with many other artists – editor Hervé Schneid, set designer Aline Bonnetto, and actors Dominique Pinon and Rufus, among others. Working with much this same team over the years, he developed a distinctive approach.

Jeunet's feature films continue, in some sense, his earlier fascination with outlandish characters, often established through relationships to the minutiae of prop and set design. Other scholars have enumerated these formal characteristics elsewhere, so a quick review should suffice here. In terms of cinematography, Jeunet's style exhibits a systematic use of wide-angle lenses, close-ups, and vibrant colour schemes, all used to overlay setting and performance with a ludic, almost otherworldly texture that has been likened to 'impressionism' (Bergery 2004: 60). Many shots are taken with the actors less than two feet from the camera, an approach that also permits an exaggerated depth-of-field, ideal for showing environs that are full of ornate objects and meticulous details. *Amélie* cinematographer Bruno Delbonnel remarks that working with Jeunet is almost always a question of showing 'as much as possible in the frame' (Bergery 2004: 60). In most cases, this also leads to the adoption of certain editing patterns and sound techniques, as objects are established and then associated with the characters or situations involved. In *Delicatessen*, for example, each character is given a dwelling space populated by a variety of objects associated with him or her. For the circus clown Louison, it is his circus paraphernalia; for the ill-fated grandmother, a ball of knitting yarn; for the butcher, his gleaming knives.

Amélie can be seen as a continuance of these stylistic preoccupations, but it is also a self-conscious departure from them. A deceptively simple, upbeat story about a young woman who solves her neighbourhood's problems through well-intended guile and creative craftmaking, the film shifts away the macabre atmosphere of Jeunet's prior work. Gone are the sewer-dwelling troglodytes and the childhood nightmares of the Jeunet-Caro films, replaced here with a cast of characters who seem – at least by comparison with their predecessors – somehow more rooted in the particularities of demarked national and cultural space. As Graeme Hayes suggests, one actually has to work rather hard to parse any concerted political or historical message from *Delicatessen*'s Occupation-era iconography – basking as it is within a more general spirit of post-apocalyptic, Goldbergian tomfoolery (Hayes 1999). To the contrary, a big part of what made *Amélie* more popular and controversial than the two earlier Jeunet-Caro collaborations was that it seemed to move that same, idiosyncratic universe several notches closer to saying something more specific about the conditions of contemporary France and its cinema.

Despite a career-long attachment to national iconography, Jeunet has never been one to stir the pot in overtly political ways. Yet what made the politics of *Amélie* a more complicated case than his prior films were the connections it seemed to draw between his signature style and a powerful (if ambiguous) evocation of the present. *Amélie* retains significant echoes of his earlier work with Caro, but Jeunet's first solo project is also more assertively meta-textual than either *Delicatessen* or *The City of Lost Children* (Jeunet and Caro 1998) At the same time, the story that emerges is incrementally more mundane and 'authentic' than the earlier Jeunet-Caro films – folding similar visual and sonic techniques into a more upbeat, but also somehow more colloquial sense of nationality and lived, cultural experience. All in all, these features form a deceptively simple combination that scholars are still working to unpack.

Part of the pleasure, for those who enjoy *Amélie*, is the sense that the film constantly comments on its own materiality. The energetic mix of image qualities, voice-over narrations, special effects, fast-paced editing, handheld camera, and direct camera address suggest a fascination with the surface of images. The opening of the film trades joyously in the small objects and daily rituals that populated the earlier films but rarely overwhelmed them entirely.[2] In this case, Jeunet flaunts his fascination with small elements of mise-en-scène in a bravado opening, first by anchoring the film (and Amélie's birth) in a pre-credit set of happenstance events (a man erasing his late friend's name in an address book; wine glasses fluttering on a windy tablecloth), and then introducing the dramatis personae via their 'likes' and 'dislikes' – a laundry list of details that both draws on an earlier Jeunet-Caro short, *Foutaises* (1991), and references his own 'autobiographical' predilections as well as a cluster of national cinematic and artistic influences, including (in no particular order): a venerable cast of French actors in French-speaking parts; a story invoking the colourful specificities of present-day Montmartre; an accordion-infused soundtrack by Jan Tiersen; and winking nods to the styles and preoccupations of luminaries like Renoir, Prévert, Carné, Clair, Malle, Doisnos, Tati and Truffaut (Andrew 2004).

In this vein, *Amélie*'s image track also embraces an aggressive formal eclecticism that Elisabeth Ezra likens to the post-modern 'play of surface' signalled in the interpretive work of Frederic Jameson and others (Ezra 2008: 101–103). Indeed, Amélie's adventures seem to stem from a rather frank rapport with their own 'fabulous' digital enhancement. The film's French title (*The Fabulous Destiny of Amélie Poulain*) portends these umpteen playful elements, all of which are inserted throughout to interrupt the diegesis or at least to push its overtly constructed nature to the fore. The most gregarious of such moments include: the 'likes and dislikes' sequence (strung along by the rich voice-over narration of André Dussollier which returns only sparsely after introducing the dramatis personae and their lovable ticks); two animated sequences in Amélie's apartment (portraits of birds on the walls speak to each other; a pig-shaped lamp turns itself out at night); and several direct addresses to the camera (Madam Poulain screams 'enough' at the fourth wall when her new baby cries; Amélie professes her love of watching for 'things no one else sees' during a screening of *Jules and Jim*; Amélie and Nico briefly smile at the audience during a handheld sequence near the end). There is also a certain textural variation to the cinematography which, while perhaps hard to label as overt reflexivity, still makes some of the film's more banal moments stick out as constructed. Amélie's travel on the metro to find three 'Brédoteau' names from

died in a car crash last night

Figure 3.1   Amélie (Audrey Tatou) reacts to the news of Princess Diana's death. Screen grab from *Amélie / Le Fabuleux Destin d'Amélie Poulain*. Film: France/ Germany, 2001

the phonebook, for instance, is accompanied with a jiggly, handheld camera and a longshot of the train whizzing by.

A particular sequence of *Amélie* registers as a sort of meeting point between the stylisation of Jeunet's world and the authenticity of a 'real' one. The arrival of this crucial moment is signalled as such by the voice-over narrator, who opines in the present tense about the approach of an event that he claims 'will change Amélie's life forever'. Though this cue sounds, on initial encounter, much like the prescriptive descriptions of the 'likes and dislikes' sequence that open the story, it also blatantly falls short where those others have succeeded – doing little to prepare the viewer for what follows. In the frames in question, Amélie readies herself for bed in her apartment when the offscreen voice of a television news reporter interrupts her solitude, announcing that Princess Diana has been involved in a tragic car accident. Tautou responds to this brief sound bridge in medium-closeup, whirling around with noticeable concern (Figure 3.1). The image track then responds with a point-of-view shot of the screen of her television. Despite this punctual moment, Diana's death – and the unplanned 'reality' implied by the image associated with it – does little to hold Amélie's attention. Rather, she quickly diverts her eyes to the cap of her perfume bottle, which has just fallen from her hand with a loud clunk. Not only that, she also abruptly shuts off the television, literally turning her back on its mediated 'reality' to pursue the cap as it rolls against the baseboard of the bathroom wall, knocking a tile loose to reveal a small hole, and – eventually – the tin box full of knick knacks that will map out her eventual destiny.

Jeunet himself seems to have been aware that Amélie's loving relationship with present day Paris would be the film's eventual selling point, but he could not have anticipated the extent to which that element would dominate later discussions of the film. Many of his statements actually suggest that he himself was, at best, lackadaisical about this aspect of the film's formal texture. In the DVD commentary, for instance, he briefly notes that he chose to insert a few references to Princess Diana so that the viewer could 'understand that the events of the film were meant to take place in something like the present day' (*Amélie* 2001). Likewise, his statements to the press around the film's release suggest only a passing awareness that some people would object to his 'picture postcard' aesthetics as little more than a 'tourist's view' of the real Montmartre ('Interview' 2001). Whatever the director's original intentions, there seems no avoiding the fact that Amélie's disavowal of the Princess Diana footage also shoehorns a great many of the film's thematic and stylistic tensions into one fateful moment. Here it thematises, as Ezra points out, a concise articulation of what will later become a full-fledged meditation on the status of iconicity – one that might be seen to work against, or at least to complicate, claims about the film's dubious politics (Ezra 2008: 109). On a denotative level, the discovery of Brétodeau's time capsule is what launches Amélie's altruistic quest to heal others' afflictions. On a connotative level, however, it is much more than that – as it opens the film's discursive field to a rather more complex exploration of the status of imagery and its variant relationships with reality.

Indeed alongside their overt constructed-ness, the film's events revel in the indexicality of Parisian locations as filmed – something that Jeunet's previous work eschewed in favour of creating almost entirely self-sufficient, imaginary realms. While this element should not be overstated – no one would confuse Amélie's Paris with a form of cinéma vérité – it is also safe to say that the film's two hours of screen time often seem to purposely conflate the 'fabulous' elements of Amélie's world with a multiplicity of more deliberately anchored, 'real' French milieux: Monsieur Brétodeau strolls in the vibrancy of Montmartre's outdoor markets in search of a phone booth; Nico (Mathieu Kassovitz) kneels at the metro Abbesses as the viewfinder dwells on the scratched-but-still-shiny floors; Amélie and Nico chase each other around the spiral walkways of Montmartre in handheld following shots; the closing sequence rejoices in the spontaneity of the new couple's refreshingly ad hoc play on a motor bike.

Ezra catalogues these visual layers in her auteur study of Jeunet, arguing that the film, rather than a simple cooption to the global flows of image seduction, becomes about the process of that seduction itself (Ezra 2008: 102). From this perspective, she suggests, while the film's narrative can be seen as a moral fable about preserving forms of daily, human contact and contingency, the form of the film itself seems to revel in the surface effects of language, images and icons. That reading gains even more clout considered against the other ways critics and scholars have laid claim to the formal characteristics of *Amélie*. The space between the different interpretations has often been rather startling. All the film's fun and play would be well and good, the film's detractors suggest, if it did not also exhibit clear pretentions towards capturing something more authentic and French about that 'reality' that it actually expunges from its image track.

THE INITIAL DEBATE

The film's mixed stylistic agenda was greeted, at first, with what seemed like a chorus of excitement and praise. Initial reviews lauded its optimistic tone, its charismatic lead actress and its catalogue of playful references to French cinematic heritage. As both the film's popularity and the strength of this critical consensus escalated, an equally nationalist backlash brewed. Several critics telegraphed the lines of attack early on, dismissing its celebrated features as bric à brac primarily aimed at popcorn-gorged Americans. While an initial round of fireworks sparked when the film was left off of the Cannes programme, the real controversy exploded with the first thoroughly negative critique – a scathing editorial by *Les Inrockuptibles* editor Serge Kaganski, published in the Left-leaning newspaper *Libération*. After debunking the value of both Jeunet's style and the film's supposedly 'national' aesthetic charms, Kaganski became particularly vitriolic in his conclusion, suggesting that Jeunet's white-washed view of Paris promulgated a form of xenophobia worthy of an advertisement for the Right-wing *Front National*.

The ensuing debate was both old and new. In many ways, it was a reminder of the long-standing fissures between French commercial cinema and film criticism (Vanderschelden 2007: 96). Kaganski's complaints about an 'aestheticised' cinema echoed other canonised conflicts, including the 1950s complaints of proto-New Wavers against the 'Tradition of Quality' and the 1980s criticisms of the *cinéma du look* (later countered by Bassan and then reclaimed by Jameson as exemplary of post-modern pastiche). More proximately, the exchanges about Jeunet's film drew on animosities from the late 1990s spat between Patrice Leconte and the critical establishment (discussed in Chapter 2). A late contribution to that debate by Kaganski actually foreshadowed his eventual attacks on *Amélie*, as he wrote in defense of film criticism as a 'subjective' enterprise that ought to rail with targeted emotion against mainstream media outlets, which themselves are guilty of a 'feigned objectivity that ultimately only serves advertising and marketing' (cited in O'Shaughnessy 2001: 75).

Whatever the significance of earlier parallels, Kaganski's later attack on *Amélie* should also be seen as a response to a specific context. For this time he was railing not only against Jeunet's film, but also against the larger socio and politico-economic realities he saw operant in 2001 – eventually issuing a nearly point-by-point exceptionalist rebuttal to the pragmatist leanings that dominated the initial press coverage. Amidst the outpouring of ecstatic box office reports and positive reviews of Jeunet's film were a few common narratives about how *Amélie*'s success should be received as both redeemably 'local' and smartly 'global'. Almost immediately after *Amélie*'s release on 23 April, and while it was still drawing record attendance, a variety of voices sounded off on the film, claiming its aesthetic achievements as a 'national' triumph and speculating about what its success meant for the future of French cinema. Jérôme Larcher's May 2001 review in *Cahiers du Cinéma* offers a succint example:

> Unlike many of its contemporaries, [*Amélie*] is not haunted by any fantasy about Hollywood. It's actually difficult to imagine a film more French than this one. That might be a result of the fact that this filmmaker, unlike his colleagues (Kassovtiz, Kounen . . .), has already directed a Hollywood film – the fourth episode of the *Alien* franchise. Whether his experience working with the studios was traumatising or enriching, Jeunet is now back, four years later, with a film completely stripped of all references to Hollywood. He is also, maybe, the only director of his kind who has never been seduced by the American sirens – even though he is also the only one who really understands how to make a French film in an American style, a cinema of digitally enhanced, picturesque imagery. (Larcher 2001: 112)

Much like Larcher's, the other initial reviews of *Amélie* fostered a rather heroic account of what the film's box office success could mean to France and its national cinema. At the same time, they exhibited a range of rather different reactions to the film's stylistic qualities. On one hand, they often lumped Jeunet's film in with the other successful commercial films of the year – *Brotherhood of the Wolf*, *Le Placard*, *Yamakasi*, *Belphegor*, *La Vérité Si Je Mens 2*. On the other, they seemed to quite enjoy finding just the right language to describe what made this film so different (and more successful) than its peers. In the process, two intertwined arguments began to emerge about why Jeunet's film should be critically lauded. The first of these posited that *Amélie* was a unique formula for international and national success, one that did not compromise its artistic vision or cultural particularity for the mere sake of box office. The second subjected any hesitation about this cultural value to a politico-economic reality check – pointing to *Amélie*'s commercial potential, emphasising its stylistic distance from other recent popular films, and opining about the harsh realities of the French audiovisual market.

One article, entitled 'Occupons-nous d'Amélie' and published in *L'Express* five days before *Amélie*'s release, made perhaps the most overtly nationalist appeal of them all. Fresh off a pre-screening, film critic and novelist Jean-Pierre Dufreigne wrote that 'something marvelous [was] happening' that should be embraced because of its obvious distance from the other so-called 'French cinema' currently on screens (Dufreigne 2001). He wrote, 'We're not just talking about the current 50% market share for national production (let the bugles sound!), due to a lucky combination of successful films – some more merited than others (see opposite)' (Dufreigne 2001). The parenthetical reference guides the reader's eyes to a sidebar column on the same page that reports on the box office success of action films like *Brotherhood of the Wolf* and *Kiss of the Dragon*. Dufreigne is not specific about which of these success stories he deems 'more merited', but his overall position is clear – Jeunet's film offers a chance for even a discerning critic (like himself) to embrace popular French cinema anew (Dufreigne 2001).

Embedded in this take on the film is another line of rhetoric – one that subordinates stylistics to political-economics. Dufreigne concludes his plea by claiming the film should be recognised above and beyond several apparent flaws, which include a 'weak screenplay hidden behind the film's inventiveness'. He writes:

> We should not split hairs here [. . .] no, we should instead take up Amélie's cause. Amélie has a mission that has fallen from the sky like a suicidal Québecoise: to heal the problems of peoples' lives. She is inventive, child-like and obstinate. And she is alone. Out of this same solitude, amidst a crowd of excellent actors, stride Jeunet and Audrey, wiping away our tears and painting a sunny smile on Paris – a happy, nostalgic celebration *chez* Tati (Jacques Tati, that is). (Dufreigne 2001)

Steeped as it is in rhetorical ambiguity between the story of the film, the story of the French public and the story of French cinema in general, the passage offers a sort of knowing mission statement for all three. Nitpicky critiques ('We should not split hairs') should not have a place in view of a film that stands for something much larger. In Dufreigne's language, it is almost as if the film itself both represents and incarnates France's exceptional past ('inventive', 'obstinate' and 'alone'). Even so, the author's choice to 'take up' this film is not always a comfortable one – even for him – as beyond his sincere admiration for Tatou's eyes ('the most beautiful in the cinema since Lillian Gish'), his tone also often verges on the ironic or even the backhanded. *Amélie*, he writes in one passage, has 'fallen from the sky like a suicidal Québecoise', embracing a mission somewhere between the path of a revered French cinematic stylist (Tati) and the chain of bric-à-brac stores that shares his last name. This language here then both invokes the film's at times grotesque sense of humour (Madam Poulain does meet her fate in such a way) and dramatises the ironic conflict between two possible ways of seeing the same set of textual features – one immersed in its commercial, sentimental, nostalgic appeal, and the other maintaining an educated, sardonic detachment from their lures.

As *Amélie* took the box office by storm, more and more reviewers piled on with similarly split affiliations to its style. Few approached Dufreigne's level of hyperbole, but many followed a similar logic – lauding the film's optimism, its energy and its nostalgia. *Marianne* reviewer Danièle Heymann, for example, called it 'the sunshine that has been missing in this rainy spring' (Heyman 2001: 1). Others agreed that the film had popular merit and national appeal, but remained a bit less laudatory of its methods. Marie-Noëlle Trenchant of *Le Figaroscope*, for instance, called the film 'charming like the melody of an accordion', noting that it did well to revive 'a somewhat forgotten tradition of popular imagery' but then pointing out that Jeunet sometimes used 'a mise-en-scène a bit too emphatic for such a simple story' (Trenchant 2001). Along the same lines, a few, like Michel Boujut in *Charlie Hebdo*, dismissed the film for creating a 'very artificial' universe where 'the picaresque rules, accompanied by a few pretty visual motifs of which none, alas, ever amount to a real idea'. Boujut drives home this point by spending only one full paragraph on *Amélie* before launching into a celebration of Stephen Frears' *Liam*, which he claimed (in apparent opposition to Jeunet's film) 'eluded simple description' through a set of performances 'anchored in a terrifying reality' (Boujut 2001).

As has often been its practice, the *Le Monde*-owned magazine *Télérama* staged a virtual debate between two competing viewpoints. In his argument 'against' *Amélie*, François Gorin wholeheartedly embraced the sarcastic brand of mockery only hinted at in the other accounts mentioned so far, writing several paragraphs worth of elliptical phrases beginning with 'Ooh' and 'Aah', ('Ah, colored postcards, Sunday paintings for those who it is always Sunday, the supposedly "philosophical" side [. . .] Ah, the fusion of different eras, Lepine races and video clips, little practical jokes . . .') (Gorin 2001). In response, Jean-Claude Loiseau's 'for' column argues back, somewhat limply, that Jeunet's film is 'not really concerned with reality' and that the film '[will] probably remain a prototype' since 'overusing such happiness is risky in a cinema so unused to it' (Loisseau 2001).

Between the collective lines of these initial reviews, two rhetorical positions had already formed – one that embraced *Amélie*'s imperfections in the name of its populist appeals and another that rejected those very same features as little more than retrograde schlock. In a larger sense, the former was happy to emphasise a broadly nationalist vision of how the film's aesthetics fit into the growing, global mission of French cinema. Jeunet's true achievement, for this framing at least, was to have made a film neither too conceptually rarefied for global audiences nor too flagrant a sell-out for domestic ones. On 5th May, *Le Figaro* ran a cover story that made that stance an even more militant one. Beneath a title proclaiming 'Everyone is crazy about *Amélie*', it suggests that one reason for the film's success was the abject failure of other forms of locally produced cinema:

> It is as if these million spectators, most of them young people, are reacting against the current tendency of auteur cinema, which has recently been so often ugly, depressing and claustrophobic. ('Quatres millions' 2001)

Few other accounts were so openly antagonistic, but by mid-May the main-stream media was reaching a sort of collective agreement that the film's cultural value was as a rare successful – yet also 'national' – departure from both standard low-budget arthouse fare and sell-out blockbusters. The so-called 'Amélie effect' had added an intellectual thrust to its wave of box office support.

As *Amélie* broke box office records, media coverage also began to hypothesise about what its future relevance would be to other spheres of life. A spate of new articles reported on the lively discussions about the film that were taking place all over – while chatting in cafés, lingering in cinema lobbies, or even stopping just outside in the street to share a cigarette and some thoughts about the film's larger message.[3] This shift featured the appearance of formal statements to the press by most of the country's visible politicians (Chirac's request of his own private screening was big news). Meanwhile, other articles began to respond to what was now clearly becoming a wider-ranging discussion about the politics of popular media practices in France's expanding audiovisual industries. A front-page story for *Le Monde* some two weeks into *Amélie*'s run describes the enthusiastic responses of selected audience members and then offers some hypotheses about what the film's success should mean for French culture. At one point, the author, Robert Belleret, seems even to argue with an implied skeptical reader, suggesting that 'no one dreams of critiquing this film for not being militant enough because everyone accepts the premise that it is a fairy tale of sorts, where reality is reconstituted'. Later in the article, however, he makes an apparently contradictory suggestion – that the film's loving portrayal of 'the little people' (*les gens du peu*) and its cheery, apolitical stance might actually also be a bit politically 'subversive' in the way they 'turn their back radically against the sentiment of our day, which tends to be so terribly sordid, trivial and cynical' (Belleret 2001). Part of the author's warrant for these claims is an evaluation of how Jeunet fits into the geo-political context of the cinema. Earlier in the article he cites Jeunet's *Alien Resurrection* experience as proof of why the director is actually up to something much more savvy than a simple feel-good comedy. It is because Jeunet 'understands [those big fat Hollywood machines] from the inside' that he can weave his knowledge of his own culture into a marketable film, referencing France's greatest auteurs and visual artists. As Belleret puts it, 'What we've got here is an *auteur* film without any big stars, kitschy but still well thought-out, as difficult to classify as it is to predict' (Belleret 2001).

Two days later, three authors in *Marianne* grasped for an even broader cultural explanation, comparing *Amélie*'s popularity to that of *Loft Story*, which that month had also become wildly popular as the first French-produced reality show on TF1. Though the article begins by citing a contrast between the film and the show ('good' French cinema versus 'bad' American-influenced television), it concludes that the two products might actually be closer in spirit than most viewers are inclined to think. Implicitly rejecting Belleret's claims about the film's 'realism', the *Marianne* authors instead highlight its digitally-enhanced cleansing of the gritty Montmartre details – its 'erasure of the graffiti from walls' and 'obscuring the covers of the porno cassettes in the sex shop' ('La France d'*Amélie Poulain*' 2001). Their larger point, however, is that the significance of both products ultimately lies in an appeal to the sensibilities of a new generation of viewers, those at ease with having television and internet access to a variety of commercialised forms of entertainment, and also with maintaining a safe distance between their thirst for learning and the type of '"learning" that takes place on *Loft Story* and other audiovisual spectacles' ('La France d'*Amélie Poulain*' 2001). Indeed, the most telling aspect of the *Marianne* article is how it charts the perspectives of the younger generation, which it suggests remains askance from the ideology critiques levied against much of what they watch. This claim is briefly supported by some anecdotal testimony from a young *internaute* who reports that while watching *Amélie* with a 'room full of professors', she was horrified to hear some denounce the film as 'Vichyiste' and 'conformist' only to be accused by their peers of a worse crime – 'preferring *Loft Story*'. ('La France d'*Amélie Poulain*' 2001). Although it refrains from a full evaluation of the points it raises, the *Marianne* article debunks the apparent contrast between two popular texts, neither of which can claim to be very 'authentic' or 'real'. In one of their more obscure passages, the authors suggest that the new media environment might mean accepting what they call the 'Dr. Jekyll and Mr. Hyde in all of us' – ostensibly a reference to a contemporary spectator that finds few contradictions in navigating very different types of media, from 'vulgar' to 'elitest' forms and back again. What the comparison of *Amélie* and *Loft Story* really reveals, then, is a discussion about how the French audiovisual industry has changed to accommodate new styles of viewership –and about how two recognisably national products have succeeded in drawing in an audience long monopolised by Hollywood and its televisual partners.

Though these articles often seemed to be staging their celebrations against an implied skeptical reading, an outwardly antagonistic view of *Amélie* was a bit slower to make its presence known – at least in print. As we have seen, one subtext of the writing by even the film's biggest supporters was a keen awareness of how the film's kitschy appeal would also ruffle some feathers. But beyond a few sarcastic asides (Boujut's in *Charlie Hebdo* or Gorin's in *Télérama*), there had still been few articulations of exactly what was objectionable about Jeunet's vision of Paris. Perhaps other negative reviewers were unwilling to publish their most pointed criticisms, resigned to the fact that they would not be heard amidst the excitement. A few weeks later, that would change.

AMÉLIE PAS JOLIE

Kaganski's intervention in the proceedings belongs, as Vanderschelden notes, to a second stage of public discourse on *Amélie*, after the Cannes brouhaha in mid-May and among a spate of articles that grasped for the larger cultural implications of the film's popularity (Vanderschelden 2007: 96). His words appeared as an open response to *Libération* critics David Martin-Castelnau and Guillaume Bigot, who two days earlier defended Jeunet's film, claiming that it 'evoke[d] the "simple people" with tenderness and respect' and that it offered the French 'a mirror quite different from the deformed glass we often see ourselves reflected in – one where we can actually bask in pleasure, insouciance and – imagine that . . . hope' (Martin-Castelnau and Bigot 2001). Perhaps surprised by such support for the film in the pages of his favourite left-leaning newspaper, Kaganski offered his own take two days later, in direct response to Martin-Castelnau and Bigot:

> It is perhaps time to offer a contrasting view, for the sake of making an argument [. . .] a right that has become, at this point, an obligation given the almost total agreement among the entire French media, apparently anestheitized and blinded by the 'event,' and now completely stuck in poulin-esque genuflection. (Kaganski 2001a)

Kaganski's review objects not only to the film's directorial style but it also offers a concertedly exceptionalist objection to what the film represents on a larger scale – aesthetically, economically, politically.

'*Amélie*, pas jolie' is full of memorable, snarky lines. Kaganski argues that Jeunet's visual debt to a 'postcard' Montmartre sabotages whatever other claims to cultural authenticity it might have. He divides these complaints into a user-friendly, three point format. First, he lodges his aesthetic complaint that the film is 'anti-cinema', and that Jeunet is more 'visual virtouso than cinéaste' in that he exerts 'such absolute control over his images that they no longer breathe'. Second, Kaganski claims, the supposedly 'national' elements of the film are little more than clichés. For 'behind this so-called "poetic" crust' and its 'inoffensive retro elements' we find a 'particularly nauseating vision of Paris and of the world', and one that offers a 'postcard that never existed except in the imagery and collective unconscious created by Carné, Prévert and Doisneau' and hence offers 'a populist film more than a popular one'. Finally, Kaganski closes the article by noting that the film does not actually represent Paris but one local area of it – Montmartre – which in present day terms is actually quite ethnically diverse. It is here that he lodges his most acerbic criticism, that the film has 'sympathy for the people' only if they are 'monmarto-rétro-franco-franchouillard' and that it 'cleanses [the city] of its ethnic, social, sexual and cultural polysemy'. *Amélie*, he concludes, embraces a cheery ambivalence to ideology that makes it the 'ideal candidate' for an advertisement for the *Front National* (Kaganski 2001a).

Kaganski's essay travelled quickly in the national media, propelling his name to a notoriety beyond the level he could have imagined when he wrote it. Over the next several weeks, responses spilled forth, with both *Libération* and *Les Inrockuptibles* publishing a sample of reader letters taking positions on his claims. As Kaganski himself would be the first to argue, the words of one critic should not be overblown. Nor (in this case) should the creativity of what he wrote. As Ginette Vincendeau points out, in the context of cultural criticism in France today, the accusation of any film (or really any other cultural product) of far rightest or neo-Vichyiste sentiments should be taken with a grain of salt, given that such moves often represent more a well-trodden polemical maneuver more than a genuine claim (Vincendeau 2001: 25). Moreover, Kaganski's accusations about 'aestheticisation' reiterate familiar refrains from older debates about the *cinéma du look* some twenty years earlier. Finally, the racial tinge to his *Amélie* critique did not seem to hold up for long. As the satirical newspaper *Le Canard Enchaîné* suggested, Kaganski could hardly be serious about his allegations unless he meant for some sort of quota system to be put in place in order to 'count the number of ethnic minorities' in each and every film made in France (*Le Canard Enchaîné* 2001).

Although the racial debate about the film may have been responsible for the initial brouhaha, it is Kaganski's larger argument that has now stood the test of time. As Vincendeau begins to demonstrate in her early analysis of the film, both *Amélie* and the discourses around it deserve further scrutiny for how they lay bare deeper seeded divisions. In the lively subtext of *Amélie* 'pas jolie' is a view of a national industry that has become the victim of new business practices that are increasingly tied to the profit margins of television stations. In this sense, Kaganski voices an ardently exceptionalist slant on the much longer and still ongoing 'conversation' about the fortunes and foibles of French cinema under pressure from the global market, recalling previous controversies (the Leconte affair of 1999) and anticipating future debates (the Club of Thirteen report) (see Chapter 2). Kaganski himself reflected on this fact in the later entry for *Les Inrockuptibles* that preceded a selection of reader letters on the subject. He there addresses the debate in its larger politico-economic context, writing that he expected to have his review be controversial: 'That the rest of the media is lynching me symbolically doesn't surprise me at all: we are living in an era that is governed more than ever by advertisements and commercial transactions, which celebrates success as an absolute value' (Kaganski 2001b). Whatever the merits of his claims about Jeunet's politics, Kaganski is more concerned with the larger picture – a critical establishment that blindly backs up a film financing and distribution culture increasingly at odds with the type of national cinema he supports.

In the months that followed, Kaganski and other critics fortified their exceptionalist critiques of the film by bringing to the fore the political-economic assumptions that had always lain thinly below the surface of the initial exchanges on the film. Although he backed off his accusations of LePenism, Kaganski deepened his investment in an ideological critique, reiterating the stakes of his argument that the film was 'anti-cinema' in the Bazinian sense. The title of his follow-up *Inrocks* article – 'Comment je me suis disputé à propos d'*Amélie Poulain*' – refers explicitly to Arnaud Desplechin's 1996 film *Comment je me suis disputé ... (ma vie sexuelle)* and later lists several other titles he deems more warranted of praise for their 'authentic' look at 'simple folks', including *Ressources humaines* (Laurent Cantet 1999) and *Rosetta* (Dardenne brothers 1999) (Kaganski 2001b). In a defence of his colleague published in *Libération* about a week after the letters to the editor, Phillipe Lançon dropped the racial and ethnic angle of the original argument in order to further pursue the film's (to his mind) dubious links to corporatism, which he likened to 'Disney in Montmartre' (Lançon 2001).

A more developed rethinking of the *Amélie* phenomenon followed in various film journals and publications, questioning the relative value of the film's box office receipts, and proposing that its success should inspire a more in-depth conversation about the health and prospects of an industry. In many cases, while the film's success was deemed worthy of celebration, that account was accompanied by a cautionary lesson. Later in the year, *Cahiers du cinéma* editor Jean-Michel Frodon reflected on the film's significance for French film culture, compiling a dossier for *Cahiers du cinéma* entitled 'The downside of all this success' [*La face cachée de l'embellie*], which scrutinised the ill health of an industry lying just behind all the fuss about the success of *Amélie* and other films of 2001 (see Figure 3.2). A number of other economic studies of the industry have followed suit since then, often citing *Amélie* as the 'prototype' that provoked their initial concerns. Although such accounts rarely concern

Figure 3.2   Cover of *Cahiers du cinéma*,
No. 564: January, 2002. Reproduced with
permission from the journal

themselves with the aesthetic qualities of Jeunet's film itself, images from the
film have sometimes been used in an ironic fashion – as if to evoke the temporary mirage of good fortune and feeling from an artificial boost of attendance
figures – even while the true benefits of the 'cultural diversity' umbrella were
becoming much harder to see. That initial *Cahiers* cover, for instance, featured
an extreme closeup of the by-then famous poster of Tatou's face, this time
showing just her smile and chin. A cropping of the film's omnipresent poster
campaign thus stood for the critique that would be contained inside the journal.

Later takes on *Amélie* rarely risk a direct attack on Jeunet or his film.
Rather, they use the film's title and its images as a signal for certain tendencies
in contemporary French cinema. As Ezra suggests, the images of *Amélie* the
film soon became a veritable mise-en-abyme for the *Amélie* phenomenon and
the excitement of 2001 – a rare moment when France became enamoured
with its own cinema's untapped potential for appealing to mass audiences
at home and abroad. In many intellectual circles, what had begun as a wave
of optimism soon came full circle, ending with an energetic re-assertion of a
particular take on the structural disadvantages of 'truly' French cinema in a
globalised economy. Indeed, many of the voices that most counted would soon
aim to rewrite the legacy of *Amélie* – making the intellectual memory of the

film today a constant source of shrugs, sardonic wit and vigilance about the existence of a creeping corporatism, hidden behind the all-too humble attitude of an 'endlessly reiterated icon' (Ezra 2008: 109).

THE CONTINUING LIFE OF THE DEBATE

Since the weighty initial response to *Amélie*, a number of scholars have worked to provide an account of the blend of cultural and cinematic influences that place *Amélie* so tantalisingly between the 'global' and the 'local'. Among these accounts, several recent ones by Anglo-American critics stand out, both as works in their own right and as scholarly manifestations of the interpretive tendencies discussed in Chapter 3. To directly align these more removed writers within the fray of the original debate would be misleading. Yet it is fair to say that all of them share the curious distinction of acknowledging Kaganski's charges against the film without directly tackling the ideological questions he raises. Even so, in their attempts to sidestep, nuance or rethink the earlier reception literature, their readings also end up positioning the film vis à vis the larger politico-economic questions at stake in '*Amélie* pas jolie'.

Dudley Andrew's short but incisive *Film Comment* article on *Amélie* offers perhaps the best exemplar of what we might call an exceptionalist tack on the film's aesthetics. Throughout his argument, Andrew adroitly navigates the multiple cinematic reference points in the film – Prévert, Carné, Truffaut – pointing out connections between Jeunet's artistry and his national heritage:

> From my perspective, French cinema has been most compelling and complex when, as in *Jules and Jim*, it both acknowledges and strips away its makeup. Smudges mark a rift between face and soul that, ever since the New Wave, has been traced by significant French films, such as *Passion*, *L'ami de mon amie*, *A nos amours*, and *Sans toit ni loi*. *Amélie*, by contrast, is pure face, albeit a face that makes you smile. (Andrew 2004: 35)

The implication, then, is that the film – no matter how self-aware it might be – occupies a lower order of national film aesthetics precisely because of its planned, rigorous format.[4] On this view, a particular type of lensing makes the film somehow less worthy of supporting as 'French' in the first place.

Albeit with softer words than Kaganski's, Andrew's critique is similar, as it demerits Jeunet's vision because of its fast-cutting and fastidious mise-en-scène – a bias that Rosalind Galt traces throughout the reception of the film, and holds up as an exemplary case study of how aesthetic judgments contain an implicit 'claim on what kinds of texts are aesthetically and intellectually valuable as well as proper to the medium' (Galt 2011: 24). Along similar lines, I have been outlining here how value judgments about the 'morality' of the film's transnational ambitions can be read between the lines of the ways scholars and critics have approached – and continue to approach – Jeunet's film. Vanderschelden's monograph on *Amélie*, for instance, introduces the polysemic nature of the film's features, rooting out and summarising its multiple economic, cultural and artistic sources. Her conclusions about the film's value, however, tend to hover in an agnostic middle ground about the debates that this compendium of elements eventually incited in the film's home country. That stance becomes most clear when she treats the Kaganski controversy:

> Whether we agree or not with the opinions voiced is irrelevant. More interestingly, in our society, which is often considered consensual and reluctant to enter ideological debates, for once, a controversy sparked from what, after all, was only a provocative comment made by a critic known for his bias for *auteur* cinema (Vanderschelden 2007: 85)

These attempts to minimise ideological interpretations of the film are even stronger earlier on in the book, where Vanderschelden seems to want to pull the film out of discourse altogether, claiming that '*Amélie* is not an ideological manifesto, it is just a French film that overtly asserts its nationality' (Vanderschelden 2007: 81).

It is, for our purposes here, the point where this account pulls back that it verges on a rhetorical positioning similar to what we earlier termed a professionalist discourse of transnationalism. Vanderschelden, in this case, deliberately minimises the vital socio-cultural conflicts raised by a text in order to think beyond them, either by advocating for a higher agenda of 'globality' or by pleading that the plan is 'just to make films' under the given circumstances of unequal exchange between Hollywood and France. Much as Luc Besson claims on occasion, transnational French films are 'innocent objects' that '[don't] want to harm' – and the goal should simply be to establish a French presence of any sort on global screens, whatever the costs of doing so (O'Shaugnessy 2001: 68).

A third recent tack on *Amélie* does not seek to redeem the film's status so much as to complicate the mainstream reception of it by showing how it engages or plays reflexively with the very textures of commercial imagery it offers up. This line of argument first emerged in 2001, when Vincendeau rebutted Kaganski's critiques by aligning the film with the 'postmodern heart' distinctive to Jeunet's *oeuvre* (Vincendeau 2001: 43). In the first book-length study of Jeunet's career, Ezra reads the director's entire filmography in a similar light, pushing against common critiques of aestheticisation by drawing attention to how his films revel in their own constructed representations and mediations of 'history' and 'nation'. If Ezra's book represents a pragmatist scholarly discourse on *Amélie*, that is because she both resists measuring the film's value against established aesthetic models (Andrew 2004) and maintaining its ideological 'innocence' (Vanderschelden 2007), instead validating Jeunet's offering of a consumable product that succeeds at 'conceal[ing] and convey[ing] a great deal of information about contemporary cultural preoccupations' (Ezra 2008: 7). A pragmatic measure of *Amélie* is then one that engages not only with how the film plays with the past, but also with how it is in itself a knowing reference to the stakes of how French culture – in all its ambivalence – enters the channels of a transnational marketplace.

CONCLUSION

This chapter has worked to show how the textual features of *Amélie*, often read as 'ambivalent' or even 'innocent' of concerted ideological statement, are anything but that. Although the film operates within the confines of an identifiable, national iconography and authorial signature, it also contains a variety of other elements – both stylistic and thematic – that suggest a larger sensibility, one capable of thinking beyond the restrictions of a national cinematic framework. This combination of discursive features in the film is evidenced by the important variety of responses from critics and scholars since its release – from the initial *Amélie* debates around Kaganski's polemic to more recent efforts to position the film as a 'global' or 'transnational' text.

By conducting an analysis both of *Amélie* and of the discourses that continue to accrue around it, we see how different stylistic interpretations of the film continue to sag with the weight of value judgments about the strategic questions currently at play in any diagnosis of popular French cinema. As Moine suggests, 'the *Amélie Poulain* phenomenon derived in large part from the powerfully different forms of identity that the reception of the film managed to invest in its variously 'national' features' (Moine 2004). Ultimately, this perspective sheds a far different light on the importance of Jeunet's film. Rather than a neutral arbiter of some standoff between the denizens of 'cultural diversity' and the moguls of global Hollywood, *Amélie* emerges here as a provocative combination of features – one that both evokes preoccupations and provokes insecurities in a national image culture long seduced and repulsed by its own image abroad. In other words, the formal design of one film took on heightened importance in the French public sphere in 2001 because its 'bigness' exacerbated longer standing tensions between the divergent interests that formed – and continue to form – the incipient transnational 'project' of the French industry itself.

Notes

1. According to CNC data, when the film was released it was given a comparatively modest 432 copies. After 1.2 million spectators saw it during the first week alone, 110 more copies were put into circulation, bringing the total to 542 (Belleret 2001).
2. Michelle Scatton-Tessier has likened this element to a larger societal move towards *le petisme*, which places a focus on small, everyday pleasures in French life as a way to advance an advertising culture associated with globalisation (Scatton-Tessier 2004).
3. An article in *Le Point* 11 on May 2001 actually did reference the widespread phenomenon of discussing the film, offering a caricature of the kind of conversation that was taking place all over: 'On s'offre une cigarette, on se parle. Vous croyez au miracle aujhourd'hui?' This same passage was later cited again in an article reassessing the film's popularity in the aftermath of the Kaganski and Cannes controversies ('Quatre millions d'adhérents au parti d'Amélie Poulain.' *Libération* 2 June 2001). See also Belleret 2001 and Vincendeau 2001.
4. Andrew's more extended consideration of the film in *What Cinema Is!* (2010) suggests that his initial generosity towards the film may have waned somewhat in the intervening years, especially by comparison with his enthusiasm for the rough-hewn texture of the Romanian Cannes winner *4 months, 3 weeks, 2 days* (Mungiu 2003) (Andrew 2010: 48–56).

Works Cited

Amélie (2001), DVD Commentary Track, Directed by Jean-Pierre Jeunet, New York: Miramax.

Andrew, Dudley (2004), 'Amélie, or le fabuleux destin du cinéma français', *Film Quarterly*, 57: 3, Spring 2004, pp. 34–45.

Andrew, Dudley (2010), *What Cinema Is!: Bazin's Quest and its Charge*, London: Wiley-Blackwell.

Austin, James F (2004), 'Digitizing Frenchness in 2001: On a 'Historic' Moment in French Cinema', *Yale French Studies*, 15:3, pp. 281–299.

Belleret, Robert (2001), 'L'edifiante histoire du fabuleux succes d'Amélie Poulain', *Le Monde*, 9 April.

Bergery, Benjamin (2004), 'Cinematic Impressionism', *American Cinematographer*, December, p. 60.

Bonnard, Frédéric (2001), 'The Amélie Effect.' Alice Lovejoy, trans, *Film Comment*, Nov/Dec, <https://www.filmcomment.com/article/the-amelie-effect/> (last accessed 4 February 2019).

Boujut, Michel (2001), 'Destins contrariés', *Charlie Hebdo*, 1 May.

Dufreigne, Jean-Pierre (2001), 'Occupons-nous d'Amélie', *L'Express*, 19 April.

Ezra, Elizabeth (2008), *Jean-Pierre Jeunet*, Urbana: University of Illinois Press.

'La France d'*Amélie Poulain* contre la France de *Loft Story*' (2001), *Marianne*, 14 May

Galt, Rosalind (2011), *Pretty: Film and the Decorative Image*, New York: Columbia University Press.

Gorin, François (2001), 'Contre: . . . ou étouffant', *Télérama*, 15 April.

Hayes, Graeme (1999), 'Replaying History as Farce: postmodernism and the construction of Vichy in Delicatessen', *Modern & Contemporary France*, 7:2, pp. 197–207.

Heymann, Danièle (2001), 'L'amie Amélie repeint la vie aux couleurs du bonheur', *Marianne*, 30 April, p. 1.

'Interview with Jean-Pierre Jeunet' (2001), *Le Figaroscope*, 25 April.

Kaganski, Serge (2001a), 'Amélie pas jolie.' *Libération*, 31 May, <https://next.lib eration.fr/cinema/2001/05/31/amelie-pas-jolie_366387> (last accessed 4 February 2019).

Kaganski, Serge (2001b), 'Comment je me suis disputé à propos d'Amélie Poulain', *Les Inrockuptibles*, 12 June.

Lançon, Philippe (2001), 'Le frauduleux destin d'Amélie Poulain', *Libération*, 6 June, <https://www.liberation.fr/tribune/2001/06/01/le-frauduleux-destin-d-amelie-poula in_366569> (last accessed 4 February 2019).

Larcher, Jérôme (2001), 'Le cabinet de curiosités', *Cahiers du cinéma*, May, p. 112.

Le Canard Enchaîné (2001), 'Amélie Poulain', 6 June.

Loisseu, Jean-Claude (2001), 'Pour . . . savoureux.' *Télérama*, 15 April.

Martin-Castelnau, David and Guillaume Bigot (2001), 'Le secret d'Amélie Poulain', *Libération*, 28 May, <https://next.liberation.fr/cinema/2001/05/28/le-secret-d-ame lie-poulain_366103> (last accessed 4 February 2019).

Moine, Raphaëlle (2004), 'Vieux Genres? Nouveaux genres? Le fabuleux destin de quelques films français', *Cinéma contemporain: état des lieux: acte du colloque de Lyon (2002)*, pp. 151–167.

Moine, Raphaëlle (2007), 'Genre Hybridity, National Culture and Globalised Culture', *France at the Flicks: Trends in Contemporary French Popular Cinema*, Cambridge: Cambridge Scholars Press, pp. 36–50.

O'Shaugnessy, Martin (2001), 'Republic of Cinema or Fragmented Public Sphere: The Debate Between Film-makers and Critics', in John Marks and Enda McCaffrey (eds), *French Cultural Debates*, Melbourne: Monash University Press.

Parra, Danièle (1991), 'Rencontre avec deux tronches de l'art', *Revue du cinéma*, 471: May, pp. 30–32.

'Quatre millions d'adhérents au parti d'Amélie Poulain' (2001), *Libération*, 2 June.

Scatton-Tessier, Michelle (2004), 'Le Pétisme: Flirting with the Sordid in *Le Fabuleux Destin d'Amélie Poulain*', *Studies in French Cinema*, 4:3, pp. 197–207.

Stringer, Julian (2003), 'Introduction', *Movie Blockbusters*, London: Routledge, pp. 1–15.

Trenchant, Marie-Noëlle (2001), 'Le Fabuleux Destin d'Amélie Poulain: Merveilleux Populaire', *Le Figaroscope*, 25 April.

Vanderschelden, Isabelle and Sylvie Waskewicz (2002), 'Le Fabuleux Destin d'Amélie Poulain', *French Politics, Culture & Society*, 20:1, pp. 151–155.

Vanderschelden, Isabelle (2007), *Amélie*, Urbana: University of Illinois Press.

Vincendeau, Ginette (2001), 'Café Society (the 'Amélie Poulain' phenomenon)', *Sight & Sound*, 11:8 August, pp. 22–25.

4. *VALERIAN* AND THE PLANET OF
A THOUSAND CRITICS

In the opening passage of *Valerian and the City of a Thousand Planets* / *Valérian et la cité des mille planètes* (Luc Besson 2017), the EuropaCorp company logo cedes the screen to grainy stock footage of a Russian space station in orbit. As our eyes rest on interior shots of chipper cosmonauts greeting grinning astronauts, our ears register the lyrics of 'Space Oddity' (1969), David Bowie's playful response to Stanley Kubrick's *2001: A Space Odyssey* (1968). The first few seconds of this sequence could evoke the sort of existential wonder typical of more 'serious' sci-fi ('. . . and I'm floating in the most peculiar way . . .') but then Bowie's raucous guitar riffs arrive just as we accelerate through a montage of diverse space station crews greeting one another. Several millennia of inter-stellar collaboration collapse into a few minutes of screen time, detailing the construction of Alpha – the titular 'city of planets' – first by the diverse human cultures of 2020 and later by various speculative life forms of the 28th century. There is an initial solemnity to the bridging of cultural difference (European crews seek handshakes before bowing in deference to Japanese colleagues) but this quickly gives way to bawdy slapstick, as human crews engage awkwardly with various creatures – some lacking identifiable appendages, others all-too eager to drench them with gooey ectoplasm.

While this goofy homage may not please all palates, it does suggest other possible readings of the film's prelude. It is as if *Valerian* also wishes to signal its own precariousness, tonal and otherwise – 'floating', as it were, 'in a most peculiar way' – as a big-budget, sci-fi blockbuster that defies both the economic and the cultural expectations of a French-made film. The film's reported pro-duction details certainly seem to support this reading. At a reported €198 million ($160 million) budget, it generated pre-release headlines as both the most expensive French film and the biggest budget 'independent' production ever made outside the support of Hollywood's major studios. It is at once more audaciously effects-driven than Besson's 1998 *The Fifth Element* (to which it is often compared) and more financially daring than the recent line of other English-language EuropaCorp star vehicles – *The Transporter* trilogy (2002, 2005, 2008), the three *Taken* films (2008, 2011, 2013), or *Lucy* (2014). Shot primarily on the green screens of EuropaCorp's self-avowed 'Hollywood-style' Cinéma Cité in Saint Denis, the film stars two lesser-known Anglophones (Dane DeHaan and Cara Delavigne) amidst a host of more recognisable ones (Clive Owen, Ethan Hawke, John Goodman and Rihanna). It flaunts digitised effects achieved in collaboration with George Lucas's Industrial Light & Magic (ILM) and New Zealand's WETA digital; an international marketing campaign managed by distributors-for-hire in the US (STX) and Asia (China's Fundamental Films); and cross-platform promotional materi-als aimed at product convergence (a cartoon series and a mobile game were released prior to the film). Like previous EuropaCorp titles, *Valerian* opened in North America a full week before its European release; unlike them it steered directly into competition with Warner Brothers' more conventionally financed multi-national tent-pole – Christopher Nolan's World War II epic, *Dunkirk* (2017). In North America, early trade press reports often revolved around the question of how to categorise the production itself – an 'independent' block-buster financed by a French company without help from major US studios but shot almost entirely in English. Some saw it as a courageous attempt to face up to Hollywood, while others claimed these same attributes made it 'the biggest cinema gamble of 2017' (Goodfellow 2017), wagering that a meager box office would doom EuropaCorp altogether.

What these immediate responses generally neglected to mention is that *Valerian* is also just the most recent flashpoint in a much longer story. Besson has been at the forefront of commercial French cinema for the past three decades, but he has been far from alone. As shown in the previous chapters of this book, the sorts of ambitions incarnated by this particular film in 2017 find their roots in the late 1980s and early 1990s, when a series of government reforms changed France's media landscape. By mandating a variety of new ways for television broadcasters (and later other media platforms) to invest in domestic film production, French film authorities infused their industry with a slew of new investment resources aimed – among other things – at stimulating a new kind of crowd-pleasing genre movie. Over the three decades since, a generation of directors, producers, executives and actors have become infatuated with the goal of making France not only the home to renowned auteurs, but also to audacious filmmaking practices that compete with global Hollywood in other ways, both by imitating its spectacular lures and striving to find meaningful variation from them.

All this to say that measuring the cultural valences of a film like *Valerian* means dealing with the imaginative aspirations that exist within a domestic context that has not always been of one mind about producing films like it. Consequently, this chapter aims to account, in broad fashion, for the bundle of concerns that emerged around the film at the time of its release. If Besson's cinema frequently generates a sort of nervous energy in French film culture, that is because more than any other contemporary figure, his work embodies the hopes and fears that lie at the heart of French cinema's current 'mixed-economy' blend of art and commerce. To unpack the complexity of the *Valerian* moment, this chapter places the film and its reception in several different contexts and time scales. It begins by tracing Besson's evolving position amidst the cultural politics of popular cinema over the past two decades, sketching a broad sense of how he has cultivated his reputation by drawing freely from the different rhetorical and ideological repertoires contained within the consensual discourse of 'cultural diversity' currently in use in the French film industry. This back-story then sheds light on how we should understand the extended production and reception coverage – and criticism – of a film he pitched for years as a hypothetical 'French *Star Wars*' franchise.

THE PROFESSIONAL

French coverage leading up to the release of *Valerian* felt a bit like an industry holding its collective breath. There was also no shortage of humour. A political cartoon in *Le Film Français* published three days before the film's opening in France captured these dynamics rather succinctly (see Figure 4.1). In a recasting of the cover of the film's source material – a 1971 *Valérian et Laureline* graphic novel by Pierre Christin and Jacques Mézières – a surly-looking Besson takes the hero's spot, looming behind a vexed, wide-eyed Laureline. She meets our glance here as she queries her companion: 'Didn't you say you were going to stop directing films?' Some of this humour, of course, is of a jovial 'Besson bashing' sort.[1] The artist – a certain 'Monsieur Kak' – pokes fun at the director's romantic past with lead actresses, his frequent claims to be abandoning the director's chair and his own accounts of youthful fantasies about seducing Laureline. Yet the cartoon also reserves a satirical edge for a more diffuse target, evoked most by Besson's dour repost to his heroine – 'It's just a small personal project'. Placed beneath the words '*Valerian*: Blockbuster of the Year', the punch line resonates with the self-deprecating humour of a culture industry that continues to balance its numerous creative strengths on vastly different economic and cultural planes.

Figure 4.1   Cartoon published in *Le Film Français*, www.lefilmfrancais, 26 June 2017. Reproduced with permission from the artist

Figure 4.2   Cover of *Valérian et Laureline, Tome 2: L'Empire des mille planètes* (1971). Reproduced with permission from Editions Dargaud

The loaded subtext of the cartoon relates to numerous broader cultural dynamics at play in *Valerian*'s reception. Since the founding of EuropaCorp in 1999, Besson's 'go-it-alone' company has become the most prolific Gallic source of exportable entertainment. As a brand name most known abroad for action thrillers shot in English like *The Transporter* (Yuen/Leterrier 2002), *Taken* (Morel 2008) and *Lucy* (Besson 2014), EuropaCorp often gets labelled by critics as the 'unintended consequence' [*effet pervers*] of Jack Lang's audio-visual reforms of late 1980s and early 1990s. Indeed, the firm's very name seems fashioned as a kind of cross-cultural provocation – ending with an awkward 'r' and 'p' combination that twists the latter half of the word in vernacular French pronunciation.[2] Bemused critics and scholars continue to find new ways to caricature Besson's role in the French film industry. He has been, among other things, a 'Don Quixote' (Sojcher 2005), a 'spy' (Brown 2007), a 'big game hunter' (Bénabent 2010), a 'pharaoh' (Joyard 2012) and a 'nabab' (Schaller 2017). Meanwhile, Besson's own reclusiveness from the media only tends to fan the rampant rumours about his production methods, which have generated a series of scandals and lawsuits recently gathered in a scathing (and unauthorised) 'tell all' biography by former *Les Inrockuptibles* critic Geoffrey Le Guilcher with a dark silhouette gracing the cover (Le Guilcher 2016b).

In the academic literature, Besson's name has long been equated with the 'aestheticisation' of French film style in the 1980s and 1990s. While his putative prostration to an 'aesthetic of advertising' and the so-called *cinéma du look* is well documented by now (and has drawn eloquent rejoinders from Raphaël Bassan (Bassan 1989) and Marie-Thérèse Journot (Journot 2005)), academic research on Besson's *oeuvre* remains scant beyond Susan Hayward's path-breaking *auteur* study (Hayward 1998) and her follow-up edited volume with Phil Powrie (Hayward and Powrie 2006). As Hayward points out, the director's fraught relationship with the critical establishment dates to the beginning of his career, when perceived slights by prestigious journals like *Cahiers du cinéma* and *Positif* eventually led him to limit press access to his films, and to only grant interviews to 'sympathetic' magazines and journalists (Hayward 1998: 4). The founding of EuropaCorp in 1999 only amplified these antagonisms, as Besson's determination to compete with Hollywood brought undeniable success at the box office and a barrage of law suits too numerous to detail here.[3] As the company grew in influence, academic interest began to accelerate as well, though mostly in article form.[4] In the final chapter of her book *Beyond Auteurism*, Rosanna Maulé describes Besson's cultural bearing as 'calculated professionalism' (Maulé 2008: 175). Given what we know about more recent events, that characterisation seems only more apt ten years down the line.

For an ambitious entrepreneur like Besson, the meaning of 'cultural diversity' often shifts as a function of his strategic goals. In many cases, he uses the term as a way to champion market-driven forms of corporate strategy that have begun to flourish in France since Lang's tenure. As suggested in Chapter 2, he commonly uses a repertoire of professionalist refrains to support his approach to film aesthetics. His work should be evaluated, he suggests, in terms of an up-front economic calculation, since film franchises like *Taken* (Morel 2008) or *The Transporter* (Yuen/Leterrier 2002) play a specific role in a geopolitical context where French cinema is currently 'in survival mode' (Gonzalès: 2003). For Besson, this means dispensing with intellectual pretension in favour of efficient production methods. As he puts it, 'I have never set foot in the *cinémathèque*, I have never been hooked on that sort of cinema. What attracted me was not 'the film' but to *make* them.' (Powrie & Hayward 1999: 9). In other words, whatever their qualities, these are movies that play a role in keeping Besson's productions grounded in the Hexagon, allowing French domestic talent to 'make do' with the resources available, and depriving Hollywood of monopolising all of the long-term financial victories.

In the 1980s and 1990s, Besson became a mainstay at Gaumont just as the erstwhile French major was revamping its finances to profit from a sweeping government reform initiative. During that time, he also came to occupy an extreme position in domestic discourse around the internationalisation of the film industry. In 1985, a new Gaumont management team led by Patrice Ledoux specified the firm's strategic approach, focusing on dependable national genres (often comedies) while developing an agenda for making exportable films (Bonnell 2006: 240). A rising star since his independent debut *Le Dernier Combat* (1983), Besson's first feature at Gaumont – *Subway* (1985) – was an immediate hit, attracting attention in the press and the particular interest of house producer Pierre-Ange Le Pogam. Subsequent collaborations between the two men resulted in even greater commercial heights – *The Big Blue* (1988) and *Nikita* (1990) – as well an even more ambitious agenda later on. In 1993, the same year that the General Agreement on Tariffs and Trade (GATT) negotiations popularised the notion of a French 'cultural exception', Gaumont chairman Nicolas Seydoux orchestrated a high profile merger with Buena Vista Entertainment (Disney's European arm) to form Gaumont Buena Vista International (GBVI) with the express purpose of pursuing the company's commercial interests on a national and international stage. Over the next few years, Besson became the highest profile member of a small group of Gaumont directors recruited to the cause of making international products (Bonnell 2006: 241). *Léon / The Professional* (1994), a co-production with Warner Brothers, profited from the arrangement, but the film's €16 millon budget would pale by comparison with Besson's next project, a freewheeling €75 million science-fiction pastiche featuring set design by Mézières, special effects from the American company Digital Design, and flamboyant costume design by Jean-Paul Gaultier – all while maintaining enough French production credentials on the technical side to qualify for state aid. With dialogue almost entirely in English and lead roles for Bruce Willis, Chris Tucker and other American stars, *The Fifth Element* (1997) became a landmark for French filmmaking – shattering box office records on national ($54 million), US ($63 million) and worldwide ($263 million) markets but also stretching the conventional wisdom of what could credibly be called a 'French' film in CNC terms (Hayward 1998).[5] Although it performed slightly better with critics, *The Messenger / Jeanne d'Arc* (1999) barely surpassed its €67 million budget at the box office, casting Besson's credibility in question just as Seydoux and his management team were considering his next proposal – an action-heavy buddy comedy about a cab driver in Marseille called *Taxi* (2000).

When Gaumont refused to back this idea, Besson and LePogam formed an independent company to make the film, first called Leeloo Productions (Ragot 2010). Largely on the strength of *Taxi* – and the promise of its potential sequels – Besson and Le Pogam forged on alone, vigorously pursuing just the sorts of vertical integration practices that Jean-Denis Bredin had foreseen in his report to Socialist minister Jack Lang twenty years earlier. In constant search of film products they could control from conception to distribution, the duo rebranded their venture 'EuropaCorp' in 2001, adding the logo of a dolphin that morphs into an angel (inspired from *The Big Blue*). The new name would appear for the first time in the opening credits of *Kiss of the Dragon* (Nahon 2001), bringing to fruition the Franco-European Jet Li vehicle shot in Paris that Besson had coveted for years (Michael 2005: 64–67). Using methods widely called for by the prior generation of reformers, EuropaCorp sought to spread financial risk across multimedia properties, reinvesting its profits from box office and ancillary sales to support a larger budget 'tent-pole' every few years. Besson and Le Pogam touted this approach regularly in the media throughout the 2000s, claiming they would only 'green light' productions that were 80% financed in advance through television pre-sales, foreign distribution contracts and product placement opportunities like the Peugeot deal that funded the first *Taxi*, or the Audi contract that paved the way for making *The Transporter* (Le Guilcher 2016a). In the 2000s for instance, approved 'transnational' action films like *Taken* were usually given a €20 to €25 million budget and adopted a rapid, no-frills production schedule that allowed them to be made for a fraction of the cost of their Hollywood competition. While these practices did allow Besson's company to come in consistently under budget, they were not without substantial risk. During the shoot of *Taxi 2* (2000), for instance, a cameraman was tragically killed during the rush to film an action scene according to Besson's demands (Le Guilcher 2016b: 169–181).

A relative novelty for the French film industry at the time, EuropaCorp's speculative business model was touted frequently in the trade press during the 2000s and 2010s. Only by paying attention to 'the entire life of a film',

Besson and LePogam argued, could a contemporary French-based studio hope to maintain a business model properly acclimated to a global economy dominated by Hollywood franchises (Ragot 2010). Isabelle Vanderschelden suggests that their practices eventually played out in three separable strategies – production of English-language 'post-national' films (*The Transporter*, *Taken* and *Lucy*); production of locally-oriented French-language films (*Taxi* and *Banlieue 13*); and distribution of auteur and independent films in France and Europe (Vanderschelden 2009). By pursuing these diverse practices, the studio could spread its financial risk across different properties, reinvesting the profits periodically in the service of more ambitious projects. On the strength of this strategy, the firm experienced rapid growth throughout the 2000s, announcing its entrance on the stock exchange in 2006, and mounting bigger budget films every few years – €65 million budget for each installment of the animated *Arthur et les Minimoys* series (2006, 2009 and 2010); €67 million for *From Paris with Love* (2010); €40 million for *Lucy* (2014); and €48 million for *Taken 3* (2015). By 2010, the studio was annually producing or distributing an average of fifteen feature-length films on the French market, as well as launching North American television series derived from the most successful of its ventures (primarily *The Transporter* and *Taken*) and supporting a growing media arm for tie-ins – books, DVDs and video games. Attention to so many ancillary interests separated Besson's company from its major domestic competition (Pathé, Gaumont, UGC and MK2), all of which owned exhibition chains but continued to have little else in the way of ancillary interests (Ragot 2010). As of 2010, EuropaCorp was producing five films per year on average with the largest per-film budget average in the country (€15.5 million).

Amidst his busy work schedule, Besson rarely takes time to make pronouncements about cultural matters. In 2001, he gave a rare extended interview with *Studio* magazine months prior to the infamous Messier affair (See Chapter 1). During the conversation, he outlined his position a bit further:

> There is no cultural exception. We have to keep the word 'culture.' That's all. Culture is the identity card of a country. Period. We don't say 'the passport exception.' We say 'passport.' With culture it's the same, we don't even have to fight over this. The culture is in us, in our heart. It won't be possible to take it out of us. Or it will be necessary to kill us.
> (Cited and translated in Maulé 2008: 174)

Though his remarks are clearly not intended as cultural theory, Besson's wording here merits some pause. Though he steers clear of Messier's 'death' pronouncement, his position does sound strikingly similar to his erstwhile Vivendi colleague (with whom he had just signed a contract), making culture sound like a 'natural' outcome of economic strategy, much like Motion Picture Association of America (MPAA) president Jack Valenti did at GATT in 1993. The overall implication here seems to be quite similar to that of books written by American neoliberal intellectuals like Thomas Friedman (*The Lexus and the Olive Tree*) or Tyler Cowen (*Creative Destruction*), who in the 2000s argued that the supposed 'crisis' of economic globalisation was actually a boon for cultural diversity, as it permitted greater circulation of cultural goods than ever before.

In the early 2000s, Besson's nascent economic argument began to link up more clearly with an aesthetic one. As EuropaCorp began to have more commercial success, his commentary to the press was no longer phrased in terms of the individual treatment of his films, but rather as a producer of a diversity of products gauged to compete internationally. His frustration with his own country's critical establishment, he argued, was not simply from negative reviews (as was often reported) but from the structural biases of a system that failed to recognise the value of different approaches to filmmaking. 'It's a little painful', he says, 'because [I'm] trying to do something for [my] country, and they don't get it' (Gonzalès 2003). These sentiments echo not only the views of many executives and entrepreneurs of his generation (see Chapter 1), but also of director Patrice Leconte and the *réalisateurs en colère* (see Chapter 2), with whom Besson joined in 1999 to urge French critics to evaluate popular cinema on its own terms. On this view, film criticism should also adapt its practices to the challenges of a new era of filmmaking in France, where multimedia distribution and accelerated globalisation make the consumption of products a tremendously fragile game of finding niche audiences – one that can be sabotaged by the loathsome words of just a few domestic critics. As Besson put it trenchantly, 'why would a newspaper send a 70-year-old guy to review *Transporter* or *District B-13*? They're not for him!' (Eagan 2007: 15).

The Exceptional Opportunist

Besson's typically a-political (hence no less ideological) professionalist take on the role of critical practice never fails to infuriate his critics. Lately he has also found a more palatable bent to complement that stance. This new line of argumentation places EuropaCorp at the centre of a commercially revived resistance movement against Hollywood hegemony. Adding a more devout exceptionalist tinge to his rhetoric has benefited Besson politically by clarifying the nationalistic role that his filmmaking practices play in the industry's mission of promoting 'cultural diversity'. To this end, he has spearheaded at least two recent initiatives that have resulted in major changes to how his home country produces films.

In 2012, Besson realised a long-term goal with the completion of the *Cité du Cinéma*. An enormous, state-of the-art production studio culled from the remains of a gas factory outside Paris, the *Cité* is equipped with a post-production lab (Besson's own Digital Factory), nine sound stages with green screen capabilities, office space, a multiplex, educational facilities and a high-end restaurant. These facilities positioned the studio to both anchor EuropaCorp's ongoing projects and to attract high profile foreign productions to Paris. Three years later in 2015, Besson successfully lobbied the government for a reform to the CNC's tax rebate programme (*crédit d'impôt*) to allow English language films to profit from it. The combination of these two events arguably put Besson and his company closer to the paradoxical heart of the French film establishment than ever before. In a decade-long campaign to garner financial support to build the *Cité*, Besson deployed multiple rhetorical tactics. At the inception of the project, for instance, he appealed to centre-right representatives of the Chirac administration by highlighting the domestic economic advantages of having a vertically integrated production hub in Paris. He touted this well-nigh exceptionalist bent in an interview with the right-leaning newspaper *Le Figaro*:

> It is clear that American cinema will attack us by any means possible and that it intends to annihilate our little pocket of resistance. It does this through funding co-productions, by distributing films and by buying up cinema venues in Europe. I do not intend to let this happen and I will do everything in my power to continue producing films in France. [. . .] French cinema has a survival instinct but we need all our talent to keep it alive. I like American cinema and I know it well, but it has a way of eating everything in the world and leaving no opportunities for anyone else. (Gonzalès 2003)

Many of Besson's public pitches for the *Cité* hung on a similar strategy of creating a popular cinema in (but not of) the more 'modernised' filmmaking practices associated with Hollywood. He later supplemented that line of reasoning with another one devoted to the preservation of a more localised sense of 'cultural diversity' founded in the geographic fabric of Paris itself.

By 2007, the planned studio had been confirmed for a site in Seine-Saint-Denis, one of the city's most historically underserved suburbs. Since the project qualified for aid from the city's wider urban revivification initiative, Besson quickly made this fact into a rallying cry – trumpeting the new studio as a way to integrate the excluded populations of Paris into a new centre for film production. Drawing on his own story of exclusion from *La Fémis* and other elite film schools, Besson amplified an egalitarian sense of 'cultural diversity', especially with his vision for *L'Ecole de la Cité*, an onsite academy for 'passionate would-be filmmakers' between 18 and 25 who could not find 'a place for themselves in the system' (Besson 2012). Later that year he reinforced his position during Cannes, announcing that EuropaCorp would provide outdoor screenings in various outlying neighbourhoods of the banlieue to 'encourage the participation of people who are normally excluded' by 'mounting a cultural event in a stigmatized neighborhood' (Bureau and Agoudétsé 2007). During the long construction phase of the *Cité*, the irony of this newfound exceptionalist slant was not lost on media coverage, most notably because it coincided a bit too neatly with the rise of Nicolas Sarkozy – the corporate conservative president whose hyperactive platform was broadly sympathetic to practices of just this sort. A scandal to this effect first broke in 2008 when *Le Parisien* reported that then EuropaCorp marketing head Christophe Lambert (former star of Besson's *Subway* and *The Highlander*) had intimate connections with the Sarkozy administration, with whom he found a juridical loophole to allow the *Caisse de dépôts* (a government public works agency) to 'rent' educational space at the *Cité* to house the troubled state-run film school *L'Ecole Louis Lumière*. For the hefty sum of 2 million Euros per year, Besson's own *Ecole* would now be housed next to one of the 'elite' institutions from which he had previously sought to distance his own training programme (Le Guilcher 2016b: 261). Citing broad ideological differences with this new agenda, Le Pogam left EuropaCorp in 2011 and was officially replaced by Lambert (Henni 2011). Although Lambert passed away from cancer in 2015, there is no sign that this particular controversy will end soon. At the time this chapter was written, a court case was still pending regarding the legality of EuropaCorp's particular arrangement with the *Caisse de dépôts* (Le Guilcher 2016b: 245–262).

At the time the cartoon cited at the beginning of this chapter appeared, readers of *Le Film Français* would also have been quite familiar with the same magazine's ongoing coverage of *Valerian*'s drawn-out pre-production phase, which featured its own mini-drama of cultural policy reform. Besson aimed early to position his new film as a 'French touch' blockbuster fighting the uphill battle against American franchises. His first public mention of the project was arguably on 12 May 2015, with a mysterious tweet during Cannes: 'You know how difficult it is to exist in between giants like Marvel and DC Comics' (Dumazet 2017). Armed with storyboards, concept art, and the recent international success of *Lucy*, he then took DeHaan and Delavigne with him to pitch the new idea to international distributors at the festival, emerging a few days later with some €80 million of pre-sales commitments: €10 million each from three French sources (BNP, Orange, TF1) and €50 million from China's Fundamental Films (Dumazet 2017). He then lobbied François Hollande's second Minister of Culture, Fleur Pellerin, on behalf of a potential science fiction franchise that he and Lambert promised would offer France the chance to mount its 'own *Star Wars*' (Crété 2015). His main target was the *crédit d'impôt*, a tax rebate programme created in 2004 to lure Hollywood filmmaking to the Hexagon while keeping French productions from leaving it. The initial version of the rebate offered a 30% tax refund to foreign-funded productions (generally not shot in French) and 20% to French-produced ones (which had to be in French).[6] However, as an English-language, French-produced genre film, *Valerian* was poised to fall through the cracks of that initial system, which nevertheless backed many of its aspirational global peers. A mini-drama subsequently unfolded in the press. Besson argued that the arbitrary linguistic restrictions of the programme would force him to take his production elsewhere despite a desire to stay 'at home' and offer employment for his French-based technicians and crew (Weickert 2015). The consequences, he claimed, would be dire – causing French cinema 'to die within the next fifty years' (Dumazet 2017). In response to that plea, Pellerin eventually proposed the reform he sought, allowing French-produced films shot in other languages to qualify for a 20% rebate and – more consequentially – for a 30% threshold if they featured (like *Valerian*) the need for 'strong visual effects' (Arrighi de Casanova and Léger 2015). These new guidelines became law in 2016, garnering broad support across the industry, and harkening a new status quo.

The apparent broad support for Besson's agenda needs to be contextualised. In recent years, the French industry has spent considerable time differentiating between 'good' and 'bad' uses of film investment. The very same year the *crédit d'impôt* was created, for instance, the funding methods of Jean-Pierre Jeunet's *A Very Long Engagement / Un long dimanche de fiançailles* (2004) stirred controversy when the news broke that Warner Brothers France – a newly-created Paris affiliate of the Hollywood major – stood to make windfall profits from Jeunet's second collaboration with Audrey Tatou. In response to the news, the press irrupted with reports about how a 'Trojan Horse' was stealing money from the CNC. That scandal, which eventually sent Jeunet's producer Francis Boespflug to court, seems rather quaint in light of the institutional support for more recent initiatives, recent CNC *Bilan* (a summary of the 2016 year in French cinema) for instance displayed a still from the production stage of Christopher Nolan's *Dunkirk*, shot in France in part due to the tax incentives made possible by the reforms to the rebates (CNC *Bilan* 2016). Ironically, while hosting a Warner Brothers' World War II epic clearly represented a victory for the industry's agenda to use the *crédit d'impôt* to lure more transnational film productions, Nolan's film would later be released the same weekend as *Valerian* – greatly compromising the box office fortunes of the domestic production that the programme had initially been revised to make possible in the first place.

At the same time, discussions around Besson's success at changing the *crédit d'impôt* exposed familiar ideological divides. In response to the reform, one of France's oldest and most influential creative unions, the *Société des auteurs et compositeurs dramatiques* (SACD), expressed 'strong skepticism' about supporting 'certain French films shot in foreign languages' because of the deleterious effects they feared could arise from films with 'purely economic motivations' (Arrighi de Casanova and Legier 2015). In response, to this type of objection, producer Eric Altmayer (best known for commercially successful films like *Saint Laurent* and *OSS 117*) pushed back with a different framing entirely:

> Let's be clear about this. The defense of French cinema in general depends on just a few [big productions]. These are the films that allow for all of the others to exist. Making domestic film production stronger with these big films has positive effects for all aspects of our cinema, not just from an economic perspective. (Arrighi de Casanova and Laugier 2015)

These comments allude to the slippery subtext of aesthetic judgement that frequently hovers in the margins of such exchanges in the French public sphere. For Altmayer, big-budget productions (in English or otherwise) should be supported for all the benefits they contribute – as he puts it, 'not just from an economic perspective'. Meanwhile, his SACD colleagues remain worried that an onslaught of titles reeking of 'purely economic' motivations will mean eventually abandoning the French language and, it follows, the hard-won aesthetic liberties of economic independence from Hollywood.

Like many of her predecessors, CNC president Frédérique Bredin sought to mollify these disagreements by offering diplomatic language that could characterise the new regulations as an olive branch for all sides of the debate. 'Our industry cares about jobs' she claimed '[and] of course, also about artistic creation' (Arrighi de Casanova and Laugier 2015). Later, the CNC's webpage itself touted Besson's most ambitious film ever as a 'symbol of the success of the *crédit d'impôt* and of the successful expansion of French cinema policy to include the ambition for genuine 'superproductions' (CNC 2017). Clearly Besson's success as a lobbyist on behalf of *Valerian* failed to convince all of the industry's skeptics. Yet the eventual press coverage and reception of the film in France also suggests a new stage of consensus around Besson's value to his home industry – and perhaps even the beginnings of a different framework for considering how his professionalist approach to film aesthetics might fit within it.

Launching *Valerian*

On 22 June 2016, a 'behind-the-scenes' exposé on *Valerian*'s production in *L'Express* offered a first-person narrative by Christin and drawings by Mézières, recounting the duo's visit to the film set at the *Cité*. Their bias is clear; Christin's prose rhapsodises about Besson's prowess as a director while comparing the new studio to 'a gothic cathedral with blue walls for special effects' while Mézières' illustrations figure Besson amidst the bustle of set activity, as if to make the director a character from the comic book itself. Yet it is in the final paragraph of the article that we find the co-creators' most direct claim about their thoughts of the film:

> The comparatist mania of the internet will probably discover contradictions between the two stories, since the rules of making a spectacular movie meant for an international audience are not the same as those of a science fiction story anchored in the literary, graphic and even political traditions of France. But the cosmos is a place of alterity [*alterité*] where the acceptance of difference is part of the wisdom of the stars. (Christin and Mézières 2016: 3)

While the last line here is somewhat cryptic, it anticipates the sorts of attacks Besson's film would eventually face later on. In particular, Christin's quip about the 'acceptance of difference' outlines a pragmatic defense for the film's aesthetics, qualifying expectations with an appeal to the economic realities of the global film economy. More importantly, however, are the oblique references that Christin makes to a 'comparatist mania' – for which more informed fans would immediately think about the original graphic novel's place in the cross-cultural politics of blockbuster science fiction.

When Lambert and Besson trumpeted *Valerian*'s potential as France's 'own' *Star Wars* franchise, their argument was both nationalist exhortation and an implicit nod to rampant rumours in fan culture. Since the early 1980's, fans of the BD have grumbled that it was an unacknowledged inspiration for George Lucas' famous franchise. The original *Valérian et Laureline* strip first appeared as a feature in *Pilote* magazine in 1967, eventually generating its own fullfledged graphic novels. After watching the original trilogy, Mézières famously tried to contact Lucas in 1983, but never received a response. Among dozens of other online fan resources, a blog post on *ScreenMania* published the week after *Valerian*'s release recounted that episode while placing a series of stills from the *Star Wars* films next to similar frames from the *Valérian et Laureline* comics, including this one from 1983, where Mézières humorously evokes his resigned acceptance of the matter (see Figure 4.3).

While this disputed history of aesthetic influence rarely surfaced in the mainstream coverage of the film, it was also clear that EuropaCorp's promotional campaign was quite in tune with the vagaries of consumption on different levels – and most specifically with how an audience attuned to the history of the film's genre would consume its meaning in an entirely different way. Part of the launch of *Valerian* was a concerted cross-cultural attempt to introduce international audiences to a graphic novel that represents, for many continental fans, an overlooked gem of European science fiction. EuropaCorp's attempts to attract younger fans to this angle began in earnest over two years prior to the film's actual release. After his successful trip to raise funds at

Figure 4.3   A cartoon by *Valérian et Laureline* artist Jacques Mézières suggests some unacknowledged origins for the Star Wars aesthetic. Cartoon originally published in *Pilote* 113 (October 1983)

Cannes, Besson promptly hired a firm called Silenzio Interactive to head up the digital promotion of the film – a €5 million investment in the curated dissemination of information. The digital campaign began with a May 2015 tweet by Besson announcing the casting of his two star actors (simultaneously posted on Facebook, Snapchat and Instagram). A series of video teasers followed (released to YouTube on 10 November 2016, 29 March 2017 and 24 May 2017) as well as careful management of how the film's other star – pop singer Rihanna – conveyed production news to her 75 million followers on Twitter (Chenel 2017). Meanwhile, Besson himself engaged in a series of public appearances gauged to encourage online public involvement in the production. In October 2015, he announced a competition for aspiring designers to create costumes, twenty of which would eventually be chosen to appear in the film. After receiving 3,350 submissions to the hosting platform Talenthouse, he and costume designer Olivier Bériot selected a list of winners (mostly from France and Europe, but also from the US, Canada and Belarus). Perhaps the most important initiative in the promotional campaign was Besson's July 2016 trip to ComicCon in San Diego. With DeHaan and Delavigne and numerous costumes and props in tow, Besson himself introduced a teaser trailer to the audience while wearing a *Valérian et Laureline* T-shirt. The reported minute-long standing ovation he received generated significant buzz to the film's apparent advantage in North America, as influential 'geek' websites like *Collider* began to cover the story more in earnest (site founder and editor-in-chief Steve Weintraub called the teaser 'jaw-to-the-floor spectacular') (Weintrub 2016).

Meanwhile, most of the mainstream coverage of *Valerian* in France began to characterise both the production of the film and Besson's ambitious outreach attempts as a watershed moment. As the release date approached, the film's earnest social media campaign to mount a French 'rival for *Star Wars*' made a special set of appeals to its French-based audiences on social media – including a futuristic display at the Parisian metro stop Franklin D. Roosevelt (passersby could tweet selfies for a chance to win tickets) and a 40-metre fresco of Valerian's spaceship 'The Intruder' by beach artist Jben, which made its pitch to go viral with a video showing how he created it on the coastal sands of Charente-Maritime (Chenel 2017). Numerous articles prefaced their coverage by first mentioning Besson's recent infrastructural achievements for the domestic film industry – the *Cité du Cinéma* and the *crédit d'impôt*. In this light, the film was covered just as Kak's cartoon suggested – that rare 'French blockbuster' that nevertheless represented one man's personal authorial obsessions. A spread in *Le Parisien*, for instance, featured a graphic comparing the film's budget to other summer blockbusters (*Spider-man: Homecoming*, *Dunkirk*, *Wonder Woman*, and *War for the Planet of the Apes*) and an article that recounted both Besson's long-term love story for the BD and the film's unprecedented historical accomplishments: a record €197 million budget; 2,500 employees; 6,000 pages of concept art; and 2,547 frames of special effects for this 'French project carried by Luc Besson, who moved mountains to do it' (Baronian 2018).

The press coverage leading up to *Valerian*'s release takes on greater significance in light of Besson's longer career trajectory and relationship with the media. Much like the cartoon in *Le Film Français*, the run-up featured a familiar spread of different takes on his methods. While exceptionalist rumblings across the media painted Besson as an unruly capitalist taking advantage of the loopholes in French film policy to make his most extravagant film to date, these were countered by professionalist voices touting the sheer rarity and audacity of his undertaking. In the process, the features of the film itself became fodder for a host of different critical responses that betrayed important ideological and generational variances.

Even while Besson's film was still in post-production, coverage in France probed for ways to either dismiss or ratify its legitimacy as a 'French' cultural product. Reports in the media had already begun to telegraph major positions in the coverage to come. As early as March, *Le Canard enchaîné* previewed a broadly exceptionalist critique – pointing out that 'whether or not the film booms or busts', Besson's financial interests were protected, as he would make the most money of anyone involved in the production. Particularly damning was the claim that he may even cast relative unknowns (DeHaan and Delavigne) due to his own desire to make a profit ('Les recettes du chef' 2017). At the end of May, the glossy mainstream magazine *L'Express* offered what seemed like a professionalist rejoinder, arguing that while Besson's screenplays 'were not always inspired' and his methods 'not always beyond reproach', this particular film deserved a different treatment, if only because 'the temerity and energy necessary to pilot a ship like *Valerian* demands respect' (Carrière 2017). Two weeks later, the independent journal *Sang Froid* launched a new front to the culture war around the film, printing a rundown of fifteen years' worth of what it called the 'guerilla tactics' of EuropaCorp's legal team (Le Point Pop, 2017).

The most revealing pivot point in the reception of the film came in the anticipation gap between its launch in North America and France. As has become standard practice for its highest-profile English-language films, EuropaCorp released *Valerian* to French and European cinemas on 26 July, one full week after its opening in the US and Canada (21 July). In so doing, Besson's studio imitated a standard Hollywood promotional strategy, attempting to orchestrate the timing of how reviews accompany the film's releases to different audiences. Following the first screening of the film in Hollywood on 28 June, certain online critics, often affiliated with prominent fan sites, were permitted to tweet their initial responses to the screening in hopes of cultivating word-of-mouth on social media (Poucave 2018). This meant that the collective responses of niche critics like Peter Sciretta, a blogger for the website */Film* ('Slash Film') were given priority over more culturally legitimated critics. Sciretta's tweets – which extolled the film as 'visually stunning' and 'gleefully inventive' – then circulated for a full week online before more established voices could have their say (Hall 2017). Meanwhile, other media sources trumpeted from other angles. A feature from 18 July in *Vanity Fair* refrained from commenting on the film itself, but ramped up expectations in nationalist terms, arguing that EuropaCorp should be seen as 'a counter-revolution in French cinema that has now thoroughly bested the establishment' (Rushfield 2017).

When higher profile American critics did finally express their thoughts on the film, they seemed unable to explain its quirkiness without employing broadly nationalistic categories. *The Hollywood Reporter*'s Todd McCarthy was the most strident, attacking the film as 'Euro-trash' with a '50-year-old Barbarella-style tackiness' that could only hope to attract 'less discriminating' (i.e., foreign) audiences due to script flaws that 'any old hack Hollywood screenwriter' could have remedied with the help of some bourbon and that 'Hollywood studio chiefs can breathe easy that, this time, at least, they'll escape blame for making a giant summer franchise that no one wants to see, since this one's a French import' (McCarthy 2017). Even critics with more positive assessments overall agreed with some of his observations, suggesting that the film's loose approach to screenwriting allowed it to be refreshingly unique. David Edelstein of *New York Magazine* suggested a ham-fisted script was the price to pay for watching the 'unfettered visual imagination' of an artist who didn't 'worry about his corporate masters' (Edelstein 2017) while *AV Club*'s Ignatiy Vishnevetsky celebrated the film's 'lushly self-indulgent' style as a diversion from Hollywood-generated superhero films where 'trains are expected to run on time' (Vishnevetsky 2017).

If *Valerian* was carefully marketed towards youth culture that is also because Besson understood where his work is most likely to be appreciated. Vishnevetsky, for instance, made a name for himself defending the acumen of maligned 'popcorn' action directors like Tony Scott, John Hyams and Paul W. S. Anderson, and has become a model for numerous online critics who define themselves against the more culturally 'legitimated' reviews in publications compiled on *Rotten Tomatoes*, *MetaCritic* or (in the French case) *Allociné*.[7] In one of his more theoretical interventions, Vishnevetsky proposes a new term – 'workflow' – as a way to recognise new forms of intentionality in the digital age (Vishnevetsky 2013). Scholars like Steven Shaviro have recently picked up on the term as well, highlighting how it satisfies the need for a change in terminology when studying contemporary production techniques where traditional distinctions between set direction, cinematography and editing are less relevant in the ambiguous mix of multi-screen work and digital processing (Shaviro 2014). While the omnivorous embrace of media forms often attributed to Vishnevetsky and others surely constitutes part of any 'new cinephilia', there remain significant questions about the historical significance of recent de-hierarchised views in online criticism (Shambu 2014) that some critics pejoratively term 'vulgar auteurism' (Tracy 2009; Marsh 2017). For one thing, most of the individual exponents of this apparent movement remain as interested in art films as they are in blockbusters or music videos (Labuza 2013). More generally, because the search for 'new' sensibilities has been an obsession of film criticism since the beginning, the presence of a discourse does not ensure its novelty. Certainly, in the case of France, a similar distinction between critical approaches emerged in the 1980s between *cinéphilia* (love of cinema) and *cinéphagia* (consumption of cinema). Fanzines and niche 'genre' publications of the 1980s – *Mad Movies*, *Ecran Fantastique* and *Starfix* – often attempted to wrest emergent media forms away from these pressing ideological questions.

At the same time, these sorts of debates in France also tend to become wrapped in larger framing questions about how to respond most effectively to Hollywood franchises and the new media forms they mobilise in unprecedented ways (cable, video and DVD) and that 'legitimate' critics often perceive as an imperialist invasion. On one hand, this involves probing digital artifacts for architectural components that are no longer anchored in traditional separations between production and post-production. Moreover, at a certain point, any assessment of these discourses around *Valerian* finds itself propelled back into the film itself. Part of this is by savvy design – and it is here where the features of *Valerian* itself became a nexus for the film's reception.

READING VALERIAN

Since Besson's entire career evidences an almost pre-natural sense of the logics of global popular cinema, it can be no accident that a keystone of *Valerian*'s domestic marketing campaign focused on how much the film itself could be a result of the collaborative work culture at the *Cité du cinéma* – something that the 'new cinephilia' (led by critics like Vishnevetsky) has highlighted as a decisive turn in the interpretation of contemporary visual aesthetics. During the build-up to production, this involved an online competition for costume designs and other gimmicks, but the most notable feature of the film itself in this regard was the 'Big Market' sequence that follows our introduction to the two main characters, which was the result of an enormous master class at the *Ecole de la Cité*, where students storyboarded a complex action scene that prominently features two technologically adroit teenagers who navigate a topography literally suspended in a phenomenological tension between flashy consumerist 'surfaces' and the suspenseful chronology of 'making do.' As if to sardonically invoke the narrative consequences of 'workflow' practices at the *Cité*, this labyrinthine, visually ambiguous action set piece turns on the suspense of Valerian's hand becoming wedged between two digitally enhanced layers of the image track. This winking conceit about the figurative foibles of 'virtual reality' leads to some of the film's more striking frames, as DeHaan's shimmering form becomes both a reflexive vehicle for *Valerian*'s gesture towards the limits of its own world-building gestures (Figure 4.4), arguably anticipating the visual dynamics that would appear a few months later in Stephen Spielberg's *Ready Player One* (2018). In turn, the reception of the film featured a series of pirouettes between transnational and national frames, wherein these formal properties of the blockbuster itself – and France's ability to engage with them – became a sticking point for critics on both sides of the Atlantic.

The mechanics of the film's staggered transatlantic press embargo also created another (perhaps unintentional) dynamic. Just a few years ago, such a controlled release tactic might have induced critical backlash from the French establishment. This time some of the most prestigious critical enclaves became the film's most ardent defenders, rebutting American critiques by amplifying how the film's features articulated meaningful difference from the norms of Hollywood. Straining against the limits of the French press embargo, a number of publications offered what can only be termed a reception of the American reception – often using headlines made with pull quotes culled from the initial

Figure 4.4   Valerian (Dane DeHaan) finds himself trapped between two dimensions in the Big Market action sequence of *Valerian and the City of a Thousand Planets*. Screen grab from *Valerian and the City of a Thousand Planets*. DVD. EuropaCorp France: 2017

reviews. On 11 July, for instance, *Les Inrockuptibles*' critic Ludovic Béot wrote a summary of the first American reviews that had appeared the previous day, prefacing his account with a bolded headline from Stephen Whitty of *New York Daily News*, who called the film 'an enormous black hole'. The most important rhetorical move by Béot, however, was the second part of his title – 'Quand le presse US dézingue *Valérian*'. Difficult to translate to English, the use of the verb *dézinguer* here implies an exceedingly vulgar and uncalled for attack – an angle on the American reception that Béot builds on with his first paragraph, which begins 'We must admit, we were not anticipating such violence', giving McCarthy's review 'the "most mean spirited" award' and concluding in his final paragraph that a critical 'lynching' might not actually mean the film was destined to fail at the box office (Béot 2017).

As the French opening of the film drew nearer, other critics picked up on Béot's consternation. When the official embargo lifted on 18 July, Béot's *Les Inrocks* colleague Vincent Brunner published an interview with Cristin and Mézières entitled 'Visionnaires des étoiles' (Brunner 2017). Unlike the feature in *L'Express*, which vaguely alluded to the nationalist dispute about the origins of *Star Wars*, Brunner's title evokes the *Valérian et Laureline* duo as the franchise's spiritual visionaries (the original French title of the film was *La Guerre des étoiles*). During the questions, Mézières offers an account of his unsuccessful attempts to contact Lucas, while Christin expresses the film's intervention along starkly nationalist lines, as if to seek out ways in which it distinguishes itself formally from its international competition:

> These are not American heroes, they are funny and they make a sort of typically French couple [*franchouillard*]. In any case, we can tell the public

is tired of these cataclysmic blockbusters, all about massive destruction. *Valerian* is just the opposite. We see conflict and there are very pumped-up scenes, but the film is more optimistic and relativist. And the hero is the superb actor Dane DeHaan who, in my opinion, has never been a body builder. (Brunner 2017)

The next day, Yannick Nely of *Paris Match* offered an even more overtly nationalist take with his article entitled 'No, *Valerian* is not the worst block-buster of the summer'. Nely laments the overwrought influence of McCarthy's review in particular, observing that *The Hollywood Reporter* critic's words were now being 'brandished like a trophy' around the world, and suggesting that they amounted to little more than a moment of 'French bashing' (Nely 2017).

In the week gap between the two releases, French journalists prepared an equally nationalist response to the perceived American slight. The day before the film's release, an op ed by David Barroux, editor-in-chief of the financial journal *Les Echos*, spells out the film's economic consequence in no uncertain terms in an article entitled 'Quite far from the cultural exception' (Barroux 2017). After recounting the most common exceptionalist critiques of Besson's cinema and his comportment in the industry, Barroux asserts a framework for thinking about how Besson's film challenges orthodox hierarchies of 'global' film aesthetics: 'the American industry can certainly tolerate Bollywood or Parisian art cinema, but allowing others the opportunity to impose their own global blockbusters is out of the question' (Barroux 2017). He follows this assertion with a passage worth quoting at length:

> [Besson] is one of the rare heavyweights of French cinema who succeeds in actually growing our audiovisual production. In terms of budget and in terms of special effects, he pulls French films upwards. With the success of films like *Taken* or *Taxi*, he has proven that he is capable of establishing franchises and that he also has the wherewithal to turn them into television series. The audiovisual economy is in the middle of another revolution. Due to Netflix, the globalization of the industry is accelerating even more, the game is becoming even more expensive. France has everything to gain from having a larger player that can complement Gaumont and Pathé. We will all share a bit in *Valerian*'s success. And it's failure, too. (Barroux 2017)

The lines of this argument are by now all too familiar, especially coming from a finance-oriented journal that rarely if ever touches on film aesthetics. Yet it is worth noting that just as this heavily professionalist slant on the potential value of a veritable French blockbuster hit the press, the more 'legitimate' critical enclaves also seemed to be modulating their criticisms based on a similar calculus.

Much of the rest of the French coverage emerged as decidedly pragmatist in tone – balancing the aesthetic terms of their arguments with larger reflections about the rarity of the film's transnational ambitions and its uphill climb to compete against Hollywood monoliths. Perhaps predictably, a conservative-leaning *Le Figaro* critic was effusive on almost all counts, amplifying Besson's own arguments with an interview that called *Valerian* 'a humanist film with a colossal budget, quite far from American blockbusters' (Delcroix 2017). *France Soir*'s Jean-Michel Comte praised Besson for 'not being afraid of the Americans,' and lauded his ability to make a film with 'characters and action scenes that compare favorably to *Star Wars, Star Trek, Guardians of the Galaxy* and *Transformers*' (Comte 2017). *Le Monde*'s spread on the film actually offered two distinct takes on the film's consequences for France. In her feature article on the production, Mathilde Dumazet traces the film's genesis back to Besson's first collaboration with Mézières on *The Fifth Element*, his viewing of *Avatar* (Cameron 2010) and his subsequent announcement of a competition at EuropaCorp, wherein he solicited online contributions from artists to help conceive the look of the film (Dumazet 2017). Written as a jovial meta-narrative rather similar in tone to the cartoon in *Le Film Français* ('Once upon a time, there was the most expensive French film in history') the feature casts Besson as the hero of the story in a way that counterbalances Isabelle Regnier's accompanying negative review, which recalls the backlash to *Amélie* by dismissing *Valerian* as a 'parade of intergalactic postcards' that you 'can't get your eyes to focus on' (Regnier 2017).

At this early date, it remains to be seen what will become of perhaps the first 'French blockbuster' truly meriting the term in a transnational sense. In North American coverage, *Valerian*'s lacklustre opening weekend earned Besson numerous finger-wagging reprisals and only seemed to confirm predictions about EuropaCorp's imminent demise. As this account is written, trade press reports continue to surface suggesting that *Valerian*'s massive box office failure will lead to a retrenchment at EuropaCorp, which has announced layoffs, cancelled its European television production plans, and forecast a far less ambitious production slate for the immediate future. Reading immediate reports in the US media, one might think that Besson's film is destined to be indexed alongside numerous other ambitious summer sci-fi flops – *Cloud Atlas* (Wachwoksis 2012) or *John Carter* (Stanton 2012). Viewed via the transnational perspective proposed here, however, the film's legacy is likely to be far more complicated and consequential.

Towards Pragmatic Consensus?

It may well be that the *Valerian* moment represents a sign post in a longer conversation. This is a discussion that has to do with the cultural potential of French-made films that adopt digital effects and the 'look' of commercialised cinema more frequently associated with North America. Of all the coverage in established French publications, only one – by *L'Obs* reporter Nicholas Schaller – seemed to offer anything close to a the scathing words of Todd McCarthy. Beginning his account with an anecdote of actually meeting Besson (the director apparently began by exclaiming 'It's amazing how French you are!'), Schaller compares Besson's scandal-plagued career to *Citizen Kane*, quoting an anonymous former Gaumont colleague's backhanded assessment that Besson 'brings together the thought processes of a teenager and the intellect of François Mitterrand' (Schaller 2017). Interestingly, most of the other elite 'intellectual' enclaves in French film criticism did not seem to share Schaller's ongoing antagonism for Besson – even sketching the outlines of what seemed to be his auteur-based defence. Didier Péron of *Libération*, admittedly never an ardent defender of Besson or commercial cinema, offered what seemed like sympathy, first describing the agony of waiting for the press embargo to lift, then adding that the film clearly didn't deserve such venomous attacks from America since it was at worst 'totally inoffensive' despite a sense of 'never quite getting beyond the impression that it was a pale imitation of other space operas' (Péron 2017). Though less than sanguine about *Valerian* itself, Péron advances an overall argument in favour of the film at the end of his review, suggesting that a more callous capitalist than Besson would have more readily 'conformed to the market' by making *Lucy 2* instead (Péron 2017). For its part, *Les Inrocks* built on its already generous coverage with a review by Jean-Marc Lalanne entitled 'Destroyed by American critics, *Valerian and the City of a Thousand Planets* deserves far better.' Lalanne goes on to defend the film as 'a well-made yet atypical blockbuster' ready to 'seduce with a pop lightness and childish charm' despite the 'protectionist hostility' of critics like McCarthy (Lalanne 2017).

Pragmatist inflections of this sort are striking. Worth recalling that it was none other than Péron and Lalanne who joined forces sixteen years earlier to write a review of *Amélie* likening its digitised aesthetics to a child's box of retro curiosities 'dipped in formaldehyde' (Péron and Lalanne 2001) while comparing its ideological effects to Vichy propaganda in their accompanying interview of the director (Jeunet 2001; also cited in Austin 2004: 292). Given the enormous gap in scope and commercial ambition between Besson's ambitious-to-a-fault English-language blockbuster and Jeunet's retro-Parisian romantic comedy, that same duo's defence of a film like *Valerian* seems worth noting as a sign of how much the French cultural environment has changed in the intervening years.

Read from this perspective, the *Valérian* moment for French cinema could well be a reckoning point, not just for Besson's individual trajectory, but also for the mutations of a national culture industry that has long resisted embracing the sort of aesthetic ambitions and marketing methods that have become hallmarks for its most aggressive competition. Without exaggerating the importance of a few turns of phrase, we can also say that, for the time being at least, the French media industries seem committed to managing the contradictions of their most bankable, controversial and popular filmmaker – and of finding new ways to articulate the cultural legitimacy of films like his, which will continue to tantalise with their designs on the global market.

NOTES

1. This reactionary term was proposed by the late Christophe Lambert while he served as CEO of EuropaCorp.
2. Despite its obvious relevance to the company's cultural position in France, this is a nuance of language that many American researchers tend to gloss over. I am grateful to Thomas Pillard and Chloé Delaporte for emphasising this point to me.
3. Geoffrey Le Guilcher devotes nearly half of his unauthorized biography of Besson to the lawsuits against the director. See *Luc Besson: L'homme qui voulait être aimé* pp. 169–287. As this account is written, Besson has also been accused of sexual assault and harassment by five different women from various points in his career – a scandalous development that has already compromised the European distribution of his most recent film, *Anna* (2018), and may ultimately combine with the *Valérian* losses to doom the company (Keslassy 2018).
4. See Michael 2005; Brown 2007; Vanderschelden 2007; Vanderschelden 2009; Pettersen 2014; Gleich 2014; Rappas 2016.
5. See <http://boxofficemojo.com/movies/?id=fifthelement.htm>.
6. In English, the programme is known as Tax Rebate for International Productions (TRIP). Both tax rebates must not exceed 80% of total production costs.
7. A Russian-born, Chicago-based cinéphile-turned-critic, he has carved a name as a de facto leader for a rising generation of critical voices in North America. After cultivating a reputation for witty, insightful commentary on the nascent online forums *Mubi* and *Cinema Scope* during the mid-to-late 2000s, Vishnevetsky was selected in 2011 as a co-host on Roger Ebert's *Ebert Presents* at the tender age of 24, reportedly on the strength of a particular essay, in which he reclaimed legitimacy for – among other things – the action films of Jean-Claude Van Damme.

WORKS CITED

Arrighi de Casanova, Vanina and François Léger (2015), 'Crédit d'impôt: Luc Besson a-t-il sauvé le cinéma français?', *Première*, 15 October, <www.premiere.fr> (last accessed 1 February 2019).

Austin, James F (2004), 'Digitizing Frenchness in the year 2000: On a 'Historic' Moment in the French Cinema, *French Cultural Studies*, 15:3, pp. 281–299.

Baronian, Renaud (2018), '*Valérian* un film de titan', *Le Parisien*, 26 July, < http://www. leparisien.fr/culture-loisirs/cinema/valerian-un-film-de-titan-26-07-2017-7157124. php> (last accessed 1 February 2019).

Barroux, David (2017), 'Cinéma: au-delà de l'exception culturelle', *Les Echos*, 25 July, <https://www.lesechos.fr/25/07/2017/LesEchos/22493-032-ECH_cinema---au-dela-de-l-exception-culturelle.htm> (last accessed 1 February 2019).

Bassan, Raphaël (1989), 'Three neo-baroque directors: Besson, Beineix, Carax.' In Susan Hayward and Phil Powrie (eds), *Essays on Luc Besson: Master of Spectacle*, New York: Manchester University Press, pp. 11–23.

Bénabent, Juliette (2010), 'Luc Besson, le chasseur', *Télérama*, 10 February, <https://www.telerama.fr/cinema/le-chasseur,52460.php> (last accessed 1 February 2019).

Béot, Ludovic (2017), 'Le film est un immense trou noir: quand la presse américaine dézingue Valérian', *Les Inrockuptibles*, 11 July, <https://www.lesinrocks.com/2017/07/11/cinema/le-film-est-un-immense-trou-noir-quand-la-presse-us-dezingue-valerian-11964597/> (last accessed 1 February 2019).

Besson, Luc (2012), as quoted in 'La genèse du projet', *Ecole de la Cité*, <https://www.ecoledelacite.com/lecole-de-la-cite.html> (last accessed 1 Feburary 2019).

Bonnell, René (2006), *La vingt-cinquième image: une économie de l'audiovisuel*, 4th edn, Paris: Gallimard.

Brown, Will (2007), 'Sabotage or Espionage? Transvergence in the works of Luc Besson', *Studies in French Cinema*, 7:2, pp. 93–106.

Brunner, Vincent (2017), 'Visionnaires des étoiles: Entretien avec Pierre Christin et Jacques Mézières', *Les Inrockuptibles*, 19 July, <https://www.lesinrocks.com/2017/07/19/livres/entretien-avec-pierre-christin-et-jean-claude-mezieres-createurs-de-valerian-11966500/> (last accessed 1 February 2019).

Bureau, Eric and Bénédicte Agoudésté (2007), 'Luc Besson offre le Festival de Cannes à la banlieue', *Le Parisien*, 6 May, <http://www.leparisien.fr/paris/luc-besson-offre-le-festival-de-cannes-a-la-banlieue-06-05-2007-2008006094.php> (last accessed 1 February 2019).

CNC, *Bilan 2016*, <www.cnc.fr> (last accessed 1 February 2019).

CNC, '*Valérian et la cité des milles planètes*: symbole de la réussite de la réforme du crédit d'impôt', <www.cnc.fr, https://www.cnc.fr/cinema/communiques-de-presse/valerian-et-la-cite-des-mille-planetes--symbole-de-la-reussite-de-la-reforme-du-credit-dimpot_110384> (last accessed 1 February 2019).

Carrière, Christophe (2017), 'Avec Valérian, Luc Besson joue très gros', *L'Express*, 26 July, <https://www.lexpress.fr/culture/cinema/avec-valerian-luc-besson-joue-tres-gros_1930167.html> (last accessed 1 February 2019).

Chenel, Thomas (2017), 'Une campagne promotionelle très puissante sur Internet et les réseaux sociaux', *Les Echos*, 25 July.

Christin, Pierre and Jacques Mézières (2016), 'De la BD au cinéma, Valérian prend une nouvelle dimension', *L'Express*, 22 June, <https://www.lexpress.fr/culture/cinema/de-la-bd-au-cinema-valerian-prend-une-nouvelle-dimension_1804948.htm> (last accessed 4 February 2019).

Comte, Jean-Michel (2017), 'Valérian', *France Soir*, 25 July.

Crété, Geofrrey (2015), 'Luc Besson adaptera Valérian au cinéma pour concurrencer Star Wars', *écranlarge.fr*, 14 May, <https://www.ecranlarge.com/films/news/939919-valerian-and-the-city-of-a-thousand-planets-de-luc-besson-sera-notre-star-wars-a-nous> (last accessed 1 February 2019).

Delcoix, Olivier (2017), 'Avec Valérian, Luc Besson atteint son objectif', *Le Figaro*, 25 July, <http://www.lefigaro.fr/cinema/2017/07/25/03002-20170725ARTFIG00194-valerian-l-objectif-reve-signe-besson.php> (last accessed 1 February 2019).

Dumazet, Mathilde (2017), 'Besson et Valérian: une saga de vingt ans', *Le Monde*, 25 July, <https://www.lemonde.fr/cinema/article/2017/07/25/besson-et-valerian-une-saga-de-vingt-ans_5164592_3476.html> (last accessed 1 February 2019).

Eagan, Daniel (2007), 'Flight of Fantasy', *Film Journal International*, 110:5, May, pp. 14–15.

Edelstein, David (2017), 'Valerian is magical, even if the script isn't', *New York Magazine*, 19 July, <http://www.vulture.com/2017/07/valerian-is-magical-even-if-the-script-isnt.html> (last accessed 1 February 2019).

Gleich, Joshua (2012), 'Auteur, mogul, transporter: Luc Besson as twenty-first century Zanuck', *New Review of Film and Television Studies*, 10:2, pp, 246–268.

Gonzalès, Paule (2003), 'Luc Besson: le cinéma français est en survie', *Le Figaro*, 31 December.

Goodfellow, Melanie (2017), 'Luc Besson talks 'Valerian', the biggest cinema gamble of 2017,' *Screen Daily*, 20 June 2017. https://www.screendaily.com/interviews/luc-besson-talks-valerian-the-biggest-cinema-gamble-of-2017/5119067.article

Hall, Jacob (2017), '*Valerian and the City of a Thousand Planets* Early Buzz: What are Critics Saying About Luc Besson's Sci Fi Epic?' /Film: Blogging the Reel World, 28 June, *www.slashfilm.com*, <https://www.slashfilm.com/valerian-early-buzz/> (last accessed 1 February 2019).

Hayward, Susan (1998), *Luc Besson*, London: British Film Institute.

Hayward, Susan (1999), 'Luc Besson's 'Mission Elastoplast': The Fifth Element (1997)' in Phil Powrie (ed.), *French Cinema in the 1990s: Continuity and Difference*, Manchester: Manchester University Press, pp. 246–257.

Hayward, Susan and Phil Powrie (2006), *Essays on Luc Besson: Master of Spectacle*, New York: Manchester University Press.

Henni, Jamal (2011), 'Luc Besson licencie son bras droit Pierre-Ange Le Pogam', *La Tribune*, 8 Feburary, <https://www.latribune.fr/journal/edition-du-0802/technos-medias/1115644/luc-besson-licencie-son-bras-droit-pierre-ange-le-pogam.html> (last accessed 1 February 2019).

Jeunet, Jean-Pierre (2001), '"Un bonheur indescriptible à fabriquer": Jean-Pierre Jeunet détaille sa méthode, son rapport à la réalité', Interview by Jean-Marc Lalanne and Didier Péron, *Libération*, 25 April.

Journot, Marie-Thérèse (2005), *L'Esthetique publicitaire dans le cinéma français des années 80: la modernité en crise, Besson, Beineix, Carax*, Paris: L'Harmattan.

Joyard, Olivier (2012), 'La Cité du cinéma de Luc Besson, un projet pharaonique et risqué', *Les Inrockuptibles*, 22 September, *www.lesinrocks.com*, <https://www.les inrocks.com/2012/09/22/actualite/la-cite-du-cinema-de-luc-besson-un-projet-pharao nique-et-risque-11306216/> (last accessed 1 February 2019).

——'Les recettes du chef' (2017), *Le Canard Enchaîné*, 3 February 2016.

Keslassy, Elsa (2018), 'Luc Besson Faces More Allegations of Sexual Assault, Harassment', *Variety*, 10 July, <https://variety.com/2018/film/news/luc-besson-euro pacorp-allegations-sexual-assaults-harassment-france-1202869487/> (last accessed 4 February 2019).

Labuza, Peter (2013), 'Expressive Esoterica in the 21st century – or, what is Vulgar Auteurism?', 3 June, *Labuza Movies*, <https://labuzamovies.com/2013/06/03/expressive-esoterica-in-the-21st-century-or-what-is-vulgar-auteurism/> (last accessed 1 February 2019).

Lalanne, Jean-Marc (2017), 'Détruit par la critique américaine, "Valérian et la Cité des mille planètes" vaut mieux que ça', *Les Inrockuptibles*, 21 July, <https://www.lesinrocks.com/cinema/films-a-l-affiche/valerian-et-la-cite-des-mille-planetes/> (last accessed 1 February 2019).

Le Guilcher, Geoffrey (2016a), 'Les voitures qui ont fait gagner les millions à Luc Besson', Streetpress, 12 January, <https://www.streetpress.com/sujet/1452617965-biographie-luc-besson-voitures-gagner-des-millions> (last accessed 4 February 2019).

Le Guilcher, Geoffrey (2016b), *Luc Besson: L'homme qui voulait être aimé. La biographie non-autorisée*, Paris: Broché.

Le Point Pop, 'EuropaCorp: la guerilla judiciaire de Luc Besson', *Le Point*, <https://www.lepoint.fr/pop-culture/cinema/europacorp-la-guerilla-judiciaire-de-luc-besson-19-06-2017-2136447_2923.php> (last accessed 1 February 2019).

Maulé, Rosanna (2008), 'Luc Besson and the Question of the Cultural Exception in France' in *Beyond Auteurism: New Directions in Authorial Film Practices in France, Italy and Spain since the 1980s*, London: Intellect, pp. 163–188.

McCarthy, Todd (2017), 'Valerian and the City of a Thousand Planets: Film Review', *The Hollywood Reporter*, 10 July, <https://www.hollywoodreporter.com/review/valerian-city-a-thousand-planets-review-1019847> (last accessed 4 February 2019).

Michael, Charlie (2005), 'French National Cinema and the Martial Arts Blockbuster', *French Politics, Culture & Society*, 23:3, pp. 55–74.

Marsh, Calum (2017), 'Don't Hold Back, Calum Marsh. Tell us How you Really Feel about Michael Bay', *National Post*, 22 June, <https://nationalpost.com/entertainment/movies/dont-hold-back-calum-marsh-tell-us-how-you-really-truly-feel-about-michael-bay> (last accessed 1 February 2019).

Nely, Yannick (2017), 'Non, Valérian et la cité des milles planetes n'est pas le pire blockbuster de l'été', *Paris Match*, 20 July, <https://www.parismatch.com/Culture/Cinema/Non-Valerian-et-la-cite-des-mille-planetes-n-est-pas-le-pire-blockbuster-de-l-ete-1305680> (last accessed 1 February 2019).

Péron, Didier (2017), 'Valérian: Navet spatial', *Libération*, 25 July, <http://next.liberation.fr/cinema/2017/07/25/valerian-navet-spatial_1586162> (last accessed 1 February 2019).

Péron, Didier and Jean-Marc Lalanne (2001), 'Un coup de Jeunet', *Libération*, 25 April, <https://next.liberation.fr/culture/2001/04/25/un-coup-de-jeunet_362374> (last accessed 1 February 2019).

Pettersen, David (2014), 'American Genre Film in the French Banlieue: Luc Besson and Parkour', *Cinema Journal*, 53:3, pp. 26–51.

Poucave, Jacques-Henry (2018), 'Valérian: les critiques US sont tombées: déception ou massacre?', *Ecran Large*, 11 July, *www.ecranlarge.com*, <https://www.ecranlarge.com/films/news/992771-valerian-les-critiques-americaines-sont-tombees-et-c-est-un-massacre-total> (last accessed 1 February 2019).

Rappas, IA Celek (2016), 'The Urban Renovation of Marseille in Luc Besson's *Taxi* Series', *French Cultural Studies*, 27:4, pp. 385–397.

Regnier, Isabelle (2017), 'Valérian: un défilé de cartes postales intergalactiques', *Le Monde*, 27 July 27, <https://www.lemonde.fr/cinema/article/2017/07/26/valerian-et-la-cite-des-mille-planetes-un-defile-de-cartes-postales-intergalactiques_5164968_3476.html> (last accessed 1 February 2019).

Ragot, Sophie (2010), 'EuropaCorp, French Film in the American Manner', *InaGlobal*, 11 October 11 <https://www.inaglobal.fr/en/cinema/article/europacorp-french-film-american-manner> (last accessed 1 February 2019).

Rushfield, Richard (2017), 'The Future of French Cinema May be Riding on Luc Besson's *Valerian and the City of a Thousand Planets*', *Vanity Fair*, July 18, <https://www.vanityfair.com/hollywood/2017/07/luc-besson-valerian-and-the-city-of-a-thousand-planets-set> (last accessed 1 February 2019).

Schaller, Nicholas (2017), 'Luc Besson, le dernier nabab du cinéma', *L'OBS*, 25 July, <https://www.nouvelobs.com/cinema/20170719.OBS2333/luc-besson-le-dernier-nabab-du-cinema.html> (last accessed 1 February 2019).

Shambu, Girish (2014), *The New Cinephilia*, Montreal: Caboose.

Shaviro, Steven (2014), 'Workflow/Rihanna', *Shaviro.com*, 23 April, <http://www.shaviro.com/Blog/?p=1215> (last accessed 1 February 2019).

Sojcher, Frédéric (2005), *Luc Besson: Un Don Quichotte face à Hollywood*, Paris: Seguier.

Tracy, Andrew (2009), 'Vulgar Auteurism: The Case of Michael Mann', *CinemaScope*, 40: Fall 2009, <http://cinema-scope.com/cinema-scope-online/vulgar-auteurism-case-michael-mann/> (last accessed 1 February 2019).

Vanderschelden, Isabelle (2009), 'Luc Besson's ambition: EuropaCorp as a European Major for the 21st Century', *Studies in European Cinema*, 5:2, pp. 91–104.

Vanderschelden, Isabelle (2007), 'Strategies for a Transnational/Post-national Popular French Cinema', *Modern & Contemporary France*, 15:1, pp. 37–50.

Vishnevetsky, Ignatiy (2017), 'Luc Besson's space romp *Valerian and the City of a Thousand Planets* is fun if you can stand dumb', *AV Club*, 14 July, <https://film.avclub.com/luc-besson-s-space-romp-valerian-and-the-city-of-a-thou-1798191824> (last accessed 1 February 2019).

Vishnevetsky, Ignatiy (2013), 'What is the 21st Century? Revising the Dictionary', *MUBI*, 1 February, <https://mubi.com/notebook/posts/what-is-the-21st-century-revising-the-dictionary> (last accessed 1 February 2019).

Weickert, Clio (2015), 'Luc Besson déplore le système des crédits d'impôt qui l'empêche de tourner en France', 25 August, *20 Minutes*, <https://www.20minutes.fr/cinema/1672091-20150825-luc-besson-deplore-systeme-credits-impot-empeche-tourner-france> (last accessed 1 February 2019).

5. COUNTERCURRENTS IN FRENCH ACTION CINEMA

Since the rise of blockbuster franchises in the 1980s, spectacular action sequences have become a hinge point for debates about the impact of globalised cinematic forms. As Scott Higgins puts it, action films 'display the production values that enable American movies to dominate global markets' (Higgins 2008: 74). While historians tend to agree that action – and often digitally enhanced action – constitutes a primary aesthetic ingredient of globalised cinema, there is still much to be articulated about its influence elsewhere.[1] As José Arroyo points out, action and spectacle present particular problems for historicising any genre, since they play a role in so many different types of films (Arroyo 2002: viii). This is certainly true in terms of French cinema. In some sense, action *tout court* has been part of French filmmaking for a very long time. A broad definition of its influence could begin by reconsidering early Gaumont chase films or Feuillade serials, then work up through Truffaut's sprightly heroes and beyond. Notwithstanding these canonised possibilities, a French-made action cinema – in the pre-conceived industrial sense of the word genre – remains unexplored, partly because research on French cinema still tends to neglect its overtly commercialised forms, but also because French studios did not invest in the traits most identified with action films until quite recently. While action scenes do feature prominently in various *policiers* of the 1980s, the staid cutting and sclerotic spatial articulation of, for example, a Belmondo star vehicle like *Le Professionel* (Lautner 1981) or a sci-fi *policier* like *Le Prix du danger* (Boisset 1982) does not compare favourably with

Hollywood or Hong Kong films of the same period, where mobile camerawork and faster-cut editing were already visible in *Raiders of the Lost Ark* (Spielberg 1981) or *Rambo: First Blood* (Kotcheff 1982), when the exploits of Bruce Lee and Jackie Chan were widely known on cinéphiliac circuits in Paris and elsewhere (Michael 2005: 63), and when something akin to what David Bordwell calls 'intensified continuity' (more mobile camera; bipolar lens lengths; faster cutting; dependence on close-ups) was just beginning to appear in French films – albeit usually discussed as one part of the putatively 'vacant' advertising aesthetic of the *cinéma du look* (Bordwell 2002). Moreover, in terms of the French establishment, all of these tendencies usually tend to be subsumed under a broader neglected category – cinema of the 'fantastic' (*cinéma du fantastique*) – which itself has been largely repressed in mainstream criticism (Gimello-Mesplomb 2012). Just thirty years later, however, action aesthetics of the 'intensified continuity' variety have become the norm for the present generation of French directors, for whom Hollywood blockbuster franchises and Asian action genres no longer represent 'invasive species' or video store curiosities, but different options on an aspirational palette of film technique.

In other words, if we heed Randall Halle's wise warning about a transnational film theorist's obligation to compare 'like with like' (Halle 2008: 29), numerous questions remain unanswered about French cinema in action. To date, most of the scholarly work on the topic focuses on EuropaCorp.[2] Yet Luc Besson's studio also represents a bit of a conceptual stumbling block for the topic, especially since its most visible films can 'very easily be mistaken for Hollywood products' (Martin-Jones 2012) and often end with the sum effect of occluding not only the other cinematic contributions of Besson's own company, but dozens of other titles currently issuing from an industry that is just beginning to imagine what its 'own' tradition of commercialised action cinema might look like.[3]

Besson generally uses various professionalist refrains to support his argument about film aesthetics. His work should be evaluated, he suggests, in terms of an up-front economic calculation. Films like *Taken* (Morel 2008) and *The Transporter* (Leterrier 2002) are intended to play a specific role in a geopolitical context where French cinema is currently 'in survival mode' (Gonzalès 2003). As Besson puts it, 'I have never set foot in the *cinémathèque*, I have never been hooked on that sort of cinema. What attracted me was not 'the film' but to *make* them.' (quoted in Hayward and Powrie 2006: 9). In sum, whatever their qualities, these are movies that play a role in keeping Besson's productions grounded in France, allowing domestic talent to 'make do' with the resources available, and depriving Hollywood of all of the long-term financial victories. EuropaCorp may well constitute the most visible current model for 'post-national' or 'trans-national' French action blockbusters, but how to analyse the features of the films themselves remains a rather knotty conceptual problem. In an insightful recent comparative analysis of two EuropaCorp action thrillers, Lisa Purse demonstrates different forms of textual hybridity in the French-language *Banlieue 13* (Pierre Morel 2004) and the English-language *Danny the Dog / Unleashed* (Louis Leterrier 2005), suggesting that the two films constitute 'various permutations' of an 'internationalizing formula that has emerged out of the cultural exchanges between different film producers over time.' (Purse 2011: 175). Heeding the caveats of other scholars, Purse disfavours an approach that permits Hollywood to 'own' the development of action cinema, or that narrows the game of aesthetic influence to discretely nation-based traditions ('French' or 'American' or 'Asian'). While she is wise to be wary of these mitigating factors, her concurrent move – to generalise across quite different films – also risks overlooking the important nuances that emerge when we examine the textual and contextual dynamics that arise from a more historically motivated case study. Suggesting a way to think across and among the current tendencies in French action cinema, this chapter begins by looking at several EuropaCorp action thrillers, and ends by considering how other salient trends have emerged alongside Besson's influence, in many cases in contra-distinction to the cultural posture of his films.

A Very Particular Set of Skills

Perhaps no single moment crystallises the EuropaCorp 'touch' than a particular scene from *Taken* (Morel 2009). Seconds after his daughter Kim (Maggie Grace) is kidnapped by Albanian sex traffickers, retired FBI agent Brian Mills (Liam Neeson) harangues her captors in a wildly improbable long-distance phone exchange where he makes a menacing announcement – if they do not release her, he will deploy his 'very particular set of skills' to 'find' and 'kill' them. In their conspicuous resemblance to lines uttered in so many recent action movies (a villainous Phillip Seymour Hoffman in *Mission: Impossible 3* (Abrams 2006) comes to mind, among many others) Neeson's words also encapsulate the plot mechanics of a film that made Neeson a latter day Charles Bronson at the ripe age of 60, and has since spawned two sequels (in 2011 and 2014), an 'origin story' television series for NBC (2017), and multiple copy-cat productions featuring older Hollywood stars – Wild Bunch's *Blood Father* (starring Mel Gibson and directed by Jean-François Richet) and StudioCanal's *The Gunman* (featuring Sean Penn and also directed by Morel). The irony of this 'very particular' claim, of course, is that there is nothing that 'particular' at all about a character – or a franchise – that continues to generate new iterations of *24*'s Jack Bauer while reviewers everywhere remain aghast at its 'pathologically generic' qualities (Vishnevetsky 2016). As Jacques Mandelbaum of *Le Monde* puts it, the *Taken* trilogy now constitutes a sort of 'low bar' for the EuropaCorp name, with a 'mindless repetition of themes, stripped down screenplays, middlebrow branding, competent direction and a tiny droplet of familial pathos in an ocean of spectacular action' (Mandelbaum 2015).

Yet an interrogation of Besson's cultural influence on the 'Frenchness' of action cinema also begins at the meeting point between this so-called 'lowest bar' and the impressive box office results that continue to issue from it. The perceived 'independence' of Luc Besson's production company abroad is an irony of the strength and contradictions of the French government's current approach to 'mixed-economy' media management. On one hand, Besson's emergence over the past twenty years might be construed a successful result of the reforms discussed throughout this book. In other ways, English-language films like *Taken* and *Lucy* could also be seen as the 'unintended consequence' (*effet pervers*) of the Lang era that critics find most difficult to swallow. Over the past decade, four English-language action thrillers – the three *Taken* films (Morel 2008, Megaton 2011 and 2014) and *Lucy* (Besson 2014) – have expanded the international visibility of Besson's brand and exacerbated its problematic cultural status in France. So while these two pithy, one-word titles now account for four of the top ten French film exports of all time, they stoke the resentment of the French critical establishment, which bristles at their formulaic quality even as it acknowledges their significance to yearly export returns. Several scholars have sought to complicate the negative reception of EuropaCorp action films by pointing to the potential for ideological cracks in their ambiguous plot and characterisation (Pettersen 2012; Martin-Jones 2012; Archer 2015). While most accounts engage only briefly with the role that action stylistics play in generating these critical responses, a recent article by Joshua Gleich goes further, arguing that a 'taut excess' of editing patterns is what makes Besson films like *Léon / The Professional* and *The Transporter* distinctive (Gleich 2012: 263), and that these features suffer in *Taken* due to a 'dependence on the norms of the Hollywood blockbuster' that came about with EuropaCorp (Gleich 2012: 267). While this attention to technique is a welcome complement to industrial accounts (Maulé 2008 and Vanderschelden 2009), Gleich also ends by repeating the most common critical refrain against EuropaCorp – its lack of specificity in a transnational context of film aesthetics. As Julien Gester of *Libération* writes at the end of his lukewarm review of *Lucy*, 'we can't help feeling that Luc Besson is filming all of this with the indifference of a marketing campaign, as if his material is less important than the cynical alchemy of the formula that underlies it' (Gester 2014). While numerous critics on both sides of the Atlantic now refer to Besson's company with kneejerk derision, they also tend to gloss over the strategic significance of a 'house style' that straddles national and global markets.

A 2005 article by Meaghan Morris is helpful in theorising the variant global paths of EuropaCorp, and of contemporary French action films in general. She proposes two interdependent forms of global circulation for action cinema. Drawing on Gilles Deleuze and Félix Guattari's distinction between 'major' and 'minor' literature, she argues that Hong Kong action films might be re-conceptualised according to at least two distinct modes of articulation (Morris 2005: 190). The 'major' mode, most associated with Hollywood blockbusters, features internationally recognised stars affiliated with the genre (Schwarzenegger, Stallone and Cruise), high-end production values made possible by extensive shooting schedules, exotic locations and digital post-production. This version of global action maximises profits through the well-worn forms of horizontal integration that first appeared in France in the 1990s (multiplexes, multi-platform distribution, 'long tail' marketing campaigns and tie-in merchandising). They often trade on what Morris calls 'All American affirmative action' or 'Hollywood global' casting, featuring established stars and supporting character actors against a backdrop of what cultural theorist Marc Augé has called the 'non-spaces' of global commercial culture (hotels, resorts, airports, commercial centres, military bases, yachts and skyscrapers). Meanwhile, 'minor' action films, Morris suggests, circulate on a different but no less global network, produced by small-scale specialist houses and fly-by-night companies, attaining a less-mainstream (but still quite pervasive) international audience through the collective force of genre connoisseurship, niche advertising and word-of-mouth. Rather than their presence on the multiplex marquee, these films flourish first by circulating among those who frequent martial arts clubs, gyms and specialty sports stores. Instead of high production values or digital effects, their 'cost-cutting' aesthetic trades on the athleticism and kinetic charisma of key performers, often athletes or martial artists by trade, surrounded by a world of non-descript urban 'any-place-whatevers' (buses, trains, factories and wharfs). As this 'minor' mode circulates, it eventually establishes its own classic titles – *Bloodsport* (Arnold 1988) – and its own quasi-independent circuit of star performers who move on a parallel track with their major counterparts, but also intersect or even break into the mainstream on occasion, especially when a Van Damme or a Jackie Chan earns increased visibility.

EuropaCorp's various methods do seem to sketch the rough contours of a 'house style' predisposed toward certain exportable formula. Yet the results of these efforts remain strikingly diverse on their own terms, often because of the way the studio works to straddle national and global markets. Management frequently reaffirms its plan to manage long-term financial risk through the pursuit of action cinema on multiple platforms. During the first decade of the studio's lifespan, Besson and co-founder Pierre-Ange Le Pogam emphasised their disciplined approach in the trade press – only giving the 'green light' to productions '80% financed in advance' and supervising 'the entire life of a film' by spreading financial risk across multiplatform properties and reinvesting its earnings to support a veritable 'tent-pole' every few years.[5] Throughout the

2000s, they burnished a reputation for staying on schedule and under budget, thereby convincing foreign distributors to invest directly in pre-sales for future films. In general, films in the *Taken* mold are produced fast – often in less than six months total – so that they can undercut the budgets of their Hollywood competition with a start to finish budget of €20 to €25 million. As *Transporter* direction Louis Leterrier puts it, 'there is no waste. Everything is as low budget as possible. You shoot fast. All of the shots or nearly all are used in the final cut. There are almost never reshoots' (Guerrin 2010). This abbreviated schedule can also play a role in luring star performers, and the surprising success of *Taken* only strengthened Besson's pitch to other stars like Guy Peirce (*Lockout*), John Travolta (*From Paris with Love*) and Scarlett Johansson (*Lucy*), eager for the opportunity to expand their repertoires beyond their typical casting in Hollywood. As of 2015, Besson's company was the largest production studio in France, producing or distributing an average of fifteen feature-length films per year, while handling marketing costs, developing television series, and tending a growing multimedia arm for books, DVDs and video games. The variety of these strategies separated EuropaCorp from the other large French studios (MK2, Pathé, Gaumont), which owned exhibitioin chains but still had comparatively underdeveloped holdings in other media. To date, EuropaCorp's most earnest attempts to 'go global' with 'tent-pole' blockbusters have been disappointing. The three animated *Arthur* films (2006, 2008 and 2009), *Adèle Blanc-Sec* (2012) and *Valerian* all performed admirably on the domestic market, but failed to perform as desired abroad. In response, Besson urges his critics to remember the pitfalls of the entrepreneurial model he is trying to replicate with far fewer resources than his Hollywood counterparts. Mounting a film like *Valerian and the City of a Thousand Planets* (2017) is only possible due to the firm's simultaneous pursuit of localised variations on similar action conventions, including the *Taxi* and *Banlieue 13* films, but also a slew of lesser-known titles like *Go Fast* (Van Hoofstadt 2008) or *22 Bullets* (Berry 2010).

While *The Fifth Element* (1997) and *Valerian* do seem to check nearly all of the boxes on the 'major' list, EuropaCorp's other production strategies suggest a give and take between modes of action film production. Around the time he founded his company with Le Pogam, Besson reached out to Robert Mark Kamen, a veteran Hollywood screenwriter known for *The Karate Kid* (1984) and *Lethal Weapon 3* (1992), but also as a self-described 'script assassin' for action movies at Warner Brothers during the 1980s and 1990s (Goldstein 2009). Kamen had helped Besson re-write *Léon* (1994) for the American market, and his counsel on the script for *Kiss of the Dragon* (Nahon 2001) cemented a permanent role for him at EuropaCorp. After decades in the Hollywood screenwriting ranks, he rejoices at the freedom of a company where no one rewrites his dialogue, and where nearly all of his scripts gets made 'because [Luc] can't afford not to' (Goldstein 2009). Asked to describe the nature of their collaboration, Kamen claims that 'Luc thinks up about eight film ideas every day; some are good, some are horrible' (Goldstein 2009). Together, they choose which ideas are most compelling, and Kamen fleshes out character traits and a story arc ('A to B to C') while Besson sketches the rudiments of a storyboard to be handed to the film's production team when financing is assured for the project (Goldstein 2009). Most of the results are films Besson produces, delegating the shooting to experienced veterans like Gerard Kracwyck (*Wasabi* 2001) or aspiring auteurs like Leterrier (*The Transporter*) culled from EuropaCorp's informal apprenticeship system. This mode of production (which Gleich likens to that of Daryl Zanuck during the Hollywood studio age) results in a set of repeated features in all the films – Kamen lists them as 'big set pieces, practical action, martial arts, [. . .] 'crazy/ crazy' stunts' and 'very few computer generated effects' (Goldstein 2009).

Besson's 'cost-cutting' methods extend beyond film-only venues to the forms of action that populate other screens on the French audiovisual market. It is also here where we might locate, for instance, the development of EuropaCorp-produced parkour films, which developed from a urban form of physical daring, first invented in the outer districts of Paris in the 1980s alongside other forms of expression like graffiti and tagging (Platten 2013: 158). Yet it is also in the 'minor' mode that the eventual stars of *Banlieue 13* – David Belle and Cyril Raffaelli – got their beginnings, first known as regional martial arts champions or anonymous stunt men in 1990s films, and eventually becoming notable *traceurs* (the term for the most accomplished parkour performers). Over the course of the 2000s, the sport emerged from its 'minor' modality to become the best-known 'French touch' action style in recent film history. The eventual stars of *Banlieue 13* and other *traceurs* had already been hired in various capacities by Besson in the mid-to-late 1990s, also serving as stunt coordinators and action coordinators across the industry, but eventually landed more regular employment with the arrival of EuropaCorp's more dependable infrastructure, gradually surfing on the popularity of a cycle of parkour films released in France between 2001 and 2009 to become an integrated part of French and, eventually, global popular action cinema. Accelerating into mainstream visibility somewhere between Raffaelli's memorable chase sequence in the French thriller *Crimson Rivers 2* (Megaton 2004) and the widely applauded opening sequence of the James Bond reboot *Casino Royale* (Campbell 2006), parkour eventually became a household word even in North America, gaining its own MTV series *Ultimate Parkour Challenge* (2009) and even drawing parodies in more 'mainstream' contexts like a 2013 episode of *The Office* (then one of the most popular sitcoms on American television).

The main antecedent for parkour's travel to mainstream and international audiences comes, of course, from the example of Asian cinema. Morris traces the 'minor' mode of the 1980s to the 'direct to tape' market, which in France and other urban centres of Europe propagated wide circulation of videos starring Bruce Lee and Jackie Chan, among others. Cannes and other European festivals began to pick up on this trend by the early 1990s, often featuring midnight screenings of Hong Kong action films around the same time that art directors like Wong-Kar Wai were beginning to make a splash on the main screens (Michael 2005: 61–64). In this regard, EuropaCorp's production methods have always been purposefully transnational. For *Kiss of the Dragon*, Besson imported Hong Kong martial arts choreographer Corey Yuen, who later worked on other films like *The Transporter* and *Banlieue 13*. This also explains the firm's investment in other comparatively 'minor' international action stars like Tony Jaa – whose *Ong Bak: The Thai Warrior* (Pinkauw 2003) was distributed by EuropaCorp domestically – as well as its other collaborations with China like *The Warrior's Gate* (Hoene 2017) a youth-oriented film co-produced with Fundamental Films about a teenager whose everyday life morphs with a martial arts video game.

Today there are also other media forms in the equation, of course. Morris's article was published the year of YouTube's founding, but it seems well within the spirit of her argument to suggest that today's versions of Belle or Raffaelli might be just as likely be found somewhere online in cheaply produced stunt videos or television programmes that fit on the sliding continuum between lowbrow and locally-specific media production, drawing interest from global martial arts networks, most visible to fans of adjacent industries like Ultimate Fighting Challenge (UFC) or the more recent Netflix-produced *Ultimate Beastmaster* – a six-country streaming simulcast of athletes taking on a multi-tiered physical challenge course. An uninitiated web search in 2017, for instance, resulted in the quick discovery of several obscure recent action-based productions out of the Hexagon – a streaming series called *Anatomy of an Anti-hero* (2017) or a short-lived television pilot called *Marc Saint Georges* (2013), both featuring a wannabe action star called Alan Delabie, the 2011 European martial arts champion who hails from Grenoble (Papin 2017). Apparently known to some insiders in France as the 'French dragon', Delabie's current repute in specialist circles allows him to garner only low-profile roles like these so far. Whether or not Delabie eventually emerges from these 'minor' action-based circuits is less important for this exercise than his relative position on a continuum of globality, ranging between globalised blockbusters and the sorts of local-grown anonymity that performers like Belle or Raffaelli began with in the 1990s, previous to their ascendance to more visibility in the parkour cycle of the early 2000s. These two modes – 'major' and 'minor' – thus stand as contrary possibilities on a global spectrum in the French-based production eco-system for action films.

Emphasising EuropaCorp's role in these varying modes of action-based media does not absolve Besson of the cynical politics that many critics accuse him of embracing. It does, however, offer a way to re-read the stylistic inflections of the films in terms how they are 'pitched' to different demographics. For Besson, the capricious legibility of action films as they travel among media platforms is what makes them an ideal gambit for a smaller scale economy hoping to infiltrate the global industry. This means acknowledging that EuropaCorp's productions straddle the demands of domestic and global markets, maximising different forms of the genre as a way to maintain economic – if not always aesthetic – distinction from their Hollywood competition. And whatever their qualities, he suggests, films like *Taken* and *Lucy* help to preserve the independence of a national film industry 'in survival mode' (Gonzalès 2003) by priming a more viable production centre in France, which allows domestic talent to 'make do' with more up-to-date resources, and – above all – deprives Hollywood of amassing all of the long-term financial gains from popular demand.

What Besson has created, from this vantage point, is the increased infrastructural capacity for technical personnel to circulate with access to production facilities in ways that they could not do so readily in previous decades. Raffaelli, for instance, was a choreographer and stunt coordinator on various productions in the 1990s before taking on a more consistent supervisory role with Besson's company when it was founded. He finally drew a secondary part in *Kiss of the Dragon* which eventually led to *Banlieue 13* and its sequel, making him a recognised talent who can move more freely, even landing named roles in the EuropaCorp gangster thriller *Human Zoo* (Rasmussen 2009) and the French-Morrocan war-horror film *Djinns* (Martin & Martin 2010) as well as occasional gigs in Hollywood.

Minor and Major Transgressions

A comparison of *Taken* and *Lucy* – EuropaCorp's two most economically successful films to date – highlights the underestimated malleability with which the firm's production methods approach the global parameters of action cinema. Several scholars have noted the streamlined approach to narration across Besson's career, and these films seem to bear significant similarities in this regard (Hayward 1998; Hayward and Powrie 2006; Gleich 2012). Each features a tightly constructed narrative (about 90 minutes); an identifiable Hollywood star in (what was at the time) an off-cast role; and an enormous budget by French standards (an estimated €25 and €40 million respectively). Upon further examination, however, these two examples of the EuropaCorp 'formula' integrate action aesthetics in ways that suggest that quite different 'cost-cutting' methods are at work within the parameters of EuropaCorp's current strategy.

Taken's depiction of Paris suggests its protagonist's descent into a spatially ascetic underworld. Neeson readily admits he took the role just to do a 'more physical' part even though he assumed it would 'go direct to DVD' (Brady 2012). In some ways, the film's narrative premise is a perfect rendition of how Morris characterises minor genre plots: 'a white star wandering around a poverty-stricken, exotic location for some vaguely justified reason' (Morris 2004: 189). That vague justification comes in the film's first act, which flashes by in some twenty minutes. Showing off his well-preserved action chops, Mills rescues a starlet singer during a concert gig gone awry, but other than this dimly lit backstage sequence, most of the locations in Los Angeles occur in the mix of urban 'non-spaces' (restaurants, hotels and airports) most typical of mainstream Hollywood action films. After a brief power struggle with his ex-wife (Famke Janssen), Mills gives permission for his daughter Kim (Maggie Grace) to follow U2 on a trip to Paris with her friend Amanda (Katie Cassidy). Yet this is a hero haunted by loss from the beginning; as he tells his wife, he 'knows what the world is like' and that has trained him to expect the worst. Those reservations shortly prove prophetic, because in just ten minutes of screen time, the naïve duo depart a luminous LA airport terminal, share a cab with a smirking Frenchman named Peter (Nicolas Giraud), and get kidnapped a few hours after arriving at their apartment. From then on, the film's image track descends into low-key lighting and claustrophobic shot scales – so much so that the remarkably detailed Anglophone tourism blog called *Paris Movie Walks* warns readers that this version of the city is 'shot in a strange and understated way', making it difficult to identify places to go (Schuermann 2018).

There are of course multiple possible reasons for the look and feel of Morel's film. As a former cinematographer, he claims in interviews that he wanted to avoid perpetuating the 'postcard' view of the French capital seen in films like *Amélie* ('Taken') or almost any other American film shot in France. Other than a brief bird's eye establishing shot of the Arche de Triomphe while Mills' plane circles for landing, precise coordinates of the city are generally repressed. This is true of the film's action scenes as well. When Bryan tracks down Peter at Charles de Gaulle airport, a frenetic chase scene ensues outside the airport. The fast-cut mobile frames devolve into a flurry of concrete and asphalt more characteristic of the vaguely sketched locations common to the minor mode. A few scenes later, Mills crosses more definitively into a dystopian atmosphere that will dominate the rest of the film's depiction of Paris, including a construction site resembling a 'hellish lunar landscape' (Archer 2015: 191) where he first encounters the sex traffickers responsible for Kim's abduction.

The claustrophobic visuals and clipped pacing of *Taken* are arguably also a function of necessity in the film's mode of production. Morel has

Figure 5.1   Mills (Liam Neeson) harangues Jean-Claude (Olivier Raboudrin) against the vague outline of the Arche de Triomphe. Screen grab from *Taken*. DVD. EuropaCorp. France: 2008

been open about the parameters of the film's budget, which apparently had enough to lure Neeson's participation (his precise salary is not available) but not enough to give the crew many opportunities to access the streets of the capital city – much less to stage dramatic fight scenes in front of recognisable monuments ('Taken'). In many places, the film itself even seems to turn this apparent aesthetic limitation into its most distinguishing thematic feature. A rare well-lit street scene, for instance, features Mills seeking out his old friend, the former French operative Jean-Claude Pitrel (Olivier Rabourdin), now a ranking administrator at the Directorate of Internal Security. The two men are framed in medium-long shot as they wait to cross the street, an angle that highlights the emblematic red awning of a famous Paris bistro behind them. Observant spectators might notice the restaurant's name – *Fouquet's* – which, when paired with the faint outline of the Arche de Triomphe in a subsequent frame, could place the conversation near the Champs Élysées (Figure 5.1).

Back in the two-shot though, Neeson glowers over his shorter French counterpart, displaying the physical distinction between them while Kamen's script hammers home other thematic comparisons. Pitrel boasts about his newfound freedom 'behind a desk' and warns that Mills 'can't just run around tearing down Paris!'. Mills' retort is cartoonish – 'I'll tear down the Eiffel Tower if I have to!'. In a few efficient frames, we digest what has to be a purposely clichéd comparison between the 'active' American and his stereotypical opposite number – the morally bankrupt French bureaucrat. For Neil Archer, that comparison constitutes part of the film's overlooked inter-textuality, which he argues references the 'self-critical and dystopian tropes' of prior Franco-European *noir* films to the bluntest extent possible (Archer 2015: 196).

Figure 5.2   A rare domestic scene in *Taken* turns suddenly violent. Screen grab from *Taken*. DVD. EuropaCorp. France: 2008

While Kamen's dialogue is arguably reflexive to a point, it would be a mistake to exaggerate its importance to the overall texture of the film. In the end, Mills' frantic search for his daughter offers few examples of the 'knowing irony' Purse suggests contemporary Hollywood action films use to foment a 'reassuring display of reclaimed power' to their audience (Purse 2011: 9). Instead, basic spatiotemporal cues are sidelined consistently here, likely because the film was difficult to shoot within the regulations of Paris. At one point Pitrel suggests Mills might find the sex traffickers' headquarters at Rue du Paradis, but the identifiable coordinates of the locale are restricted to a close-up of the road sign. Sequences that deviate from this in even small ways seem downright ornate by comparison. In one scene, Jean-Claude returns to the Pitrel apartment with a baguette under his arm (of course), greeting two young children at the door. As he turns the corner he starts at the sight of Mills, apparently just welcomed for dinner by his wife. Tensions escalate as Jean-Claude exits the room to put the kids to bed; on the way back to the table he stops in the bathroom to grab a revolver. Pitrel's wife makes small talk as the meal begins, but soon begins stammering confused objections as the two men confront each other, screaming (Figure 5.2). Seconds later, Mills not only interrupts her, but makes her his next victim with a vicious gunshot to the arm as he demands more information from her husband about a colleague implicated in Kim's disappearance.

The dissimilarities between this scene and the rest of *Taken* are striking, if brief. Set in a domestic location with a dash of warm personal interactions, the Pitrels' apartment seems to stall the norms of Morel's editing for a moment, as the frame momentarily abandons both Bryan's subjectivity and his relentless forward progress. Further, Madam Pitrel's comportment as a hostess ('white meat or dark meat?') emphasises her exclusion from the male-centred plotline, but also from this entire story world, as if to admit the underlying potential for a different sort of film – one more typical of the Paris we see in other movies, where developed interpersonal relationships exist. That potential is, of course, emphatically rebuked just moments later. Similar to the earlier chase scene at the airport, where the feckless Peter gets crushed by a truck just as the action accelerates, this dinner scene puts *Taken*'s cost-cutting orientation on full display, bringing the action to blood-chilling heights just as our generic expectations run headlong into the film's self-imposed limitations.

The asceticism of Morel's film also seems to have become its primary selling point. In this light, Neeson's proclamation about his 'very particular set of skills' may be more a happy accident of streamlined production than a savvy marketing ploy. With no other native English overseers for his script at EuropaCorp, Kamen's dialogue remains untouched – as if to display the film's entire 'A to B to C' plot with irascible attitude similar to Besson's own frequent pleas to the press – that he has no time for interviews; that he is too busy 'making films' to reflect on their deeper meanings; that he has 'never set foot in a *cinémathèque*' (Hayward and Powrie 2006). Yet the no-nonsense forward propulsion of the film – what one critic called an 'entertaining appreciation of efficiency itself' (Borrelli 2009) – has also become what online action aficionados most appreciate, and continues to make the DVDs some of EuropaCorp's top selling items. Far from seeing the film as a specimen of mindless Bessonian production methods, some younger online critics have even embraced it as an authorial masterwork by Morel – one where the sheer visual expressivity of action 'in miniature' overwhelms the customary drive for narrative seen in most mainstream Hollywood fair. Influential 'vulgar auteurist' Ignatiy Vishnevetsky, for instance, sees the film as the best current evidence of Morel's (and not Besson's) underappreciated mode of authorship within the constraints of his role at EuropaCorp, where 'the flow of action is more important than the structure that flow creates' (Vishnevetsky 2010). For certain viewers, then, the instrumentality of the screenplay and the film's production methods seem to be a feature rather than a bug.

Lucy shares a number of features with *Taken*, but with a different admixture of the 'major' and 'minor' modes. Our titular heroine (Johansson) is an American student living in Taiwan. Coerced against her will to deliver a suitcase to a hotel for her seedy new boyfriend (Pilou Asbaek), she is almost immediately abducted by Asian gangsters who forcibly insert a bag of blue powder into her abdomen. Moments after her abduction, an overzealous henchman attacks Lucy in her holding cell, causing the bag of powder to burst inside her and release its contents, which we have learned are a chemical with the capacity to maximise brain function. What this means for *Lucy* the film, of course, is an almost unlimited platform for visual conceit. The character's brain expansion, tracked through a simple repetition of black inter-titles, offers endless possibilities for scriptural efficiency. More than *Taken*, the screenplay – credited solely to Besson – elides back-story other than a brief flashback to a rave scene (during the first few seconds) and a tearful phone conversation where Lucy recounts memories of infancy to her mother (her family is never mentioned again). The main narrative arc follows Lucy's travels from Asia to Paris as Eric Serra's score solders together crosscuts between the vastly different visual economies linked to Lucy's growing omniscience. After a digitally produced image of a cell splitting, the film begins (like *Valerian* would a few years hence) with an overt homage to *2001: A Space Odyssey* (Kubrick 1968); here Lucy's ancestral hominid namesake quietly drinks water from a stream, recalling the furry costumes in Kubrick's famous prelude. Moments later, Johansson's voiceover wonders aloud 'what we do' with our brains as a montage of cityscapes flashes by, rife with accelerated pedestrian traffic recall-ing the canonised avant-garde images of *Koyaaniquatsi* (Reggio 1982). Lucy's initial interactions with the gangsters are intercut with documentary footage of cheetahs stalking and killing their prey. Meanwhile, the film's other major casting choices invoke a whorl of global popular culture references. Alongside Johansson, our main players include the perpetually blood-spattered visage of Choi Min-Sik's Mr Jang (a clear reference to the actor's earlier Korean film roles like *Oldboy* (Park Chan-Wook 1968)); the gravel voiced gravitas of Morgan Freeman's Professor Norman (his opening lecture manages to evoke both the dolphins of *Le Grand Bleu* (Besson 1986) and Freeman's own role in *March of the Penguins* (Jacquet 2005)); and Amr Waked's overwhelmed Captain Del Rio, recognisable for geo-political thrillers like *Syriana* (Gaghan 2005) or *Contagion* (Soderbergh 2011) but also a regular hardboiled presence in Egyptian *noir* thrillers and middlebrow independent cinema like *Salmon Fishing in the Yemen* (Torday 2011). Lucy's growing cerebral prowess allows her to anticipate the future – shooting some foes before they can respond; suspending others in the air; generally bending physics to her will. In the finale, she meets with Norman and his colleagues at a lab, ready to share her insights for the good of humanity, then bathing them all in a vacuous white 'desert of the real' worthy of *The Matrix* (Wachowskis 1999).

Action scenes are paramount, but inhabit *Lucy* in a qualitatively different manner than they do *Taken*. Lucy's eventual dissolution into oozing black ten-drils may shock with its sheer absurdity, but the film generally lacks extended fight or chase scenes like those that Neeson and Morel staged and rehearsed in advance. Instead, *Lucy* replaces pre-production choreography with sheer visual invention – slow motion gunplay, amped-up following shots, filtered close-ups of Johansson's face and the plastic freedom of digital inventiveness.

Figure 5.3   Lucy's car speeds down the Rue du Rivoli. Screen grab from *Lucy*. DVD. EuropaCorp. France: 2014

A notable exception is a car chase in the third act. Desperate to meet Professor Norman before the drug takes her life, Lucy commandeers Del Rio's police cruiser and promptly accelerates in the wrong direction down the Rue du Rivoli. Besson credits *The Blues Brothers* (Landis 1980) for inspiring the scene, at once breathtaking and spatially specific. Vehicles swerve, crash and even flip, while pedestrians leap out of the car's path as it swerves down Rivoli's iconic arched commercial sidewalks. In the meantime, fleeting but identifiable Parisian monuments – the Pantheon, the Place de la Concorde – flash by as if to trumpet the merits of a set piece filmed during a week of access to one of the most densely travelled Parisian arteries (Figure 5.3).

Lucy was received in France with the mix of box office enthusiasm and backhanded compliments by now quite familiar to Besson. Glossy popular magazines were predictable in their embrace of the film's returns abroad while intellectually oriented venues voiced more muted praise. What seemed to unite the establishment in praise of the film, however, was its habile use of special effects. Before *Valerian*, *Lucy* was EuropaCorp's most extensive use of digital imagery, involving some 1,000 individual frames with enhanced graphic elements. At the time, the post-production wing for the *Cité du Cinéma* had not yet been completed, and Besson had to outsource detail work to America's Industrial Light & Magic (ILM) and New Zealand's Weta Digital. Yet the Rivoli scene in particular remains a landmark for French cinema. In 2017, it was displayed in a family-oriented exhibit at the Science and Industry Museum, complete with a making-of video and original storyboards. Midway through the exhibit, Besson himself made an appearance at the museum for a master class demonstrating how the visual effects in *Valerian* were made possible.

For EuropaCorp, seeking success with action cinema means embracing the capricious, multiplatform realities of the global culture industries. While it does not exhaust the variation of Besson's efforts, a comparison of *Taken* and *Lucy* offers a succinct demonstration of how the company successfully embraces different transnational aesthetics. In the former, a clipped approach to spatial articulation pushes certain components of the 'minor' tradition to the fore, while in the latter the compact juxtaposition of visual effects and inter-textual references seems attuned to a more 'major' echelon. What the films seem to share, however, is a sort of globalised idiom anchored in 'cost-cutting' shortcuts. Not coincidentally, this is also where their reception seemed to meet. As with *Taken* before it, glossy popular magazines and television talk shows rejoiced at *Lucy*'s success abroad, while intellectual venues offered a rehearsed skeptical take – suggesting that the film, while 'efficient' in terms of its genre, remains understudied even on its own inter-textual terms (several critics verged on accusing Besson of plagiarism in the name of achieving a 'pure product of marketing').

Besson's frustration with his own country's critical establishment, he claims, does not derive simply from negative reviews (as is often reported) but from the structural biases of a system that fails to recognise the value of different approaches to filmmaking. 'It's a little painful,' he says, 'because [I'm] trying to do something for [my] country, and they don't get it' (Gonzàles 2003). These sentiments echo those of a generation of executives and entrepreneurs before him (see Chapter 1), but also of Patrice Leconte and the *réalisateurs en colère* (see Chapter 2) with whom he joined in 1999 to urge French critics to evaluate popular cinema on its own terms ('Les cinéastes' 1999). On this view, French film criticism should also adapt its practices to the needs of a new era of film-making in the context of multimedia distribution.

Here then we return to the core tenets of what we have so far been calling a professionalist slant on producing 'globalised' films in the French industry. It is understandable how claims like these leave the critical press cold, opening EuropaCorp films to the repeated charges of capitalist instrumentalism that have plagued Besson's entire career. Yet an analysis of the films also suggest an acute sensitivity to how action cinema as a mode of film practice offers multiple possible entry points for a smaller film industry seeking different forms of engagement at home and abroad. As Besson forges ahead, action cinema remains the most efficient way to embrace the capricious, multiplatform realities of the globalised culture industry. The undeniably positive point concerning his contributions has to do with providing the technical know-how and the physical plant necessary for a generation of performers to move easily between creative modes. In this light, the closing subjective montage of *Lucy*, where Johansson sits in a rolling office chair while she 'swipes' her visualised memory banks from a prehistoric Lucy to the Eiffel Tower, could be read as the most important image of the film. Bringing the ingredients of the film's international formula (the Hollywood star, her digitised inter-textual namesake and an iconic postcard image) crashing together with an aggressive form of shorthand, *Lucy* does for the 'major' idiom what Mills' unhinged Parisian rampage does similarly for a 'minor' one.

Alt-global Dreams

As the highest-profile source of French-produced action filmmaking today, EuropaCorp remains a reference point for almost all Gallic directors hoping to attain similar levels of international visibility. A growing number of other recent French action titles adopt a posture quite like the major form, yet somehow askance of its lures, as if searching from within globalised cinema for revamped forms of continental popular culture. Accomplishing this with the hope of specificity is a daunting task, especially on a post-Tarantino landscape where a reflexive relationship to film history constitutes part of how Hollywood films use 'intelligently knowing' references to re-assert ideological mastery (Purse 2011: 9–10). As David Bordwell argues, this quandary of 'belatedness' – the creation of art in an era when all 'has already been done' – can be seen as an animus behind numerous stylistic features of much contemporary film-making (Bordwell 2006:26). Still, a number of contemporary French directors continue to trumpet their own visions of what a French action cinema might look like if it incorporates globalised influences while also drawing on more regionally specific archives of taste. Director Nicolas Boukhrief exemplifies this rhetorical dance of sorts:

> [Besson] is a genius for financing, for business. There's no doubt about that. [. . .] These are films for a specific public that he has in mind, and he doesn't care about ideology or good taste. He makes his films made for consumption, and they are completely impersonal, far from B films, or *cinéma bis*, like the ones I like. Then again, I'm not one of the people he's trying to appeal to either. Ghennam 2010)

Here Boukhrief offers an aesthetic rejoinder to Besson by elevating alternative forms of popular culture –specified by a more personal relationship to 'minor' forms of culture, and by his own attunement to them. His reference points are worth unpacking a bit further, as they reveal some important parameters of how 'cultural diversity' operates in the current French reception climate around popular cinema. His first reference to B-films should be familiar to all cinéphiles, suggesting broad fluency in Hollywood of the classic era, but also with its economic and aesthetic distinctions between prestige films, lower-profile studio 'programmers' and 'poverty row' specialist production houses of the post-war period. New Wave directors famously professed their love for these films, so an embrace of B-films by itself would not separate Boukhrief's taste repertoire from the norm. Yet his second reference – to *cinéma bis* – is far more case specific, and contains the essence of how a current class of contemporary directors express 'independence' from both an entire tradition of global film references and from the more canonically Franco-European relationships to them. An expression drawn initially from the demarcation of French street addresses that fall 'between' the actual numbers, this term is notoriously difficult to translate to English.[6] In general, it refers to an entity that dwells 'parallel to' or 'next to' mainstream cinema, yet also liberated from the usual 'alternative' reference points of established circuits in France.

If this is an attitude that is case-specific to France, that is because the New Wave and its various 'alternative' legacies of interpreting Hollywood are now also perceived as part of how the dominant mode of filmmaking practice plays out in France and Europe. In this way, just a brief reference to *cinéma bis* positions Boukhrief as a filmmaker who is open to Besson's economic professionalism ('he's an economic genius') yet unattached to his particular set of aesthetic strategies for pursuing it. And it is here – in the combination of an economic professionalism with refrains of aesthetic exceptionalism – that we can locate another tendency in contemporary French action filmmaking. Though their points of reference vary, directors implicated by this second trend – call it the 'alt-global' – share an upbringing in the sensibilities of French fanzine culture of the 1980s and early 1990s. As previous chapters suggest, those two decades were a time of transition: when French television was emerging from state control (see Chapter 1); when new pop culture magazines like *Première* (founded 1976) and *Studio* (founded 1987) covered stardom far more than critical perspectives; and when prestigious enclaves generally overlooked films like *The Terminator* (Cameron 1981) and *Videodrome* (Cronenberg 1983). To fill the gap, a grouping of periodicals sprang from fanzines circulated in a younger community who grew up watching Hollywood blockbusters, but also exchanging videotapes and reading comic books. By the early 1980s, two important periodicals – *L'Ecran Fantastique* (founded 1972) and *Mad Movies* (founded 1977) – were sating these young appetites for genres outside their domestic industry, but it was a third title – *Starfix* – that, from its founding in 1986, began to nourish a generation of alternative visions for the French industry.

The writing in *Starfix* rings, in equal parts, with sarcasm and giddiness. Drawing on various obsessions with overlooked forms of cinema circulating in an industry adapting to multiple audiovisual platforms, it anticipates the major axes of what scholars have begun to call the 'new cinephilia' flourishing online today (Shambu 2014). Targeting a young audience eager to appreciate the vast regimes of visual culture recently made more available to them, it shares with its predecessors a broad taste for the 'fantastic' – a catchall term for genres neglected by the domestic industry (horror, action, science fiction and fantasy) (Gimello-Mesplomb 2012). What distinguishes the newer magazine from its predecessors, however, is a sheer mania for distinctions between these different sub-categories, and its insistence in pushing further into obscurity. Each of the magazine's core staff members brought his or her own expertise to the table, and their collected, esoteric voices assert themselves in the magazine's characteristic mix of colourful film stills (usually a provocative combination of gore, female nudity and monsters) with pages full of information about the circulation of new generic forms in France. Next to film reviews packed into columns ten-to-a-page were regular features for genre connoisseurs (video, comic books and video games) as well as in-depth 'behind-the-scenes' reportage on recent advances in technique.

The language of almost all the writing in *Starfix* vibrates with the excitement of a broad reclamation project for French cinema. The second volume, for instance, features Rambo on the cover to symbolise its focus on action cinema (Figure 5.4). The editorial staff begins the issue with the sort of irreverent intervention that would become its hallmark:

> Sylvester Stallone is on our cover. Do you find that disconcerting? We told you that *Starfix* was going to surprise you! We told you that *Starfix* would cover everything that moves on the screen! Action! Action! And more action! No bloody monsters in this issue, but there are scenes of gunplay, chases and fights! No spaceships, but lots of gorgeous women, futuristic barbarians, and machine guns! With this second issue, *Starfix* spreads its wings and dive bombs into one of its main objectives: adventure and dreams! (Headline 1983: 5)

Targeting the tastes of a certain (primarily male) readership, these comments also promote a form of pan-European branding similar to – yet distinct from – Hollywood. This move amounts to embracing another attitude about popular culture by employing a form of studied connoisseurship that elevates both obscure 'minor' and neglected 'major' forms of cinema to greater levels of prestige, or at least critical visibility, in the French context. *Starfix* stopped publication in 1993 as three of its editors – Christophe Gans, Boukhrief and Doug Headline – moved into film production, while a fourth (François Cognard) became an influential producer. Since then, the 'alternative' position they advocate in the pages of their publication has further infiltrated the culture of popular French cinema, especially since the turn of the new millennium. As if to concretise this nascent cultural status as a sort of heir to *Cahiers du cinéma*, a curated retrospective collection of *Starfix* reviews and covers was published in 2017 as *Starfix: Memories of the Future*.

Figure 5.4   Cover of *Starfix* 2: March, 1983. © Starfix Productions

One film in particular – *Le Pacte des loups / Brotherhood of the Wolf* (Gans 2001) – remains perhaps the most iconic exemplar of the alt-global trend. Conceived by StudioCanal at the height of the Messier-led Vivendi era as a response to 'the champion Besson,' the film self-consciously embraces the idiosyncratic visual pleasures of *cinéma bis* that Gans defended as an editor at *Starfix*. At the same time, as François Xavier-Molia argues, it is a film in the major mode, something normal for American franchises and yet largely absent from French campaigns before 2001 (Molia 2007). Employing a self-described 'mulatto' approach to film style, the film mixes costume drama aesthetics, an elite cast of French actors, Hong Kong inspired action sequences (choreo-graphed by Yuen), bullet time digital effects (two years after the first *Matrix* film), references to Italian gore and horror, and a giant mechanised wolf. All of this is wrapped into a convulsively self-reflexive package and loosely based on a well-known French legend, *La Bête de Gevaudan*. The brief opening sequence of the film serves as a sort of mission statement, as a retrospective voiceover by an imprisoned aristocrat after the French Revolution frames our tale, while the image track embarks on a vertiginous, digitally enhanced tracking shot that accelerates through verdant landscape, eventually resting on the frantic form of a young girl in period dress, whose scramble up a dirt embankment evokes equal parts costume drama and horror film. As she is slammed against the rocks by an invisible, growling assailant, the film packs flamboyant flourishes into a few minutes that become difficult not to read both as a function of the narrator's own lamentations and as an exhortation about film style itself: 'the world is going to have to change'.

Of course, to those viewers 'in the know', all of this had been telegraphed for years in the pages of *Starfix*. As one of the magazine's founding members, director Gans cultivated a loyal following in French cinephile culture for some twenty years, regularly covering Hong Kong action cinema and Italian goth-horror, and frequently defending both of them on account of their sheer visual excess. Shortly after *Starfix* ceased publication, Gans began filming on his first feature film *Crying Freeman* (1996) in Canada, working with martial arts expert Marc Dascoscos, who would later incarnate the kung fu fighting Native American sidekick Mani in *Brotherhood of the Wolf*. A special issue of *Starfix* released around the time of the film, celebrated the success of their own and announced that at last' French cinema is baring arms! (*Starfix* 2001).

Le Pacte des loups remains rare in the extent to which it overtly attempts to Gallicise the blockbuster formula by injecting it with the vigour of a cinephilic sensibility idiosyncratic to late 1990s France. Yet there clearly also remains a significant push for action genre films that adopt the norms of the major action mode while also aiming for cultural and aesthetic distinction from within them – as if to be in the aesthetic norms of the major form while maintaining a stance that is not entirely adherent to those same features. A similar 'alt-global' calculus is clearly at work, for instance, in the recent co-production *Largo Winch: The Heir Apparent* (Salle 2008) and its sequel *The Burma Conspiracy* (Salle 2011). As loose adaptations of a Franco-Belgian comic book series by Philippe Francq and Jean Van Hamme, both films are co-productions financed by Pan-Européene, a studio that in its current 'independent' status illustrates how a more 'typical' Franco-European production firm approaches the 'cul-tural diversity' of popular cinema in France. At first a distribution affiliate for the short-lived UK 'major' Polygram Entertainment in the early 1990s, Pan-Européene started its own domestic production agenda with the dissolution of

PolyGram later in the decade. Like many similarly situated outfits in France, the company's initial production slate ranged widely – from a fringe project like the controversial feminist road film *Rape Me / Baise-Moi* (Despentes and Trinh-Ti 1999) to an establishment auteur film like *The Comedy of Power / L'Ivresse de pouvoir* (Chabrol 2006) to the ensemble romantic comedy *Le Prix à payer / The Price to Pay* (Leclère 2006). Among these efforts on various scales, the two Winch films were by far the most ambitious financially, receiving expansive budgets by European standards (around €25 million each).

In terms of action, the films are clearly inspired by recent stylistic movements in the major mode. Unlike the striking narrative economy most associated with EuropaCorp, the storytelling here is labyrinthine, punctuated by jolts of exuberant visual extravagance. Winch himself is characterised as a superhero of sorts. Unlike Mills (who is just angry and vengeful) or Lucy (who barely has character traits), this character has a complicated back story revealed in an ornate series of overlapping flashbacks and cued by different cinematographic textures akin to what we see in multi-protagonist Hollywood films like *Traffic* (Soderbergh 2000), *21 Grams* (Innaritu 2003) or *Babel* (Innaritu 2006). For Salle, cutting and mise-en-scène here function as a way to forge a place of distinction for a Francophone amidst other globalised franchises – especially Bond, but also other global 'major' franchises centred on charismatic heroism. Some of these features derive from the film's source material, but the primary one – the ambiguous cultural identity of the protagonist himself – was invented for the film adaptation. Whereas in the comic book Winch is a white orphan born in Turkey, Sisley's hero is a multiracial, multilingual world traveller whose exploits evoke the self-assured mastery of Schwarzenegger or Stallone, but do so with the constant assertion of his own Francophone singularity as a globalised citizen.

The opening sequence of *Largo Winch* resembles the overall address of major action cinema, yet inflects it with resonances geared to its status as 'not quite' Hollywood. Following a dissolve from the 'Pan-Européene' logo (a colonial-era exploration ship, no less), the film immediately adopts an evocative style of forking narration that, while inspired by its comic book source material, communicates the alternative parameters of its 'global' idiom in stark terms. First, a conspicuous bipolarity of focal lengths: several seconds of disorienting, hand-held frames accompanied by screaming voices; a close-up of a hand we subsequently learn belongs to Nerio Winch (Predrag Manojlovic) as he answers the phone call, responds to a menacing voice, furrows his brow, bites an apple. The scramble for basic expositional information continues with three discontinuous vignettes, each signalled by fleeting inter-titles, varying cinematographic textures and Alexandre Desplat's shamelessly Bond-esque theme music. As if to trumpet the production's access to 'exotic' location shooting, a loping travelling shot encircles Nerio's luxury yacht, displaying the iconic nocturnal Hong Kong skyline as it denotes the same with an intertitle – 'Hong Kong Island 2008'. Nerio is pulled into the water moments later, floating on the surface just long enough for his drowned features to register as we cut again, this time to the sepia-toned visage of his younger self, gazing through a car window – 'Yugoslavia 1981'. Nerio and his assistant, Freddy (Gilbert Melki) arrive at an orphanage, the car pulling up in another crane shot before Nerio signs a check to management (a flamboyant overhead framing), exchanges warm glances with a giggling toddler, and then takes the boy to what appears to be a working class coastal shipyard. After briefly observing the kind countenances of Hannah (Anne Consigny) and Josip (Ivan Marevich), we learn that they will be the boy's adoptive parents, and we cut yet again – this time to another coastal landscape –'Moto Grosso, Brazil, 19 December 2008'. At this point, it should be clear that written prose falls somewhat short of capturing the fluid density of Salle's film, which spasmodically flexes its multi-national muscle quite early and often. This not even to mention the spoken dialogue, which fluctuates constantly here – from Nerio's stilted English (during his phone conversation on the yacht) to exclusively Serbo-Croation (during the flashback to the orphanage) to a mix of Serbo-Croatian and French (when Nério meets with Hannah and Josip).

This is all a prelude for the arrival of our cosmopolitan hero – master of all linguistic lexicons, and driver of the cinematic one as well. In his first appearance, Sisley's face is obscured by an initial following shot on the beach, then hidden by low-key lighting when he converses with a Chinese tattoo artist before uttering the line that seems to officially crown him ('Largo ... just Largo'). Promptly demonstrating his heroism, Largo bursts from the tattoo parlour before the symbolic 'invincible' tattoo on his shoulder is even complete, responding to frantic female screams of distress – in French ('Lache-moi!'). To the sounds of a lilting samba, madcap antics ensue in the first major action sequence, in which Largo takes on several uniformed men who appear to be corrupt Brazilian militia members harassing Léa (Mélanie Thierry) – a French double agent who will soon enough be his primary love interest (and the film's femme fatale). The density of expository details packed into the opening five minutes all become pertinent here, as they have already established Largo's versatile, cosmopolitan skill set. Freeing Léa from her aggressors, he calmly exerts his physical skills almost as easily as he switches languages: 'Don't take this personally,' he quips to Léa's main aggressor, 'I don't think you're her type'. Moments later, after being thrown violently through (what appears to be) an adjacent pile of wood and supplies, Largo emerges unscathed, exchanging witticisms with the tattoo artist ('Invincible, eh?'), stabbing his opponent through the hand, and bantering with Léa as they hop on the back of a (heretofore never seen) getaway motorcycle ('Alors, vous vous debrouillez toute-seule?'). Later sequences introduce other taglines to Largo's repertoire.

Figure 5.5   This brief high-angle shot of our hero (Tomer Sisley) battling his foes accentuates the 'intensified continuity' of the opening action sequence in *Largo Winch*. Screen grab from *Largo Winch: The Heir Apparent*. DVD. Music Box Films: 2012

During his escape from a prison, for instance, Largo first manoeuvres around foppish Brazilian guards and, in the chase sequence that follows, navigates their escape car away from the aggressive pursuit of a truck all while maintaining sangfroid in the face of Freddy's panicked grimaces – 'jai mes méthodes', he quips periodically.

In terms of action film poetics, the film's flux of motion remains, for the most part, character-centred. The opening fight sequence described above features a master long shot midway through, showing Largo combating the men, and then cutting in to the action. When surrounding details do leap into the frame, they are consistently at the service of Largo's moment-by-moment needs. So while we do witness vaguely place-specific details through the master shot (a modest, rural beachfront town square?) and intermittent reaction shots (a mixed ethnic crowd gasps at the combat), we are provided little else in the way of precise coordinates – let alone details of place (Figures 5.5, 5.6). Instead, the roving camera circles the action, fluctuating with the bipolar focal lengths characteristic of 'intensified continuity', and subordinating subsequent spatial configurations to the manoeuvres of a proactively cosmopolitan hero, who is duly 'rewarded' in the very next scene when he and Léa consummate their flirty repartee with a sultry, low-lit sex sequence that arrives a mere ten minutes into the film's run time.

For our purposes, what emerges strongly here are the attitudinal dimensions of a film that indexes itself as slightly askance from the 'major' form qua Hollywood. All of the details enumerated from the packed opening sequence

Figure 5.6 Largo (Tomer Sisley) escapes with Naomi (Mélanie Thierry) in *Largo Winch*. Screen grab from *Largo Winch: The Heir Apparent*. DVD. Music Box Films: 2012

work together to promote a prolonged tension in terms of transnational 'readability' that in the end suggests the pre-eminence of Winch's Francophone outlook. Despite the use of multiple other languages throughout, it can be no accident that the rapidity of the montage subsides with the longer takes of Largo and Léa's intimate moments, and that their post-coital conversation takes place in French. So while the action sequences in *Largo Winch* do operate within many of the recognisable codes of 'major' filmmaking, they also exist in commensurate tension with their own enduring 'minor' resources. As if feeding the film's constant need to declare its 'not-minor-ness' by amplifying the overlooked globality of a continental cultural form (the *bande dessinée*) while carving a new space for a cosmopolitan hero who reclaims this type of screen exploits as eminently Franco-centric.

In light of the broader discursive outlook proposed in this book, 'alt-global' action films like *Largo Winch* offer a combination of features that qualify as 'transnational' – and yet define themselves as quite distinct from EuropaCorp. Despite the variations in their cinematic output, contemporary filmmakers like Gans and Salle share in a current trend towards finding ways to produce culturally distinctive yet exportable French-language films that manifest a relationship to both a 'global' stylistic idiom and detailed references to the nuances of local Franco-European cultural production. These are films that define themselves from within the norms of global popular culture, yet push to find new Franco-European traditions that can resonate with audiences. In this light, their various stylistic tendencies offer an idiosyncratic mix of linguistic and aesthetic traits that do not slot quite as imperceptibly into the 'global' realm as do most of Besson's English-language thrillers. Whether their exceptionalist sensibilities derive from the avowed fetishisation of *cinéma bis* (Gans) or the Bond-ification of a Franco-Belgian graphic novel (Salle), the weft of what we have called an 'alt-global' tendency in French-made action helps to further define another variant in the current state-of-play.

<h2>NEO-LOCAL REALISM</h2>

In many ways unlike the 'alt-global' strand, which asserts the commercial potential of Franco-European popular culture, another recent trend in contemporary French-made action cinema embraces fast-paced aesthetics as a function of geographic locality in a more concrete sense. For the artists who approach action cinema from this standpoint, action filmmaking offers a chance to merge different mainstream traditions rather than to seek out new forms of Franco-European globality. Several characteristics are typical of this tendency. These are generally films produced for a smaller budget than either the 'major' or 'alt-global' varieties. Among the most well-known are a trio of titles by Fred Cavayé, all produced for substantially less than their EuropaCorp (and Hollywood) counterparts. Each film gained in funding as Cavayé's reputation advanced during the 2000s, but the price tag of all three of his films – *Pour elle* (€8.6 million) to *A Bout Portant* (€10.8 million) and *Mea Culpa* (€18.4 million) – combine to equal the price tag of one lower-tier Hollywood (or EuropaCorp) production like *The Next 3 Days* (Haggis 2010), a remake of *Pour elle* as a Hollywood vehicle starring Russell Crowe. The trade off, in general, for directors working in this mode, is a cost-cutting aesthetic that combines hallmarks of intensified continuity with a more naturalistic embrace of geographic and cultural reference points. These techniques are couched in terms that are still far more common to French filmmaking – set in the present day, or what would pass for it, and starring actors who generally lack currency on a global scale.

To this point almost exclusively French-language, the films in this vein tend to reject the overtly 'global' packaging and aesthetic lures of the major mode beyond their basic embrace of the genre. In interviews, directors like Cavayé draw on a very different set of influences than Boukhrief or Salle do. At one point, he calls it 'a combination of something like a Claude Sautet film plus the Bourne trilogy' (McCracken 2011). While this comment may be intended in jest, it goes some way to explaining the manifold distinctions between the 'neo-local' and the 'alt-global' approaches prominent in recent French action films. These are features that tend to adopt a handheld 'low-fi' aesthetic similar to how *Bourne* operates. While the *Winch* films do also intermittently display similar characteristics, the 'neo-local' variant makes use of them in a

Figure 5.7   The familiar geometric confines of a TGV become a source of action and suspense in *Mea Culpa*. Screen grab from *Mea Culpa*. DVD. Metrodome Distribution: 2015

qualitatively different manner, inflecting the conventions of the aesthetic with the concrete geographic and physical terms of how bodies occupy space. In this sense, Cavayé's reference to the *Bourne* films is no accident. As Nick Jones suggests in an artfully argued recent book, these are films that occupy similar physical locations to other global action films, but do so in a different manner from other current trends, as we see Matt Damon and other actors take advantage of the readable specificity of public spaces like office buildings and subway stations, making them more than the 'non-space' ephemera typically advanced in major action grammar (Jones 2015: 70–95).

'Neo-local' action set pieces are often orchestrated around the phenom-enological specificity of space and place. In some cases, they reference rather minute textural details, as in the climactic scene of *Mea Culpa*, which occurs in the claustrophobic confines of a high-speed train (TGV). Making use of a milieu distinctive to the Franco-European landscape, the sequence gives notable pride of place to the sophisticated geometry of the cars themselves, turning the characteristically high-backed seats and narrow aisles into both the physical obstacles for the protagonists and sources for the passage's rhythmic editing patterns (Figure 5.7). So as Simon (Vincent Lindon) and Franck (Gilles Lellouche) fire their weapons and combat their assailants, diving back and forth amidst screaming passengers, the sequence also establishes an elegant syncopation with the pneumatically activated sliding doors between cars, puffing and sighing in a manner that eventually helps Simon's wife Alice (Nadine Labaki) to forestall her attackers for crucial seconds as she flees them by using her knowledge of an intractable feature of bullet-train technology.

Other 'neo-local' action sequences draw on more extended, sensuous localisations of spatial specificity. In the climactic scene of the overlooked political thriller *Une affaire d'état* (Valette 2009) our heroine Nora (Rachida Brakhni) chases panicked hit man Michel (Thierry Fremont) up the streets of Montmartre that lead to the Sacré Coeur. The sequence deftly modulates its stylistic approach according to both geography and human limitations, as both characters grow weary on the inclined streets, stopping periodically to catch their breath, with Nora noticeably limping and falling behind after she collides with a cyclist. A climactic moment of the sequence occurs on the steep flight of steps leading to the monument itself (Figures 5.8, 5.9). Here the image track draws on audience knowledge of the locale as Michel, panicked and in the

Figure 5.8   The flight of stairs at Montmartre become an obstacle for Michel (Thierry Frémont) as he flees capture in *Une affaire d'état*. Screen grab from *Une affaire d'état*. DVD. Studio 37: 2009

Figure 5.9   Nora (Rachida Brakhni) surveys her options as she chases Michel towards the Sacré Coeur. Screen grab from *Une affaire d'état*. DVD. Studio 37: 2009

Figure 5.10   A mobile point-of-view shot reveals both the physical obstacles and geographic particularities of the art market that will host the climax of a Montmartre chase scene. Screen grab from *Une affaire d'état*. DVD. Studio 37: 2009

lead, chooses the steps, but struggles visibly to continue at each landing, and he vomits when he finally reaches the top.

Meanwhile, Nora closes the distance between them by choosing the funicular instead, glowering in medium shot as she squeezes into the cable car among chatty tourists. The sequence then concludes with a penultimate tracking shot that begins with a medium-length framing of Brakhni's face as she approaches the crowd of vendors and artisans typically gathered in front of the iconic church. As the frame leaves her face, implying point-of-view with an extended eye-line match, it wanders with frantic precision in the dusk, searching for Michel in the crowd, then pushing slowly forward as if to accommodate the bustle of artisanal commerce associated with one of Paris's most iconic churches and tourist attractions (Figure 5.10).

Perhaps the most audacious example of the 'neo-local' trend to date occurs in a bravura chase scene in the metro during Cavayé's *A bout portant*. Here the truncated narrative premise actually resembles the 'minor' inflections of *Taken*, as the image track plunges into breathless action within a mere fifteen minutes of screen time. We have scarcely met Samuel (Gilles Lellouche), a male nurse and expectant father, when violent intruders knock him unconscious in his apartment, kidnapping his pregnant wife Nadia (Elena Anaya). As Sam desperately tries to find her, he uncovers the complicated reasons for her disappearance, stumbling on an elaborate cover-up by a corrupt police department that soon frames him for multiple murders that ensue. This is the elaborate set-up for the film's centrepiece, a frantic chase scene shot in the Paris metro that makes full use of its innumerable, crowded idiosyncrasies – the grey-toned platforms, cascading staircases, bustling escalators and winding tiled hallways. Left as a mere spatial backdrop for action, these scenes could have easily been

Figure 5.11   Samuel (Gilles Lellouche) frantically navigates the Opéra metro platform. Screen grab from *A bout portant*. DVD. Sony Pictures Entertainment: 2011

made readable in a less specifiable way. Yet Cavayé's approach is as concrete as it is kinetic here, intercutting the paired shots of Sam and his pursuers as they sequentially overcome each particular architectural configuration in the same order that Parisians would in a more quotidian sense (Figure 5.11). Not only that, but as the images spasmodically flip back and forth to follow the police as they are chasing their prey, actual geographic locations of their whereabouts are tracked and reinforced through dialogue, as Capitan Vogel (Moussa Maaskri) both corresponds with his charges via walkie talkie and demands that metro personnel update him continuously on Sam's whereabouts, which they relay to him as he reaches each destination (Figure 5.12). So as we hear the excited voices tracking his progress with lines like 'It's

Figure 5.12   Captain Vogel (Moussa Masskri) requests precise updates on Samuel's whereabouts. Screen grab from *A bout portant*. DVD. Sony Pictures Entertainment: 2011

Figure 5.13   Samuel's progress is tracked on surveillance monitors. Screen grab from *A bout portant*. DVD. Sony Pictures Entertainment: 2011

the hallway of line 8, direction Balard!' or 'Opéra sur le quai là, direction Gallieni!' ('Opéra on that platform! Headed towards Gallieni!'), Cavayé also injects our consumption of action aesthetics with the verifiable coordinates of the shoot itself, as Vogel oversees the chase on grainy surveillance monitors. Unlike *Largo Winch*, this is not a sequence where action is subordinated to the hero's charismatic wherewithal. Rather, the suspenseful elements here emerge from our envisioning of an actual milieu, how it is laid out, and how Samuel navigates it from moment-to-moment.

In places, the 'neo-local' mode also connects the concrete features of action cinema to a more abstract form of cultural knowledge. For its part, *A bout portant* is littered with other references to French-specific cinematic culture. Just to mention a few dimensions – we see here a sort of localised version of the 'affirmative action' casting that goes on in 'major' genre, but anchored in the moment-to-moment socio-political resonance of Lellouche's Franco-Français 'wrong man'. At one point, he is actually handcuffed to Roschdy Zem's *beur* villain for an entire sequence, forced to be literal 'brothers in arms' as they flee the police. Meanwhile, Zem's character is also named 'Sartet' for Alain Delon's iconic character in *Le Clan des Siciliens* / *The Sicilian Clan* (Verneuil 1969), while Gerard Lanvin, long a charming star of French policiers, is cast against type as the villain. Finally, the film's climactic sequences end with brutal violence enacted on Lellouche's pregnant wife's body in a way that draws on the shock value (and perhaps even the aesthetics) of the *cinéma du corps* that Tim Palmer and others have argued becomes a vehicle for connecting the overlapping sensibilities between avant-garde and popular cinema that characterise the current specificity of the French film ecosystem (Palmer 2011). Here a form of spectacle derives not only from the sheer kinesis of intensified continuity norms, but also from the ways that the characteristically 'global' formal features of action filmmaking dovetail with the on-screen depiction of precise Parisian coordinates. In other words, this is a nascent mode that subscribes neither to the 'undifferentiated fabric' of the 'minor' animus (as in *Taken*), nor to the 'non-space' vagaries of the its 'alt-global' opposite number (*Largo Winch*), but rather to the specificity of an identifiably French landscape, rife with geographic and socio-cultural details, eminently readable as such.

CONCLUSION

Action scenes offer a fruitful illustration of how the behind-the-scenes changes in the French film industry manifest themselves on the screen today. Scrutiny of the difference between the nascent trends in French action style lays bare how a group of popular film texts have been read and – in many cases – *made to be readable* by a culture that houses markedly different views of its own potential for bringing thrilling spectacle to the screen. Moreover, the action genre, with its emphasis on specific technical competencies (athletic performances, stunt choreography and multiple cameras) and post-production processes (rendering, digital effects and editing) tends to exacerbate the gaps between different 'global' aesthetic modes. Rather than 'various permutations' of one 'internationalising formula' then, the films considered in this chapter are forms that issue from a set of productive tensions between the current French approaches to a 'globalised' style of filmmaking. Attention to how these 'major' and 'minor' variations play out in various cases helps further conceptualise the dimensionality of a media industry maximising the potential of different transnational flows of culture.

NOTES

1. Some early scholarly reflections on the topic took a pejorative slant, suggesting that an over-dependence on spectacle wrested filmmaking away from more venerable narrative roots (Wyatt 1994; Dixon 2001). Recent accounts tend to be less polemical, instead relating contemporary action trends to cycles of industrial change (Thompson 1999; Bordwell 2006; King 2000), identity formation (Tasker 1993; Tasker 2004; Tasker 2015; Buckland 1998; Purse 2011), authorship (Buckland 2006), and special effects (Whissel 2014; Rehak 2018), expanding on their geo-cultural dimensions (Bordwell 2000; Gopalan 2002; Choi 2010) or probing their early antecedents (Higgins 2016).
2. See, for instance, Vanderschelden 2007; Vanderschelden 2009; Brown 2007; Archer 2010; Archer 2015; Purse 2011; Gleich 2012; Pettersen 2014; Rappas 2016.
3. A recent roundtable of online critics, for instance, gathered at the *Forum des Images* to accompany a weekend film series entitled 'Does "French touch" action cinema exist?' In nearly two hours of discussion on the topic, however, they were derailed halfway through by a discussion of Besson's company – which pushed them out of their previous consideration of action aesthetics and into a more general conversation about the

uphill climb faced by nearly all popular cinema in France today. (Forumdesimages. fr) <https://www.youtube.com/watch?v=CcptpT9127Y> (last accessed 6 February 2019).
4. With its €75 million budget, the film drew over €7 million in France. More impressive than that, it garnered over $63 million on the American market and over $200 million worldwide – both all-time records for a French-produced film (http://boxoff icemojo.com/movies/?id=fifthelement.htm).
5. These include €65 million for each installment of the animated *Arthur et les Minimoys* series (2006, 2009 and 2010); €67 million for *From Paris with Love* (2010); €40 million for *Lucy* (2014); €48 million for *Taken 3* (2015) and finally the unprecedented €180 million for *Valerian* (2017).
6. As in the difference between 2 rue Michel-Ange Auteuil and 2 *bis* rue Michel-Ange Auteuil, this term is notoriously difficult to translate to English.

WORKS CITED

Archer, Neil (2015), 'Paris je t'aime (plus): Europhobia as Europeanness in Pierre Morel's Dystopia Trilogy', in Mary Harrod, Mariana Liz and Alissa Timoshkina (eds), *The Europeanness of European Cinema: Identity, Meaning, Globalization*, London: I. B. Tauris, pp. 185–197.

Archer, Neil (2010), 'Virtual Poaching and Altered Space: Reading Parkour in French Visual Culture', *Modern & Contemporary France*, 18:1, pp.93–107.

Arroyo, José (2002), 'Introduction' José Arroyo, ed. *Action / Spectacle Cinema: A Sight and Sound Reader*, London: BFI, pp. vii–xiv.

Brady, Buzz (2012), 'Liam Neeson admits he thought Taken would go direct to DVD', *Irish Central*, 5 June, <https://www.irishcentral.com/culture/entertainment/liam-neeson-admits-he-thought-taken-would-go-straight-to-dvd-video-1571874 35-237508351> (last accessed 4 February 2019).

Bordwell, David (2002), 'Intensified Continuity: Visual Style in Contemporary American Film', *Film Quarterly*, 55:3, pp. 16–28.

Bordwell, David (2000), *Planet Hong Kong: Popular Cinema and the Art of Entertainment*, Cambridge, MA: Harvard University Press.

Bordwell, David (2006), *The Way Hollywood Tells It: Story and Style in Modern Movies*, Berkeley: University of California Press.

Borrelli, Christopher (2009), '*Taken* by the lunacy of the script', *Chicago Tribune*, 30 January, <https://www.chicagotribune.com/entertainment/movies/chi-0130-taken-reviewjan30-story.html> (last accessed 4 February 2019).

Brown, Will (2007), 'Sabotage or Espionage?: Transvergence in the Works of Luc Besson', *Studies in French Cinema*, 7:2, pp. 93–106.

Buckland, Warren (1998), 'A Close Encounter with Raiders of the Lost Ark: Notes on the Narrative Aspects of the New Hollywood Blockbuster', in Murray Smith and Steve Neale (eds), *Contemporary Hollywood Cinema*, New York: Routledge, pp. 166–178.

Buckland, Warren (2006), *Directed by Steven Spielberg: Poetics of the Contemporary Hollywood Blockbuster*, London: Bloomsbury.

Choi, Jinhee (2010), *The South Korean Film Renaissance: Local Hitmakers, Global Provocateurs*, Middletown: Wesleyan University Press.

Danan, Martine (2006), 'National and Postnational French Cinema.' In Valentina Vitali and Paul. Willemen (eds), *Theorizing National Cinemas*, London: BFI, pp. 172–185.

Dixon, Wheeler Winston (2001), 'Twenty-five Reasons Why It's All Over', in Jon Lewis (ed.), *The End of Cinema as We Know It: Film in the 1990s*, New York: New York University Press, pp. 356–366.

Eagan, Daniel (2007), 'Flight of Fantasy: Luc Besson Discovers an Angel in Paris', *Film Journal International*, 20 April, <http://www.filmjournal.com/flight-fantasy> (last accessed 4 February 2019).

Gester, Julien (2014), 'Lucy: Besson charge le mule.' *Libération* 5 August, <https://next.liberation.fr/cinema/2014/08/05/lucy-besson-charge-la-mule_1076011> (last accessed 4 February 2019).

Ghennam, Michael, (2010), 'Entretien avec Nicolas Boukhrief', *Fiches du cinema*, 4 April, <https://www.fichesducinema.com/2010/04/entretien-avec-nicolas-boukhrief -2/> (last accessed 4 February 2019).

Gimello-Mesplomb, Frédéric (ed.) (2012), *L'Invention d'un genre: Le cinéma fantastique français*, Paris: L'Harmattan.

Gleich, Joshua (2012), 'Auteur, mogul, transporter: Luc Besson as twenty-first-century Zanuch', *New Review of Film and Television Studies*, 10:2, pp. 246–268.

Goldstein, Patrick (2009), 'Screenwriter Kamen is taken with director Besson', *Los Angeles Times*, 10 March, <http://articles.latimes.com/2009/mar/10/entertainment/ et-bigpicture10> (last accessed 4 February 2019).

Gonzalès, Paule (2003), 'Luc Besson: le cinéma français est en survie', *Le Figaro*, 31 December.

Gopalan, Lalitha (2002), *Cinema of Interruptions: Action Genres in Contemporary Indian Cinema*, London: BFI.

Guerrin, Michel (2010), 'Luc Besson, capitaine de l'industrie', *Le Monde*, May 10, <https://www.lemonde.fr/festival-de-cannes/article_interactif/2010/05/10/luc-bes son-capitaine-d-industrie_1348902_766360_3.html> (last accessed 4 February 2010).

Halle, Randall (2008), *German Film after Germany: Toward a Transnational Aesthetic*, Urbana: University of Illinois Press.

Hayward, Susan (1998), *Luc Besson*, London: BFI.

Hayward, Susan and Phil Powrie (2006), *Essays on Luc Besson: Master of Spectacle*, Manchester and New York: Manchester University Press.

Headline, Doug (1983), 'Edito.' *Starfix*, March, p. 5.

Higgins, Scott (2008), 'Suspenseful Situations: Melodramatic Action and the Contemporary Action Film', *Cinema Journal*, 47:2, pp. 74–96.

Higgins, Scott (2016), *Matinee Melodrama: Playing with Formula in the Sound Serial*, New Brunswick, NJ: Rutgers University Press.

Hjort, Mette (2009), 'On the plurality of cinematic transnationalism', in Kathleen Newman and Natasa Durovicova (eds), *World Cinema, Transnational Perspectives*, New York: Routledge, pp. 12–33.

Jones, Nick (2015), *Hollywood Action Films and Spatial Theory*, New York: Routledge.

King, Geoff (2000), *Spectacular Narratives: Hollywood in the Age of the Blockbuster*, London: I. B. Tauris.

Mandelbaum, Jacques (2015), 'Taken 3: troisième volet de la franchise bas de gamme de Luc Besson', *Le Monde*, 24 January. <https://www.lemonde.fr/cinema/ article/2015/01/24/taken-3-troisieme-volet-de-la-franchise-bas-de-gamme-de-luc-be sson_4562902_3476.html> (last accessed February 2019).

Martin-Jones, David (2012), 'Colombiana: EuropaCorp and the Ambigious Geopolitics of the Action Movie', *Senses of Cinema*, 62: March, <http://sensesofcinema.com/ 2012/feature-articles/colombiana-europa-corp-and-the-ambiguous-geopolitics-of-the-action-movie/> (last accessed 4 February 2019).

Maulé, Rosanna (2008), 'Luc Besson and the Question of the Cultural Exception in

175

France', *Beyond Auteurism: New Directions in Authorial Film Practices in France, Italy and Spain since the 1980s*, London: Intellect Press, pp. 163–188.

Michael, Charlie (2005), 'French National Cinema and the Martial Arts Blockbuster.' *French Politics, Culture & Society*, 23:3, pp. 55–74.

Moine, Raphaelle (2007), 'Generic Hybridity, National Culture, and Globalised Cinema', in Isabelle Vanderschelden and Darren Waldren (eds), *France at the Flicks: Trends in Contemporary French Popular Cinema*. Newcastle: Cambridge Scholars Publishing, pp. 36–50.

Molia, François-Xavier (2007), 'Peut-être à la fois Hollywoodien et Français? French Superproductions and the American Model', in Isabelle Vanderschelden and Darren Waldren (eds), *France at the Flicks: Trends in Contemporary French Popular Cinema*. Newcastle: Cambridge Scholars Publishing, pp. 51–62.

Morris, Meaghan (2005), 'Transnational imagination in action cinema: Hong Kong and the making of a global popular culture', *Inter-Asia Cultural Studies*, 5:2, pp. 181–199.

Papin, Arnaud (2017), 'Le rêve américain d'Alain Delabie en version websérie', *La Voix du Nord*, 5 July, <http://www.lavoixdunord.fr/187339/article/2017-07-05/le-reve-americain-d-alan-delabie-en-version-webserie> (last accessed 4 February 2019).

Palmer, Tim (2011), *Brutal Intimacy: Analyzing Contemporary French Cinema*, Middletown: Wesleyan University Press.

Pettersen, David (2012), 'American Genre Film in the French Banlieue: Luc Besson and Parkour', *Cinema Journal*, 53:3, pp. 26–51.

Platten, David (2013), 'Why Popular Films are Popular: Identification, imitation and critical mortification', in D. Holmes and D. Looseley (eds), *Imagining the Popular in Contemporary French Culture*, Manchester: Manchester University Press: pp. 123–161.

Purse, Lisa (2011), *Contemporary Action Cinema*, Edinburgh: Edinburgh University Press.

Rappas, IA Celek (2016), 'The Urban Renovation of Marseille in Luc Besson's *Taxi* Series', *French Cultural Studies*, 27:4, pp. 385–397.

Rehak, Bob (2018), *More than Meets the Eye: Special Effects and the Fantastic Transmedia Franchise*, New York: New York University Press.

Schuerman, Michael (2011), 'Where Taken was Shot', *Paris Movie Walks*, 22 March, <http://parismoviewalks.co.uk/update-taken/> (last accessed 4 February 2019).

Shaw, Deborah (2013), 'Deconstructing and Reconstructing Transnational Cinema', S. Dennison (ed.), *Contemporary Hispanic Cinema*, Woodbridge: Tamesis, pp. 47–66.

Shambu, Girish (2014), *The New Cinephilia*, Montreal: Caboose.

Starfix: New Generation 16, January/February 2001.

Tasker, Yvonne (ed) (2004), *Action and Adventure Cinema*, New York: Routledge.

Tasker, Yvonne (2015), *The Hollywood Action and Adventure Film*, New York: John Wiley and Sons.

Tasker, Yvonne (1993), *Spectacular Bodies: Gender, Genre and Action Cinema*, New York: Routledge.

Thompson, Kristin (1999), *Storytelling in the New Hollywood: Understanding Classical Narrative Technique*, Cambridge, MA: Harvard University Press.

Vanderschelden, Isabelle (2007), 'Strategies for a 'Transnational'/French Popular Cinema', *Modern & Contemporary France*, 15:1, pp. 36–50.

Vanderschelden, Isabelle (2009), 'Luc Besson's ambition: EuropaCorp as European Major for the 21st Century', *Studies in European Cinema*, 5:2, pp. 91–104.

Vishnevestky, Ignatiy (2010), 'Morel vs. Besson,' *MUBI*, 10 February, <https://mubi.com/notebook/posts/morel-vs-besson> (last accessed 4 February 2019).

Vishnevetsky, Ignatiy (2016), 'The Neeson-less Taken turns a hit movie into a TV dud', *AV Club*, 27 February, <https://tv.avclub.com/the-neeson-less-taken-turns-a-hit-movie-into-a-tv-dud-1798190580> (last accessed 4 February 2019).

Whissel, Kristen (2014), *Spectacular Digital Effects: CGI and Contemporary Cinema*, Durham, NC: Duke University Press.

Wyatt, Justin (1994), *High Concept: Movies and Marketing in Hollywood*, Austin: University of Texas Press.

6. SERIAL (BAD?) FRENCH COMEDIES

When it was translated for distribution in the UK and the US, *Qu'est-ce qu'on a fait au bon dieu?* (Philippe De Chauveron 2014) acquired the rather awkward title *Serial (Bad) Weddings*. The literal meaning of the original French certainly could have been preserved in a more straightforward way in English (perhaps as 'What in God's name did we do wrong?'). Yet the phrasing that was eventually selected also offers an instructive point of departure for interrogating a significant dimension of how contemporary French cinema internalises its current relationship to global popular culture. A multi-generational farce about a well-to-do Catholic couple struggling to cope with the interethnic marriages of their four daughters, De Chauveron's film offers a feel-good message of nationalist solidarity out of a script that pounds rather relentlessly on well-worn racial and religious stereotypes. The most immediate irony of the English title, of course, is that Anglophone audiences outside the French market barely saw it at all; US and UK distributors almost unanimously turned it down, deeming its content inappropriate for the more 'politically correct' tastes of their target audiences (Fourny 2014). As one Hollywood executive put it, 'American audiences these days would never allow themselves to laugh at blacks, Jews or Asians' (Mulholland 2014). Yet that rejection is also a response to a 'politically incorrect' form of localised humour that must now count as one of the foremost ways in which the French industry is responding to the current challenges of globalisation.

As the breakout comedy hit of 2014 with over 12 million tickets sold in

France, *Qu'est-ce qu'on a fait au bon dieu?* was immediately received as part of a recognisable, repeatable and perhaps even 'serial' (if not predictable) strategy we might tentatively call the 'localised comedy blockbuster'. While the economic influence of films in this mode may no longer be in doubt, there remain pressing questions about what to do with them as cultural objects. Academic work on French comedy remains sparse overall,[1] but there has been a notable recent uptick as scholars probe how popular culture relates to larger questions of belonging and identity in France, often in response to said hit films. Raphaëlle Moine, for instance, likens popular French comedy to a 'social laboratory' (Moine 2014) that trades on the constant 'deployment, reversal, mockery and reiteration of stereotypes' (Moine 2018: 36). Her warning – as echoed by Phil Powrie and Mary Harrod in a recent special issue of *Studies in French Cinema* – is that there is also 'a delicate balance to be struck between the enunciation of stereotypes and their denunciation' (Harrod and Powrie 2018: 4). In a similar vein, Mireille Rosello highlights how what she calls 'communitarian comedies' ('*les comedies communitaires*') function to both 'expose the limits of how different communities *become readable*', and, paradoxically, to 'try to anticipate how we will *read* them' (my emphasis, Harrod and Powrie 2018: 22).[2]

Building on the energy of these recent contributions, this chapter argues that the ambivalence that flows through several recent French comedy hits also derives from how they engage with – and are engaged by – the broader forms of transnational rhetoric currently circulating in the French film industry and critical establishment. I would suggest that we see this dynamic occurring on at least three levels with respect to this genre. Most conspicuously, in a denotative sense, recent popular comedies from France are frequently 'about' the various localised consequences of global capitalism in France or the French-speaking world. Many of them draw explicitly on the comedic potential that occurs between the uneven cultural responses to global flows in contemporary France. *Bienvenue chez les Ch'tis*, for instance, tells the story of Philippe (Kad Merad), a well-to-do public servant from sunny Provence forced to accept a job in the obscure, dreary (and overtly fictionalised) Northern town of Bergues. As he adjusts to his new environs, befriending colourful working class locals like postal worker Antoine (Dany Boon), Philippe finds an abiding affection for 'the North' and its people, embracing a way of life (and a local dialect) that he previously found incomprehensible. On a second, more connotative level, these are also films that are increasingly recognised as a grouping or cycle, wherein each new success story regenerates a 'conversation' between critics, journalists and online fans, who ruminate on the implications of formulaic – even 'serialised' – films that continue to generate visible depictions of how a country's immigrant population interacts with the ethnically French middle class (*les français de souche*). Meanwhile, these conversations about the diversity of the depictions within French comedy also eddy in another long-term discussion of interest in this book – about how French cinematic culture adapts to transnational flows of capitalist consumption. Here, once again, we see familiar patterns of rhetoric, as some voices highlight how comedies and their 'localised' features offer evidence for a distinct, mainstream French cinema facing down Hollywood hegemony (professionalist), while others read these same features as the perverse consequences of an increasingly corporatised media industry (exceptionalist) and still others seek to forge consensus between the ideological extremes (pragmatist).

Without espousing any one of these dueling angles on the cultural legitimacy of contemporary French comedy, we can see how several of the most visible recent 'comedy blockbusters' from France actually contain a pronounced tendency to 'speak back' to all three. They do this by using their stylistic and thematic features to lampoon the codified movement of transnational discourse in a French context. Though reflexivity is a pervasive feature of post-modern cultural production in general (whether as pastiche or parody) we can also see that this dimension of 'double voicedness' (Hutcheon 2000: 114) takes particular forms in the cultural politics of contemporary French comedy. In the case of *Les Ch'tis*, for instance, it arrives as a sort of recursive satirical edge, wherein the film's credibly 'present day' depictions of localised Gallic culture (Arneuil's blue and yellow *poste* getup and delivery bicycle) clash with an ongoing game of winking hyperbole, which celebrates France's internal 'cultural diversity' by exaggerating its features and their consequences – here via the accented histrionics of Boon and other performers, but also through formal features like the map in the opening act, which traces with mock gravity the putative 'vastness' of French geography (Figure 6.1). That the graphic is later echoed by a well-nigh apocalyptic voiceover about 'the North' (complete with a Godfather-esque shot angle and low-key lighting to accentuate the speaker) only redoubles the second transnational generic register of a film that jabs good-naturedly at any viewer who might overly dwell on its 'authentic' depiction of localised cultural specifics.

It is amidst the interpretive energy around comedic features like these that the dimensionality of a word like 'blockbuster' becomes most relevant. After a brief sketch of the historical and rhetorical stakes involved in evaluating the cultural politics of popular French comedy, we turn more focused attention to three of the most visible exemplars of the recent trend towards big comedy hits: *Intouchables* (Toledano and Nakache 2011), *Qu'est-ce qu'on a fait au bon dieu?* (De Chauveron 2014) and the now three deep *Les Tuche* franchise (Baroux 2011, 2015 and 2017). In all three instances, we find narratives that draw quite self-consciously on their own potential for interpretive ambivalence, staging in their features – and provoking in their reception – a standoff between domestic attitudes about the cultural effects that global

Figure 6.1   A graphic map in the titles of *Bienvenue chez les Ch'tis* emphasises the geographic distance between the South and the North of France. Screen grab from *Bienvenue chez les Ch'tis / Welcome to the Sticks*. DVD. Pathé: 2008

media culture is having on the countenance of contemporary France and its cinema.

Framing the French Comedy Blockbuster

If the past two chapters offered a more intuitive approach to the historical question posed by our titular concept – French blockbusters – then the booming market for 'localised' comedy represents its apparent obverse dynamic. Like any such couplet, it can never simply be 'one' with itself – or, rather, takes on different meanings relative to cultural practices and historical particularities. French cinema's long history of principled refusals to conform to market-based practices has spawned an entire history of creative ambition, righteous indignation and infighting (see Chapter 1). It has also generated a slew of notable recent incursions in – and on – the comedy genre. Though equally tied to the sea changes brought about by the reforms of the late 1980s and early 1990s, these films are arguably tied to the more localised and risk-averse norms of the industry.

Of course, the dimensions of this genre also have much deeper roots. France has a long tradition of film comedy that runs from silent star Max Linder up through the numerous legendary crowd pleasers that continue to play to great success at home but with scant visibility elsewhere – *La Grande Vadrouille* (Gérard Oury 1966), *Les Bronzés* (Patrice Leconte 1978) or *Les Visiteurs* (Jean-Marie Poiré 1995), to name just a few (Jäckel 2013: 243–250). Moreover, there is an abiding conventional wisdom in the industry that a genre that depends on untranslatable nuances of language and cultural comportment stands ill-equipped to make the journey to foreign audiences. Those comedies that do eventually manage to travel abroad tend to do so more successfully via remakes than subtitled runs in North America – hence qualifying the genre as perhaps the most properly 'national' cinema of all (Mazdon 2000: 92). Yet while many executives and critics justifiably complain that the remake phenomenon is a de facto consequence of North American political-economic protectionism, it is also clear that the confined linguistic and cultural realities of making comedy have become an exploitable strength for French studios – especially in an age when global Hollywood franchises dwarf domestic competition like never before.

In a longer-term sense, then, the split between 'globalised' genre films and 'localised' comedies over the past two decades could be seen as the Gallicised rendition of a well-worn Hollywood game of risk avoidance. A major part of US film strategy since the 1990s revolves around risk management – prospecting for 'tent-pole' films, but also panning for 'sleeper hits' that might eventually become 'blockbusters' through the unpredictable alignment of market caprice and word-of-mouth (Schatz 2003: 40–41). Economic historians of French cinema tend to agree that the recent increase in comedy production is a salient long-term consequence of the Lang reforms of the 1980s, but there had also been significant movement in this direction prior to the Socialist victory. In 1979, noted film historian Jean-Pierre Jeancolas cited bloated Gaumont comedy productions (many starring Louis de Funès) as a wayward symptom of the free-market mandates of the Giscard administration (Jeancolas 1979: 270). In a remarkably similar assessment published after the results of *Amélie* and other films in 2001, economic historian Claude Forest argues that by depending so heavily on comedies, France and other European national cinemas mismanage their resources by '[abandoning] the segments of the market that are quantitatively the most important' and 'leaving the public in a state of dependence [on Hollywood]'. (Forest 2002: 78).

Today, statistically speaking, comedy still stands out as the domestic force of contemporary French cinema. According to a 2014 report by Unifrance, since 1995 comedy (of either the 'pure' or 'dramatic' variety) has accounted for two thirds of France's domestic takings (67%), but only a third of its international box office takings (35%). While it does follow the inflationist budgetary trends of the past two decades, comedy looks like a stalwart of budget diversity compared with the bipolarisation that grips other genres. Over the report's twenty year span, just 6% of comedies crossed €15 million in production budget, far less than animated films (15%), policiers (17%), historical films (24%), fantasy films (26%), thrillers (27%) and biopics (32%). Meanwhile, two other genres stand out on the other end of the spectrum, as 22% of dramas and an incredible 77% of documentaries are made for less than €2 million (Deleau 2016). So, if over the past two decades comedy has outpaced all other types of filmmaking, it has done so not by investing in glossy 'blockbuster' type films,

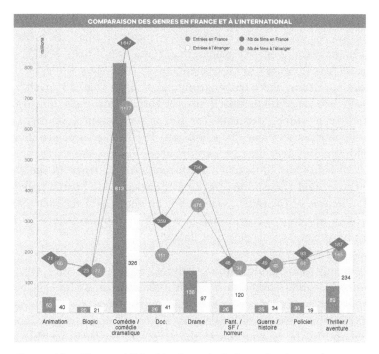

Figure 6.2   Chart published in Quentin Deleau, *Quels sont les genres du cinéma français qui s'exportent le mieux?* (Deleau 2016: 11) © Unifrance

but by dominating the mid-range budgets that used to be far more equitably distributed. Even more striking, these figures also seem to correspond with the roles that different genres have come to play in the industry's current transnational commitments. A quick glance at the above chart (Figure 6.2) reconfirms the genre's domestic affiliations, as a far greater proportion of tickets to French comedies are sold at home than abroad. Meanwhile, the opposite is true of fantasy films or thrillers, which tilt noticeably towards international audiences. Yet while accelerating investment in other genres leaves a noticeable mark on these figures, the most 'typical' French film today remains a mid-budget, locally oriented, French-language comedy.

For risk-averse executives, the popularity of comedies tends to constitute a primary example of how French cinema can best defend itself from Hollywood while maintaining a form of cultural specificity. In recent years, both national television giants – M6 and TF1 – have emphasised localised production techniques played 'close to the vest', which means using a combination of known television stars and predictable formulae to funnel resources back to their multimedia parentage with relatively low upfront financial risk. So for every successful comedic title that crosses the hallowed two million-ticket benchmark (often cited as the economic threshold for a 'blockbuster' in the CNC's local market terms) we see dozens of other titles featuring familiar cast members and similar generic packaging, yet gracing marquees only briefly before shuffling off to the relative obscurity of other media platforms. Meanwhile, on the other end of the spectrum, the narrow grouping of films that do reach audience benchmarks are more frequently than ever turned into multi-film franchises. Though there is some precedent for this phenomenon (notably Louis de Funès's *Gendarmes* series of the 1960s and 1970s) the sheer proliferation of serialised franchises over the past two decades is unprecedented for the French industry.[3] Whence the untroubled professionalist tendency in the discourse that hovers around these films, likening the success of French comedy to a 'natural' outcome of the public's desire for laughter, as if the genre's features derive from a one-to-one correspondence with market demand. As long-time Gaumont president Nicolas Seydoux puts it:

> A comedy corresponds to its culture. French men and women like comedies. *Qu'est-ce qu'on a fait au bon dieu?* is a film that reached a public that probably hadn't even been to the cinema since *Intouchables*, especially in those small locales that we call 'deep France,' where people rarely go to the cinema unless they are sure they will be able to enjoy themselves for two hours. For 120 years the French have loved comedy; for 120 years the biggest French hits have been comedies. That's not the case with American cinema, where the biggest hits, outside of animated films, have been action and adventure films. (Forest *et al.* 2017: 25)

As has become typical for professionalist framings of these matters, Seydoux's comments conflate the aesthetic attributes of individual films with the economic goals of the industry (and his own company). In short, comedy's value as a genre lies in its ability to 'reach a public' that does not customarily come to the cinema, and this role is the genre's self-evident populist destiny – irrespective of the aesthetic means used to do so. Not surprising, then, that Seydoux expands his claims by contrasting the role of comedy against conventional ideas of blockbuster cinema from Hollywood – the 'big adventure films', like *Titanic* which he elsewhere claims his own country generally 'doesn't have the means to make' and which, whenever it tries to do so, often 'means making an American film' (Forest 2017: 26). Paradoxically then, the professionalist warrant for producing continual comedy films becomes a politicised rhetoric of geopolitical 'smallness' – quite different from the genuinely 'big' entrepreneurial aspirations of a Bessonian action film like *Valerian* (2017).

The unexamined (and self-serving) instrumentalism of this framing often spurs reactionary responses in the other direction. Herein lies the second frequent view of contemporary French comedy, most common among cinephilic and auteurist circuits, which bemoan the sheer number of recent comedies and their repeated patterns of narrative and characterisation as symptoms of an encroaching standardisation (*formattage*) brought about by an economically conservative industry tied to the demands of television funding. On this view, popular comedies become the primary culprits for a regrettable loss of aesthetic distinction and corresponding surrender to the globalised market tastes. Variations on this argument recur rather frequently in the press, and tend to link the aesthetics of comedy to a callous pursuit of box office receipts. *Le Monde* critic Murielle Joudet, for instance, alludes to this view in a passing critique of the common elements behind two recent films:

> How can we explain the extreme productivity – sometimes rewarded by success – of popular comedy? Maybe it is due to a formula that is repeated from film to film, the idea that the film should start with a concept that makes the maximum number of comedic situations possible. (Joudet 2017)

Unlike professionalist views, which shrug their shoulders at broader questions of 'quality' in popular cinema (they are 'just entertainment') the exceptionalist line of reasoning does seem to briefly search for a way to defend the features of the films. However, when it does do this, it also commonly also conjures the pejorative specter of serialisation qua 'mindless' reproduction – a clear antagonist for more romantic notions of cultural legitimacy.

Of course, these tendencies are not always clearly demarcated. In numerous cases, different rhetorical slants come to cohabit the same fields, revolving in a mutual tension. As sociologist Norman Fairclough observes, this is a typical quality of how discourse circulates within a baggy monster of a concept like cultural globalisation (Fairclough 2006). As a case in point, we might point to the argument presented by the collective authors of the 'Club of Thirteen' of 2008, who spearheaded a call for renewed investment in 'middlebrow' cinema (*cinéma du milieu*), which they claimed was a primary casualty of a globalised cultural economy that stretched film budgets between the 'haves' (big budget films) and the 'have nots' (small budget films). Though sparing in details on actual films, the report alludes to several positive examples of how productions might evade the formulaic failure they observe in most mainstream comedy. For example, they point to the (then recent) collaboration between Jean Dujardin and Michel Hazanavicius on *OSS 117* (2006), which they claim retains a distinctive sensibility despite being a script-driven product of a corporatised business model (*cinéma des producteurs*) in which Hazanavicius was brought on to direct a script he did not write, yet still managed to 'author' the film (Ferran *et al.* 2008: 107). So here, while the 'Club des 13' manifesto can be read in one sense as a groundbreaking professionalist argument for a rejuvenation of commercialised forms of filmmaking (*'films du milieu'*), the aesthetic grounds on which they build their argument also falls back on long-standing exceptionalist presumptions about what sorts of socio-economic arrangements produce the best aesthetic results – dividing 'good' (auteurist, independent and cinematic) from 'bad' forms of comedy (scripted, formulaic and televisual) in a manner that resonates with how French film criticism has approached these issues since at least the New Wave. For the remainder of this chapter, we will consider another discursive context where these attitudinal postures tend to vacillate most frequently: the interpretation of the films themselves.

INTOUCHABLES

A heartwarming tale about the unlikely friendship that develops between Philippe (François Cluzet), a wealthy quadriplegic art dealer, and Driss (Omar Sy), his wisecracking domestic aide from the *banlieue*, *Intouchables* (Toledano and Nakache 2011) is now one of the most consequential French-language films in recent memory. After rising to second place on the all-time domestic box office list during its initial French run, *Intouchables* garnered the most international box office sales of any French-made film in history. It has since spurred a Hollywood remake called *The Upside* (Burger 2018), made Sy one of the most recognisable (and best compensated) French actors in the world, and catapulted his directorial collaborators, Eric Toledano and Olivier Nakache, to recognition as perhaps the most reliable sources of mainstream French comedy with a social conscience. Their next two films, *Samba* (2013, also starring Sy) and *Le Sens de la fête / C'est la vie!* (2017) both crossed the 3 million mark in ticket sales with general critical acclaim. In the meantime, analysing the textual dynamics of their breakout hit has become a touchstone for recent scholarly considerations of the representational politics of the emerging field of 'transnational' popular French cinema.

The task of interpreting the film's mélange of features has become an important sticking point in the literature on *Intouchables*. Excitement around its initial success generated enormous press coverage, as well as several early interpretive gestures. Much like *Amélie* before it (see Chapter 3), the first spate of reviews was generally positive, but as the film became a full-fledged cultural phenomenon (2 million tickets in the first two weeks), the press grasped for a wider range of interpretations. A review by *Le Monde* critic Jacques Mandelbaum, for instance, articulates a version of a reading that would soon become one consensus about the film. Crediting the production company Quad Films with renewing the vitality of popular French comedy, he claims 'the film offers a generous social metaphor that shows the benefits of contact between "old" generation of France, paralyzed privilege, and the vitality of a young generation made up of so many immigrants' (Mandelbaum 2011). A host of similarly positive initial reviews were peppered with a few scathing ones, all deriving from the most entrenched of 'elite' critical enclaves – *Les Inrockuptibles, Cahiers du cinéma, L'Humanité*. A trio of *Libération* critics summarised their objections by linking the film to a larger, troubling shift towards commercial products. Sy's performance, they argued, was a mere instrument of dominant ideology, a modern day Cinderella who 'speaks TF1'. Worse, the authors opined:

> This shows just how much the marketing cloud has enveloped mainstream cultural production, exceeding the scope of just one film and dousing the political realm in its bad faith messages. To be moved these days means to be pitiful, to laugh and cry *en masse* at a paid spectacle . . . (Lefort, Perron and Icher 2011)

Elsewhere in the December pages of *Libération*, influential activist and author Marcela Iacub wrote an op-ed accusing Toledano and Nakache of propagating Sarkozy's paternalistic anti-immigration policies (Iacub 2011). By January 2012, the initial wave of reviews offered two rather familiar templates for interpreting the film's success. For the somewhat unexamined professionalist leanings of many mainstream outlets, this was a deftly conceived buddy comedy, an inspirational remedy for the economic crisis, and a welcome boost at the national box office. For displeased exceptionalist voices, on the other hand, it propagated a nefarious faux egalitarianism, created by a conspiracy between the narrative's all-too-easy transcendence of class politics and worsened by the televisual look of its mise-en-scène.

My own early synthesis of the film's cultural and aesthetic impact focused on how its reception echoed the longer-term socio-political dynamics of primary interest in this book (Michael 2014). Crucial to my reading at that time was what I called a pragmatist 'pivot point' in the discussion. For just as the film was gearing up to consider international distribution, Jay Weissberg of the influential Hollywood trade publication *Variety* threatened to deflate export hopes by accusing it of a flagrant 'Uncle Tom-ism' that he claimed American films left behind decades ago (Weissberg 2012). In response, I argued, the French critical establishment showed a remarkable ability to 'close ranks' around the positive aspects of the film. Even the editorial staff of *Libération*, previously so adamant in their attacks on the film, seemed to walk back their earlier critique, offering a defense of its merit through the eyes of Sylvie Granotier, who responded indignantly to exceptionalist critiques ('I'm able to separate reality from fairy tales') (Granotier 2011). Elsewhere, the editorial staff responded directly to Weissberg's charges with what Powrie and Harrod describe as a 'Gallic shrug' ('. . . et alors?') (Harrod and Powrie 2018: 3).

More recently, scholars have begun to propose various ways to 'rethink' or 'unpack' the tangle of racial, political and cinematic discourses that have accrued in and around *Intouchables* and its formidable success. For David Pettersen, Sy's star turn derives from the directorial duo's conscious pursuit of a French-language variant on Eddie Murphy's 1980s Hollywood roles, which he concludes does offer a 'provisional step in generating a desire for change' even if it sinks to 'the same uncomfortable territory as the blackface and neo-minselstry tradition' (Pettersen 2016: 17). While she validates Pettersen's overall reading of the film, Emine Fisek highlights another angle of its history by excavating the complicated colonial intertexts that arise from a comparison with Philippe Pozzo de Borgo's memoir *Le Second Souffle* (2001). Specifically, by casting Sy, Toledano and Nakache sidestep a slew of possible racial and political complications inherent to a source text recounting the friendship between a disabled Franco-Corsican author and Abdel Sellou – the Algerian ex-con who became his medical aide and friend. For Fisek, the film is so challenging to interpret because 'class identity and cultural difference are blended into one another such that disaggregating their effects becomes impossible' (Fisek 2018: 197). In another recent article covering similar ground, Gemma King effectively disaggregates many of them, lauding how the film imagines a 'range of non-stereotypical paths' for its characters that 'do not conform to traditional ideas of privilege', but also lamenting that it ultimately fails to 'ask its French protagonist, or its white audience, to sacrifice the comfort of the status quo' (King 2018: 26). Finally, in a broad analysis of reception documents, Lesley Kealhofer-Kemp argues that *Intouchables* 'remains problematic precisely because it is so enjoyable, so appealing, and such a 'feel-good' movie that it does not incite viewers to scratch below the surface to think about deeper questions' (Kealhofer-Kemp year: 168). Despite their markedly different analytical frameworks, these recent contributions share in a hesitation about how the formal properties of the film match up with its ideological content. While Pettersen ultimately refrains from judging its aesthetic merits one way or another, the readings offered by King, Kealhofer-Kemp and Fisek all seem to imply that a more successful version of *Intouchables* could have 'asked' more of its audience (King 2018: 26), better 'disaggregated' its mixed features (Fisek 2018: 197) or 'incited' its viewers to question its socioeconomic difference in a more 'meaningful way' (Kealhofer-Kemp 2016: 157).

What these assessments of *Intouchables* tend to smooth over, I would argue, are the ways in which the film itself anticipates the very tenor of their arguments, even offering a deceptively simple combination of features that highlight its own contingent position at the intersection of 'serious' cultural critique and the idiom of popular cinema. In many places, the visual texture of *Intouchables* plays on a mix of references, tempting its audience with a coy game of readability. In the opening sequence, somber piano lilts on the soundtrack while two occupants of a black Maserati converse in tightly framed shallow focus. Bathed in the colourful shapes of night-through-windshield cinematography, Sy's smile and shaved scalp contrast with the ashen countenance of a bearded Cluzet, who chides his younger companion. The car weaves in traffic and small cinematographic details abound with basic questions about what we are seeing. A riverbank, a bridge, and the telltale lights of a ferris wheel denote iconic Paris, but these features are also submerged in mobile close-up shots, rapid editing and the banter between two lead actors of different races. Though these fleeting images bespeak the 'intensified continuity' of recent Hollywood action films (Bordwell 2002), they also reverberate with the flavour of action scenes in more localised cinematic inter-texts – perhaps most proximately the action thriller like *Tell No One / Ne le dis à personne* (Canet 2006) which also stars Cluzet (see Chapter 5).

The cunning twist here, of course, is that the same features that seem to promote a nascent brand of Franco-globality also conceal the most crucial narrative information. Philippe's disability and his true relationship to Driss are not revealed until several tense minutes later. Crucially, the mode of spectatorship called for in the opening of *Intouchables* is one that forestalls and then forces revised judgement. Immediately, these are two characters cast in question. Their interactions are eminently familiar and interpretable along standard generic lines for a buddy film – featuring the apprehensive, older protagonist (partner? friend? mentor? all three?) cautioning his younger counterpart (student? rookie cop? random encounter? all three?). Yet the agglomeration of generic expectations and stylistic call-outs in this sequence is also what counts most here, especially for a French-language film that self-consciously draws reference points from multiple traditions. Tempting us with possibility, then landing us somewhere we probably still didn't expect, the opening of *Intouchables* follows up this evasive opening vignette with a celebration to Earth, Wind & Fire's 'September' – as if to overtly celebrate its own interpretive liminality with the song that would become its anthem.

The film may never again approach this sheer density of narrative and thematic correspondences, but numerous other sequences of *Intouchables* expound on similar referential games. Generally, these centre on the contrasting interpretive sensibilities of the two lead characters. Notably, as Driss and Philippe grow closer, the former's appreciation of American popular culture contrasts with the latter's love for classical music, eventually intersecting with it in meaningful ways. Driss and Philippe work to expose one another to the forms of culture they love, and thereby engage in a sort of caricatured point-counterpoint about how to best consume it. The film is actually quite careful in places not to privilege one of these sensibilities over the other. For instance, in his initial job interview, a deadpan Driss responds to Philippe's reference to Mozart's Berlioz symphony by claiming that he doesn't know anyone in the Berlioz HLM (the coincidental name of a public housing project in the *banlieue*). Yet even this scene, which might otherwise have been slanted in favour of one character or the other, avoids aligning itself clearly with either Philippe's patriarchal posturing or Driss's rebellious contempt, instead leaving their miscommunication as a stark (and humourous) reminder about the ambivalence of the film's own readability. Indeed, even for those who watch the scene multiple times, Driss's actual knowledge in the interview scene remains slippery, even to those who carefully scrutinise it. For Fisek, his claims are meant to imply he only 'pretends not to know' the Mozart reference while Pettersen takes his professed ignorance at face value. The larger point, however, is less to resolve this sort of ambiguity than to relate it to the overall structure of the film. In a bookend interview scene at the end of the film, Driss saves face for his lack of preparation by charming his interviewer with not only his knowledge of a Dalí painting, but also by cross-referencing the surrealist master's name with the title of a well-known children's book. As Pettersen argues, the combination of these two scenes suggests, in the end, that Driss has become 'the educated insider who can switch between cultural registers when he needs to' (Pettersen 2016: 15).

In another memorable moment, Driss and Philippe converse about the potential purchase of a painting at an art gallery. To Driss's untrained eye, the canvas looks like 'a splotch of blood on a piece of paper', which prompts Philippe to ask what he thinks the point of art is, to which Driss offers a brusquely professionalist response ('business' / '*du commerce*'), and Philippe rebuts him with an equally caricatured elitest rejoinder: 'It's the last trace of our existence on this Earth'. In his analysis of this loaded dialogue, Pettersen dwells on its racist undercurrents, pointing to two scenes left out of the final cut. In one, Driss tries to seduce Philippe's other assistant, Magalie, with a fumbling version of the same 'intellectual' cliché about culture that Philippe feeds to him at the gallery – clearly suggesting that he is of an inferior cultural grade (Pettersen 2016: 9). Yet the eventual removal of the scene, I would add, supports a view that Toledano and Nakache were wise to the potential sensitivity of such race-based verbal gags.

Moreover, there is also a clear suggestion that the cultural exchange as presented in this film is far more nuanced than usually suggested. The directorial duo was avowedly sensitive to the complexity of how to approach the look and feel of a story of companionship like the one in *Intouchables*. Since casting Sy in a complementary role in their second feature *Nos jours heureux* (2008), the duo had been keen to give him a starring turn. Around that same time, they saw Marie Dumas' documentary *A la vie à la mort*, a made-for-television account of *Le Second souffle*. Conscious that this subject matter required a delicate approach on many fronts, Toledano and Nakache adapted the screenplay over the intervening years, only pursuing production after having success with two other films. When Sy agreed to play the role of Driss, they approached seasoned cinematographer Mathieu Vadepied – better known for his award-winning work on art house films like Jacques Audiard's *Read My Lips / Sur mes lèvres* (2002) – to help them bring their vision to the screen. In interviews, Vadepied acknowledges the perilous potential of depicting class and racial differences on-screen, as well as his own clash with the director's cultural and cinematic sensibilities ('De Pialat et Audiard').

A result of the collaboration with Vadepied is a film that treats the visual traits of the City of Lights in a strikingly bipolar manner – as if to highlight the worlds of 'have's' and 'have not's' with different cinematographic styles and forms of address. Although the primary vehicle for reading these sequences is the performances offered by Sy and Cluzet, the lensing of the film also rehearses visual contrasts of its own. Some of these have clear socio-political dimensions. In one early scene, for instance, Driss returns to the Cité from his initial interview with Philippe, beleaguered and with no apparent place to stay. As night falls, he sits and cavorts with a (markedly multiethnic) group of young companions, sharing french fries and joints, framed in mobile medium long and medium close-up shots, and photographed in muted grey-scale that accentuates his dreary, nondescript urban environs. Scenes of Driss in his adoptive mother's apartment dwell on its cramped spatial coordinates, as the actor's otherwise tall, expressive frame visibly languishes, squashed behind a kitchen table or cramped behind a shower splashguard while avoiding a crowd of small children. Shot patterns and blocking then change substantially in Philippe's home, where static, longer shots become the norm, introducing Driss and the audience to sharp, clean corners, delicate patterns, golden trim and, above all, plenty of space. It is as if this character actually shuttles between two clichéd – and eminently recognisable – visual landscapes of recent French cinema, one the gritty new 'social realist' texture often traced to 1990s films like *La Haine* (Kassovitz 1995) and the other a stagey formality and decorum far more true of a concurrent 1990s period pieces described by Phil Powrie as 'heritage films' (Powrie 1998: 481).

These are not tensions meaningfully resolved in the film, narratively or sty-listically. We never see Driss return to the Cité after making possible Philippe's romantic reunion with his epistolary lover. Instead, after setting up their union, he wanders off in a foggy long shot on a boardwalk by the sea. As the credits roll, we are jettisoned back into the makeshift closure offered by the 'real' story of Sellou and Pozzo di Borgo, who appear on-screen as the credits roll. Though critics recognised these elements, the film's abject failure to resolve them in any meaningful way was also a frequent objection. Many likened the film's strategy to a line-up of sketches for Sy's persona – already known for his hyperbolic caricatures on the Canal Plus short-form sketch comedy *Service Après Vente*. *Les Inrockuptibles* actually advanced this criticism in the first sentence of its review, arguing that the film was effectively just an extension of

Sy's television-based humour, adding a redemptive message at the end, much like the (also television-based) reality show *Josephine Ange Gardien*.

Yet there may also be reason to hesitate about embracing such an extreme, exceptionalist response. As Ginette Vincendeau suggests, criticisms of the film that advance along such severe lines also ignore the extra-textual potential of Sy's pre-established performance reputation, which goes a long way to explaining both the enthusiasm of some audiences for the film and their willingness to accept Driss as a multimodal performer who both embodies and conveys a knowing relationship to ethnic stereotypes (Vincendeau 2014: 559–560). Moreover, a significant number of other scenes in the film work to establish how cultural consumption can be a source of solidarity between the two characters. The initial sequence is a first hint of this, since after their confrontation with the officer, the two speed off in the Maserati, bopping their heads together to the beat of 'September' by the classic funk group Earth, Wind & Fire. In terms of the diegesis, the head-banging of the two characters shows their complicity, amplifying the enthusiasm of the scene while a stylish split-screen offers overlapping views of the speeding car as opening credits flit by. While many critics noted the structuring oppositions between Driss and Philippe at the time, their abiding tendency was to dismiss them as ham-fisted clichés of the genre itself. To the contrary, the characterisations of the two main characters often work to establish the readability of culture as a primary source of collective agency for its two differently marginalised protagonists – and not in an unexamined way.

Perhaps no scene illustrates these points about variable readability more incisively than one that comes right at the end of the film. Here Driss helps Philippe prepare for his long-anticipated encounter with his epistolary lover. Without an establishing shot, the scene unfolds as a montage of medium-length shots of the two characters facing the mirror. They joke as they gaze at their reflections and (by default) at us, laughing at the different configurations that Driss shaves from Philippe's overgrown beard, and displaying their reactions and sight lines to the audience. Without the common device of the shot-reverse shot to contain their interactions, the shaving sequence stands out from previous ones, both in its improvised feel and in its mode of address, comparatively more 'direct'. As Driss compares Phillippe to a series of different historical figures, shaving his facial hair in different ways, the pair are also performing for us, trying on different guises and involving the audience in the political dimensions of their jokes. On an objectively stylistic or descriptive level, this sequence stands out as different from most of the other scenes in the film. The routine the pair engages in is ostensibly motivated in the narrative – the final time Driss will work to 'loosen up' his boss for the long-awaited meeting. At the same time, the scene is nimbly and aggressively 'open' in a way that few others have been in the film. Here an overt triangulation of glances occurs (between the two main characters

Figure 6.3   While shaving his boss, Driss (Omar Sy) jokes about the iconic facial hair possibilities for Philippe (François Cluzet). First he makes him look like José Bové ...

Figure 6.4   ... and then like Adolf Hitler, thereby mixing references to figures more well-known to local (Bové) and global (Hitler) audiences.
Screen grabs from *Intouchables*. DVD. TF1 Video: 2011

and between each character and the viewers themselves). Not only that, but we once again see the two characters dealing with the permissible grounds of comedy itself, as Philippe objects to certain gags as going too far, only to finally succumb to the laughter of his friend.

The nature of the references presented in these frames is worth further pause. After all, what we are to do with this type of apparent 'opening' in the film has become a hinge point in the literature. While the immediate goal (and common result) of the film may be to incite easy laughter, the sequence also deals overtly with more serious subject matter, suggesting that the audience should reflect on the inevitable power dynamics implied by the interactions between these two differently disempowered men and, moreover, on the larger transnational exchanges and media images that their relationship – and our consumption of it – has the power to suggest.

In her reference to the portion of the opening scene where Driss plays 'September' in the car, Fisek suggests that his jovial performance sometimes works to exceed the confines of the story world, creating a 'metonym for the broader entertainment presented to the film's audience' (Fisek 2018: 193). I would argue that this closing scene does something similar, yet in a more provocative way. To start, the gag about Hitler draws on perhaps the most widely accessible negative historical touchstone for all audiences, with Driss leaving the iconically small vertical moustache on Philippe's lip, and then proceeds to play with other forms of signification on Philippe's inanimate body – pushing his hair forward, raising his hand in a 'Heil Hitler' salute, and adopting a mocking German accent – while laughing until the humour is, eventually, mutual. These extra-textual nods to the most iconic villain of the 20th century doubtlessly resonate with all audiences, but they also come after the broader moustache and lamp-chop combination of José Bové – a French agricultural activist who became known internationally in the 1990s as part of the counter-globalisation movement in France. So in this scene, packed tightly alongside the discourses of race and class so often discussed in the film itself, we also have a veritable mise-en-abîme that both signals and (potentially) demonstrates the unstable circulation of images and their interpretation.

Like *Amélie* a decade before it, *Intouchables* is quickly becoming a reference point for how any larger narrative of French film history is composed. In the process, or perhaps because of it, the film presents a deceptively simple text, continually generating implications that extend well beyond those that its authors could have possibly imagined when they recruited Sy, Cluzet and Vadepied to the cause of adapting Pozzo di Borgo's memoir. In other words, as we continue to navigate the aural and visual terms of collective laughter with Driss and Philippe, we also see that finding a consensus about where and when to laugh works in tandem with a film that repeatedly thematises the variable terms of its own readability alongside one another.

Qu'est-ce qu'on a fait au bon dieu?

Just three years after *Intouchables*, the blatantly racialised politics – and prodigious box office results – of another film made headlines. *Qu'est-ce qu'on a fait*

UGC PRÉSENTE

4 mariages, 2 têtes d'enterrement

QU'EST-CE QU'ON A FAIT AU
BON DIEU?

UN FILM DE PHILIPPE DE CHAUVERON

Leurs filles
Laure, Ségolène, Odile, Isabelle

Leurs gendres
Rachid, David, Chao, Charles

Claude et Marie

CHRISTIAN CHANTAL ARY MEDI FRÉDÉRIC NOOM FRÉDÉRIQUE JULIA ÉMILIE ÉLODIE PASCAL
CLAVIER LAUBY ABITTAN SADOUN CHAU DIAWARA BEL PIATON CAEN FONTAN NZONZI

PRODUIT PAR ROMAIN ROJTMAN POUR UGC SCÉNARIO, ADAPTATION ET DIALOGUES DE PHILIPPE DE CHAUVERON ET GUY LAURENT

Bienvenue dans la famille Verneuil

© DR.

Figure 6.5   Poster for *Qu'est-ce qu'on a fait au bon dieu?* © UGC Distribution, 2014

au bon dieu? is the story of Claude Verneuil (Christian Clavier) and his wife Marie (Chantal Lauby), a well to-do Catholic couple from the provincial town of Chinon. As the film begins, the first three Verneuil daughters are married to spouses who, as Claude puts it rather too clinically, 'derive from the flows of immigration' (*issues de l'immigration*). Isabelle (Fréderique Bel) is married to a Maghrebi muslim lawyer, Rachid (Médi Sadoun), Odile (Julia Piaton) to a Sephardic Jewish entrepreneur, David (Ary Abittan) and Ségolène (Emilie Caen) to a Chinese Buddhist banker, Chou (Frédéric Chau). The main premise of the plot concerns the imminent coupling of the youngest Verneuil daughter, Laure (Elodie Fontain). Claude and Marie are overjoyed when she announces she is engaged to a Catholic, but screwball antics ensue when they come to know that her fiancé, Charles (Noom Diawara), is also a black immigrant from the Ivory Coast. By comparison with the loud-mouthed histrionics throughout De Chauveron's film, *Intouchables* seems like a subtle character study. Their differences in overall comedic texture notwithstanding, the two films do share in an overall take away message about how race and class might fruitfully intersect through the embrace of a pragmatist connection between different types of cultural consumption.

The marketing campaign that TF1 used to market *Qu'est-ce qu'on a fait au bon dieu?* pounded brazenly on the film's abundance of ethnic and religious markers. This begins with the main publicity poster (Figure 6.5). Marie and Claude perch uneasily on a love seat in a sort of ornately staged family 'photograph'. The couple's surnames are captioned here, placed just below them in a manner that further distinguishes the elder couple from the scrum of figures to their rear. These visual demarcations are reinforced by another set of captions that designate a group of young women ('their daughters: Laure, Ségolène, Odile, Isabelle') and a group of young men ('their sons in-law [*leur gendres*]: Rachid, David, Chao, Charles'). Meanwhile, at the very top of the poster, we read yet another phrase – 'Four weddings, two buried heads' (*Quatre mariages, deux têtes d'enterrement*). The poster also deploys a mix of national and transnational reference points. For most French viewers, the presence of Clavier and Lauby alone implies the comedy genre, as do the jovial postures of the younger cast members behind them. Moreover, the arrangement of the actors themselves appears to invoke a sort of 'serialised' format, with eight young women and men splayed out along gender and racial lines as if to mimic the Benetton advert campaigns to which a derisive churchgoer actually compares them in one scene of the film. Moreover, there is a striking visual similarity between this image and any number of other recent French comedy posters, which often feature ensemble casts clustered in a grouping similar to Hollywood franchises like *American Pie* (among many others). In this case, the tagline at the top of the poster also references a landmark of the transnational rom com genre – *Four Weddings and a Funeral* (Newell 1994) – connecting the Verneuils' bourgeois consternation to the film's stylistic heritage from the Anglo-American 'elsewhere'.

Audience members who somehow miss the poster still have little excuse for misunderstanding the film's premise. The UGC logo before the opening titles stabs at a caricatured form of 'cultural diversity' by refiguring its three letters as a minorah, a yin-yang and a hammer and sickle, respectively, and the credit sequence presents a sort of primer for the antics to come. An establishing shot locates us (City Hall of Chinon, Indre-et-Loire) and we cut to a lateral tracking shot that moves left-to-right across a crowd of smiling faces while an off-screen voice announces Rachid's last name (Benasem) with exaggerated phonetic precision (Ben-AH-sem) just as the mobile frame reveals the couple and then allows scrutiny of Claude and Marie, accompanied only by their other three daughters. When the Benasem guests explode in ululation with the announcement, Clavier and Lauby adjust uncomfortably, tense grins and shifty eyes belying unease. Moments later, a second wedding scene draws humour from its explicit formal similarities to the first, offering an identical establishing shot of the City Hall, then shot patterns mimicking the previous one, culminating with another exchange of glances as the Benichou crowd ululates in an eerily similar way to their Ben-as-em predecessors. Cut to a medium shot of Claude looking again at his wife with increasing irritation.

This early moment also typifies a fundamental tension in how critics and scholars interpreted the film. Chloé Delaporte, for instance, reads the editing's clear use of Claude's reaction cues to mean that the film 'depends on the idea that the audience shares the stereotypes' with the two conservative characters (Delaporte 2017) and laughs out of sympathy for their plight among ethnic 'others'. Yet given the overt parallelism in editing and mise-en-scène here – not to mention the emphasis on similar three-syllable family names ('Ben-as-sem' and 'Ben-i-chou') – the presumption of a prejudiced spectatorial positioning is far from a given. To the contrary, the sequence could also be read to suggest that the Verneuils, in their visible discomfort and inability to parse the details of difference, are the real butt of the joke. In this vein, a pattern quite familiar to 'fish-out-of-water' plots also emerges, wherein gags induce laughter not only with but also at the expense of comic protagonists who struggle in unfamiliar circumstances. Clavier's long generic affiliation with similar plots is doubtlessly relevant here (most famously as the time-travelling medieval servant in *Les Visiteurs* franchise) as is Lauby's rise to fame on the Canal Plus sketch comedy *Le Nuls*. Moreover, given the pair's unflattering comportment in so many other scenes, its distributors, led by UGC head Alain Sussfield, anticipated that it would be far more marketable to a secular audience than a Catholic one. As Bruno Bouvet of the Catholic newspaper *La Croix* points out somewhat irritably, he and many other religious-affiliated members of the press were explicitly not invited to the film's pre-screenings in order to 'avoid likely negative critiques' while the film was road shown across the country in over seventy provincial towns prior to its release in Paris during the middle of Easter vacation (Bouvet 2014). Meanwhile, the less overtly religious conservative reviewers of *Le Figaro*'s editorial staff praised this strategic roll out, along with its multi-generational casting of comic actors, as a pragmatic 'masterpiece of marketing strategy' (Buisson 2014).

If anything, the clearest ideological affiliation here seems to be an abrasively secular form of agnosticism. The stylistic parallelism of the prelude prepares us for most of the other running gags, which constantly pit dialogue and mise-en-scène against one another, as if to short-circuit any one vantage point on scenes that string together a slew of perfunctory stereotypes. As the script trades in a parade of ham-fisted slurs and jocular banter, the film as a whole maintains careful distance, deflecting any temptation we might have to demonise a particular character. As Delaporte puts it, each member of the dramatis personae 'is conceived to invoke a larger social group for which he or she will serve as representative by serving as an ideal-type' yet also to work against it via 'anti-stereotype' (Delaporte 2017). This is particularly true of the three brothers in-law, who consistently appear as a trio and are brought to life by three comedians previously known for politically provocative acts on stand-up shows like *Jamel's Comedy Club* (Delaporte 2017). Rachid, for instance, acquires 'positive' character traits as a function of several abbreviated scenes where he is blatantly contrasted (dressed in full-on barrister clothing) against several juvenile delinquent characters that embody the frequent media clichés about Maghrebi youth, dressed in hoodies or irreverently smoking hashish (Moine 2018). Yet these affirmative depictions of the film's characters are methodically undercut with scenes that suggest their equal capacity for damaging racist attitudes. Once again, the brothers in-law are the primary example, as they routinely spout off prejudiced epithets, calling each other names like 'Arafat' or 'Jackie Chan'. A celebratory luncheon at Chou and Ségolène's prolongs this type of counterpoint, devolving into a shouting match between Claude and his three sons in-law. After an exchange of barbs about meat consumption, the 'barbarity' of circumcision rituals, and the diverse populations of contemporary Barbès, Rachid and Isabelle accuse him of racism, to which he can only affirm his nationalist affiliation ('Je suis Gaulliste comme mon père!'). And yet, as the elder Verneuils depart in a huff, any impulse to easily identify with the 'enlightened' younger characters is knocked flat by their subsequent attempts to debrief the situation, which escalate into more abusive stereotypes, culminating in an altercation where Chou fends off a charging David with a cartoonish karate chop to the throat (seeming to both evoke and mock Jackie Chan himself). Seconds later, as Claude and Marie complain about their sons-in-law while driving past the Eiffel Tower, we can't help but ponder whether they are justified in fleeing this supposedly more 'cosmopolitan' capital city.

Figure 6.6   One frame in an elevator displays multiple possible affiliations for the viewer in *Qu'est-ce qu'on a fait au bon dieu?* Screen grab from *Qu'est-ce qu'on a fait au bon dieu?* © UGC Distribution, 2014

As with *Intouchables*, individual passages of the film actually mobilise this hermeneutic ambivalence with deceptive sleight of hand. In many cases, the image track generates multiple possible affiliations via the overlapping triangulation of glances between characters that vacillate, as Rosello suggests, between 'informed' and 'ignorant' positions in the dialogue about cultural difference (Rosello 2018: 29). Claude and Marie arrive in Paris for the circumcision ceremony of their grandson, sharing an elevator with Rachid, Odile and Laure. The five are framed from above in a high-angle medium-long shot, and as Odile opines about her increasingly obvious baby bump, she and Rachid suggest possible names for the child – Xavier, Lucas and a third (offered by Rachid, his nostrils slightly flared as if about to laugh): Mohammed (Figure 6.6).

With an implicit nod to *Le prénom* (a 2011 screwball comedy about white bourgeois discomfort about the connotations of baby's name) this brief moment also forestalls our choice of any one 'correct' perspective on the awkwardness that ensues on screen. Cut-ins to Claude and Marie, for instance, could encourage sympathy for their affable state of unease, but the very next image shows the three younger characters exiting the elevator just out of their earshot, mocking the elder couple's intransigence on racial categories. Claude and Marie are ignorant here not only of the prejudicial overtones of their commentary, but also of the cultural reference points that their offspring can quickly cross-reference. The tenor of the film's gags turns on many similar moments of split identification. At Christmas dinner, for instance, Marie cites *Rabbi Jacob* (Oury 1973) as evidence that Louis de Funès was Jewish. In this case, a brief, one-off line suffices to place the film both in a longer national heritage of comedies based on ethnic stereotypes, and as a demonstration of Marie's rather layered ignorance of popular culture (De Funès was not Jewish and, moreover, the gags of the film derive from his character's attempts to disguise himself as a rabbi). The following reaction two-shot of David and Odile snickering reinforces the errancy of Marie's statement, even arguably for those viewers who do not follow the *Rabbi Jacob* reference in its full ironic form.

The missing link between these two extremes, of course, can be found in their shared reaction to what appears to be a sort of pragmatist dogma about the determinative role of cultural consumption. While no single character in the film maintains a moral upper hand in terms of racial prejudice, their eventual fates seem predicated on whether they can successfully participate in a secular, capitalist view of French national identity. The middle portions of the film move in this direction by contrasting how the staid bourgeois sensibilities of the elder characters interface with a more youthful, flexible sense of cosmopolitan cultural consumption. In many cases, these generational differences obviate other forms of possible identity formation. In one sequence, Marie seeks counsel from both a psychotherapist and the local Catholic church. The former is only slightly less helpful than the latter; his diagnosis of clinical depression sends her running to the confession box. The young priest's advice sounds sage on the surface: 'We've already spoken about this, Madam Verneuil', he says, 'What is happening to your family is not serious. It's globalisation. My family is from Madagascar. At first it wasn't easy, but now it is going much better!'. Stylistic elements again serve to undercut the apparent message, as the clergyman's whiny timbre and his furtive glances at a tablet (apparently to shop for vestments online) demonstrate both the mundane nature of her concerns ('it's not serious') and the priest's (hence the church's) callous disinterest in the Verneuil's ongoing familial plight. More than a religious figure, the priest is hence depicted as part of a younger generation who, not unlike the jocular brothers in-law, demonstrates a facility with new forms of media, yet shows little inclination to relate sincerely to his forebears.

Though fleeting at a first glance, moments like these take on heightened structural importance in a film that imagines the anatomy of a culturally diverse French society. Claude apologises to the family for his erratic behaviour after his grandson's circumcision ceremony, the three sons in-law respond with warmth, and David coins something close to the screenplay's sociological thesis ('We all have a small part of us that is racist'). Moments later, in one of the film's most cited scenes, all three sons in-law sing *La Marseillaise* in passionate unison. Yet the film's advance – symbolic and otherwise – of a multicultural nationalism also depends on these characters' relative lack of knowledge about its forms. Hence the fortunate failure of the three 'ethnic' turkeys Marie diligently researches and prepares by visiting three of Chinon's local 'ethnic' food establishments (Halal and Jewish *boucheries* and a Chinese *traiteur*). In a moment played for laughs, all three men reveal similar indifference to their 'own' culinary traditions – happily eating all three preparations because they taste good, much in the way they sing 'Il est né le divine enfant' or hymns at the midnight Christmas Eve service. Religion is hence deemphasised here, pushed aside as a mere impediment to the authentic connections available in the circulation of vaguely 'cultural' rites of passage.

By far the most conspicuous evocation of this overarching consensual pragmatism involves the newest member of the Verneuil family. A naturalised immigrant from the Ivory Coast, Charles is the only one of the four sons in-law to be shown in his 'native' land, hence making the screen depictions of Africa both a foil for the Verneuils' provincial homestead and a literal plot obstacle for the larger apparent goal of family unity. The second half of the film jockeys between several scenes at the Verneuil estate and brief glimpses of the Koffi's abode in the Ivory Coast, where bustling village life (streets filled with animals) offers a contrast to the interior spaces and verdant gardens of the provincial French estate – where a maid is shown busily working, unlike her African counterpart, who sleeps (Delaporte 2017). Yet it is also Charles, like Driss before him, who becomes the mechanism by which the film seeks to anchor its consensual depictions of racial prejudice. Unlike Sy, Noomi Diawara's character is initially placed rather squarely on the opposite end of the apparent spectrum of cultural consumption. We meet him first during a surprisingly intimate scene with Laure, who leads the viewfinder in a following shot down the hallway of their modest apartment, scantily clad as she converses with her off-screen male interlocutor. Here, simple costume choice (Fontan is shot suggestively from behind) suggests the intimate (most likely sexual) nature of her relationship with Charles, but the image track immediately diverts our attention once again, as the expected reverse-shot for her eye-line match occludes the face of her presumed lover – instead landing on a (quite large) theatrical script balanced between his knees: *Le Dindon* by Georges Feydeau. It is no small coincidence that our expected revelation about the film's worst kept secret (skin colour) becomes far less central to the mise-en-scène than the other information presented here. Like his brothers in-law, information about Charles' occupation is provided with one efficient frame – he is rehearsing for an apparent role in a 'high' French farce. In some ways, Charles' depiction is no different to what we have seen so far from this film with other characters, as we are forced to navigate a pervasive stereotype (blacks as 'performers') that plays explicitly against another one (rather than an avid consumer of American music or commercial culture, Charles is a paid participant in the tradition of classical French farce).

In a subsequent scene, Rachid, David and Chao watch Charles perform *Le Dindon* on stage. As Charles' part in the literal mise-en-scène of the play becomes the object of their (and our) scrutiny, a revealing exchange on cultural consumption also takes place. Seated in the theatre to watch their new familial 'recruit', the three young men critique and question his performance in real time. 'What's modern about putting a black guy in a Feydeau play?' asks Rachid, to which David responds, 'I don't know, I haven't been to the theater since I was five'. Other contrasts are plentiful, not least because David and Rachid avidly consume fried chicken during the entire exchange. In the context of the thread we are tracing here, it is no coincidence that two characters who previously mocked the cultural competence of their elders now reveal themselves as proud philistines. Of the three, only Chao seems even moderately aware of the minimum social norms of their surroundings, chastising his companions in hushed tones and rebutting their inane questions about Charles' on-stage seduction of a woman ('They are *acting*, guys!'). Yet the film's ideological ambivalence is more thorough still, since we should not be surprised at Chao's reproaches here, as he is married to Ségolène, the self-described 'emotive' Verneuil sister, whose artistic sensibilities are reduced to a series of oversensitive responses to familial conflicts, and whose painting ambitions thrive only on Chao's banking career and her own self-deception (her paintings are mediocre, abstract, grey-scale self-portraits). A further irony, of course, lies in the fact that their very presence at the play is motivated by Chao's own racist assertion – that black men are often known to consort with multiple women at a time.

Our diverse trio's proud ignorance of the history of cultural forms comes full circle in the very next scene. In their covert pursuit of Charles and his putative lover, they follow them to a hotel, performing a series of bumbling gaffes as they 'stake out' their targets in a stumbling, single-file line (Figure 6.6). Here the image track offers a direct gesture at any viewer's own attempts to disam-

Figure 6.7 Three bumbling brothers in-law evoke their filmic origins in Feydeau farce. Screen grab from *Qu'est-ce qu'on a fait au bon dieu?* © UGC Distribution, 2014

biguate or distribute different layers of meaning and blame. Not only does the trio's staging here recall many actual Feydeau plays, where busy casts of characters rush between bedroom doors, disentangling plots of mistaken identity that they themselves perpetuate – but the next scene both participates in that tradition and extends it, exposing their 'investigation' as a racially-loaded *fausse piste*, bound up in ironic resonances that no one character manages to read; the woman with Charles was actually his sister. Later, if Charles gains successful admission to the 'culture' of his extended family, it is not through their appreciation of his thespian predispositions, but rather his affable acceptance of their collective agenda for hybridising mass cultural consumption via 'Organic Halal' butcher shops – conceived by David, backed by Chao's bank, and predicated on Rachid's familial connections to the target market.

Larger transnational biases often subtended the French media's responses to intertextual moments like these. As with previous successful comedies like *Amélie*, more audiences for the film meant an immediate onslaught of abstract interpretation by the French press. As the box office phenomenon became clear, a heartfelt editorial from *Marianne* offered a familiar redemptive framing:

> For three weeks now, France has been celebrating its mix of cultures by watching a Chinese man, an Arab, a Black and a Jew marry the four daughters of an old, conservative, Catholic couple from Chinon, in the heart of France. It's just a movie, okay? But it's what we seem to need to escape every once in a while. *Qu'est-ce qu'on a fait au bon dieu?* is selling tickets like no film since *Bienvenue chez les Ch'tis* gave us an ode to simple people of modest means or *Intouchables* soothed our nerves with an interclass fairy tale during an economic crisis. In just ninety minutes, we watch two cultural conservatives, Christian Clavier and Chantal Lauby, overcome prejudice without forgetting who they are. We clap while basking in the warm glow of a film that rejects those contrarians claiming this country will never come together again. It is with new hope for the possible that we can learn to laugh with each other, by the thousands and the millions; French people are tired of not getting along. ('Qu'est-ce qu'on a fait au bon dieu?' 2014)

The first wave of positive reviews of the film operated with a similar ideological thrust, first applauding the 'honesty' or 'humanity' of even-handed treatment of different demographics, and then deflecting possible disagreements with a professionalist wave of the hand ('It's just a movie, okay?'). A week later, *Le Point* critics Jérôme Béglé and Albert Sebag augmented the nascent argument in industrial terms, lauding the performance of a type of French cinema that could find success 'not with blockbusters full of special effects, or tear-jerking dramas, or costly historical epics' but with modestly budgeted 'popular comedies that draw on topical, sociological issues' (Béglé and Sebag 2014). An anecdotal sampling of the most positive user critiques on online forums like Allociné finds amateur reviewers operating on similar grounds, as they ratify their admiration for the film with a common phrase: 'we had a really good time' (on a passé un très bon moment).

A collective frustration also emerged, however, when critics attempted to dig deeper into the sources of the film's comedy. Antagonists of De Chauveron's film began to emerge on all sides. On the right, a chorus of critics attacked it on a primarily denotative level. Patrick Nathan of Témoignage Chrétien, for instance, laments its emptying of the meaning of religious rituals (Nathan 2014), while Geniviève Jurgensen of La Croix regrets its portrayal of provincial Catholics as people who 'secretly share the sentiments that Jean-Marie Le Pen says out loud' (Jurgensen 2014) and iconic conservative philosopher Alain Finkielkraut (rather predictably) rages against what he sees as a false pretence for presenting a 'multiculturalist' harmony that has never existed in France (Finkielkraut 2014). The film's strongest critics on the left concur with the substance of these critiques, but also lay blame on a second level, wherein the form of the film – derived from its 'televisual' roots – dooms both its aesthetic quality and its ability to allow for 'serious' cultural critique. A review by Jérôme Momcilovic of Chronic'art, for instance, begins by cataloguing the numerous aesthetic similarities between the film's preview and its first act – comparing both to the 'perfectly terrible' formal approach of 'ordinary industrial comedy' meant only as a discussion prop for evening TF1 talk shows (Momcilovic 2014).

How much any one viewer identifies with these different levels of possible meaning is, of course, impossible to predict. As Jean-Baptiste Morain of Les Inrockuptibles puts it, 'the cleverness [of the film] is that it is difficult, at least on a first viewing, to align it with any one political message, since it gloms all of the social elements of France's problem with racism into one' (Morain 2014). Yet what undergirds this entire assessment, he makes clear in closing, is the film's overt lack of aesthetic distinction as cinema. For Morain, De Chauveron's film plays at best like a 'competent tele-film' – 'a cinema without any discernible taste, without any dimension, and with a lack of formal distinction that mirrors what it actually is and what it actually wants to be: consensual'. (Morain 2014). Since the success of De Chauveron's film, both the poetics of popular French comedy and the reception of their features seem to have taken a stark turn towards assessing just what kind of 'consensus' these films actually encourage the viewer to embrace.

TOWARDS A NEW FRENCH TUCHE?

On the heels of Gaumont's giddy box office results for Bienvenue chez les Ch'tis, Pathé set about producing a franchise along similar lines. Released in 2011, the first entry in the new franchise bore a striking resemblance to Boon's film, but also to other recent comedies like *Camping* (*Onteniente* 2006) or *Disco* (*Onteniente* 2008), which played on prevalent stereotypes of the provincial French working class (often called *les beaufs*) by contrasting their language and manners with an equally stereotyped depiction of 'elite' urban or intellectual culture. Although a blatant attempt to replicate Boon's successful formula, *Les Tuche* (Olivier Baroux 2011) reverses a plank of the film's overall narrative and tonal logic. Rather than aligning us with a sad sack mid-level executive forced to integrate the hillbilly culture of 'the North', Baroux's film focuses on a family of *beaufs* that must integrate bourgeois culture from the opposite direction. More important than this plot variation, however, is the stark difference in how the film addresses its subject matter.

While the interpretive dilemma that seemed to ensnare the popular success of both *Intouchables* and *Qu'est-ce qu'on a fait au bon dieu?* revolved around how to properly prioritise an agglomeration of features reaching for both 'authentic' and 'stereotypical' registers of meaning, Baroux's film dispenses with all such quandaries at the outset – launching instead into a parody of the very characteristics that turned its predecessors into such a locus for interpretive consternation. Here Jeff Tuche (Jean-Paul Rouve) is a recently unemployed factory worker, and his wife Cathy (Isabelle Nanty) perkily manages their home in the (fictional) Northern town of Bouzolle. They live with Jeff's perpetually inebriated mother 'Mamie Suze' (Claire Nadeau) and their three children – the saccharinely ditzy Stéphanie (Sarah Stern), the brazenly 'hip hop' Wilfried (Pierre Lottin) and the oft-neglected Donald (Théo Fernandez), who narrates the first film while bristling at the nickname ('Coin Coin') that both references the popular children's book about a lost duckling and suggests how completely his parents misunderstand his exceptional intellect. In the initial film, Jeff wins the lottery and the family uses their monetary gain to move to Monaco and fulfill Cathy's lifelong dream to meet Princess Stephanie.

Initially mocked by the uber-wealthy members of their new neighbourhood, the Tuche clan eventually manages to ingratiate themselves to their new community through their tone-deaf generosity. Cathy's sincerity and humour manage to warm the heart of her stand-offish yet lonely neighbour Mouna (Fadila Belkebla) while Jeff's unconventional coaching methods fill a paternal role for her son Jean-Wa (Sami Outalbali) and bring new life to his floundering youth soccer team. Subplots about Stéphanie's awkward romance with a black soccer player and Wilfried's gradual discovery of his latent homosexuality offer comic relief, but it is the precocious Coin Coin who eventually saves the day, finding a way to save his father from mismanaging his newfound fortune while simultaneously reeling Mouna's hedge fund managing husband Omar (David Kammenos) back to the fold, and hence re-establishing a nuclear family order just as it looks threatened to split apart.

Plot synopsis only goes so far towards assessing any film – a maxim that *Les Tuche* pushes to the extreme. While the film seems to gesture towards a message similar to that in *Intouchables* and *Qu'est-ce-qu'on a fait au bon dieu?*, offering an uplifting narrative about the transcendence of class-based divisions via cultural taste, the sheer absurdity of its machinations seems to dispense with any pretension of these previous enterprises. With his sponge-like orange mullet, stained tank-top undershirts, and knee-high tube socks, Jeff himself deploys a distinctly provincial (yet regionally non-specific) working class accent that is at the same time devoutly extra-textual – playing on a similar character Rouve developed for a popular sketch called 'Radio Beer Soccer' [*Radio-Bière-Foot*] on the Canal Plus series *Les Robins des Bois* during the early 2000s. Yet while Omar Sy's roles in *Service Après Vente* might be seen to inform his performance in *Intouchables*, the tenor of how *Les Tuche* uses Rouve's caricature is entirely different. And while the exaggerated elements of the cast in *Qu'est-ce qu'on a fait au bon dieu?* may inform its cathartic conclusion, *Les Tuche* embraces a parodic register with such gusto that it becomes impossible to distinguish between the layers of irony against which these other films couch their suggestions about the redemptive possibility of pragmatic cultural taste qua mutual understanding.

Instead, in this now three deep franchise, we follow the adventures of this particular provincial family as they become progressively overt in parodying the stylistic terms by which other recent 'localised' French comedies aim to intervene in transnational discourses about France and its cinema. Taken as a group, the three *Tuche* films become progressively detached from any investment in 'real' French culture. Interestingly, while the critical reception of the first film was largely negative due to a perceived 'shallowness' and absurdity, the second and third installments seemed to profit as critics began to understand the franchise's relative lack of pretension and overall positivity. Moreover, as the sequels grew in popularity, they only amplified this dimension of the film's representations. While the first film does offer a flicker of redemption for Jeff and his family by the end – particularly in the way their cultural tone deafness manages to break down the condescension of Monaco's elites – the second and third volumes dispense with nearly all attempts at moralising messages, instead devolving into amoral sketch comedies starring Rouve, Nanty and the others in a series of scenes. First, this takes the form of a family trip to the US, as the family's other members follow Coin Coin on a study abroad programme (*Les Tuche 2*). Next, we watch Jeff's improbable run for the French presidency, which in its elevation of his populist amateurism offers strange (though unintended) parallels to the 2016 'outsider' elections of Emmanuel Macron in France and Donald Trump in America (*Les Tuche 3*).

Certain significant questions remain about what to do with films like *Les Tuche* as cultural documents of France in the early 21st century. While on one hand, it would be a mistake to gloss over the problematic potential of stereo-types implied by many scenes in these films, it is also clear that our vantage point on those very traits depends on the spirit in which we interpret them in the first place. And without siding with any one of the pointed critiques levied against them, it is possible to see an emerging pattern in how these recent 'local comedy blockbusters' are becoming the subjects of larger, vexed, and ongoing games of transnational hermeneutics. Certainly, part of the way in which we discuss them also has to do with the poetics of an evolving genre and its norms. As Thomas Schatz and other theorists never hesitate to point out, any form of filmmaking eventually finds its most decisive evidence of existence with the arrival of a baroque ('mannerist' or 'self-reflexive') phase, wherein 'the form and its embellishments are accented to the point where they themselves become the substance of the work' (Schatz 1981: 37–38). In French critical circles, this element is still frequently referred to as a Barthesian question of readability (*degré*), wherein a 'first degree' reading would be utterly connotative, a 'second degree' reading would reflect on its own terms of enunciation, and a 'third degree' reading would parody or pastiche the common formal components of texts that operate in the second. For many critics, the parodic gesture of recent comedy has become the most objectionable aspect, as the knowingness of the films could be seen to redeem objectionable elements that nevertheless con-tinue to flourish in plain view. As *Le Monde* critic Isabelle Regnier puts it, this tendency to 'detach from the content of jokes by suggesting that they are only clichés intended to incite laughter' serves as the 'basis for a whole recent cycle of French comedy hits' while hiding 'the rancid premise of a brand of humour that promotes a cynical world view where all are reduced to stereotypes of race or gender' (Regnier 2017).

While neither the genre nor its reception have reached an equilibrium as of yet, the success of *Les Tuche* seems to have gone some way towards specify-ing what a less mean-spirited version of the form might look like – not least because the name of the franchise itself gestures at how its own brand of comedy functions as a cathartic venue for mourning the loss of certain types national particularity. As *Elle* critic Olivia De Lambertie put it in one of many recent diagnoses of the nascent trend:

> This film's absurd moral seems to be that a cultural heritage 'made-in-France' can still be stronger than the American dream. And this is perhaps one of the keys to the film's success: traumatized by the march of anxiety-provoking news, French filmgoers are now taking refuge in literal readings of these big family comedies. The arty 'French touch' may be long gone, but this more lowbrow 'french Tuche' is a deliciously regressive movement – and it is just beginning. (De Lambertie 2016)

Though they rarely share her zeal for this new comedy lowbrow, progressive-minded critics from cinéphiliac venues seem to increasingly share Lambertie's lenience for its current variations. For every reviewer who calls *Les Tuche* the 'height of a distasteful popular comedy' (Loison 2018) there are others who are more pragmatic about its social function on the contemporary cultural scene. In some cases, intentions behind that rhetoric are hard to pin down. In his review of *Les Tuche 3*, for instance, Jean-Baptiste Morain of *Les Inrocks* freely admits to liking the franchise more and more, lauding the performances by Rouve and Nanty while suggesting the film might read as a 'hymn to family relationships' except that it is 'so strange and nutty that the attempt would be ridiculous' (Morain 2016). Meanwhile, in his review entitled 'I must admit I laughed at *Les Tuche 2* (What? I'm fired?)', Aurélien Ferenczi assesses the value of its clichés with an ambivalent nationalism worthy of the genre's own mixed address:

> So *Les Tuche* learn gradually that America is not for them: any country that glorifies getting rich through hard work cannot be a match for people who want to get rich doing nothing? No thank you. I was in a good mood that morning at Gaumont Opéra. Make no mistake, this short review will not stop you from attending that Bulgarian art film that you are so eager to see. An obvious hit in the making, *Les Tuche 2: le rêve américain* doesn't need you to see it. But if you do cross paths with them, please don't discriminate. (Ferenczi 2016)

Academics, in many cases, argue that this politicised ambivalence has now become the defining feature of an emergent genre. For Rosello, the appeal of recent comedies is often a result of the way in which they simultaneously solicit different interpretive slants, playing on the moralising clichés that 'most frighten critics of communautarism' while giving them a superficial treatment that others see sorely lacking the edge needed to communicate 'any substantive difference at all' (Rosello 2018: 27). In her diagnosis of similar phenomena, Moine warns that the manipulation of broad-based clichés threatens to destabilise the ideological presumptions of films that want to champion forms of egalitarianism (Moine 2018: 47–48).

At the same time, the growing attention to the films in question implies that it would be short sighted to dismiss their sociological potential for generating constructive debate. As Laurent Jullier suggests in his analysis of online criticism of the two *OSS 117* films, probing the distinction between second- and third-degree readings on *Allociné.fr* also offers an opportunity for the poetic features of popular cinema to engage viewers in nuanced discussions about how popular film admixes the 'serious' political topics of our day (Jullier 2010). Moreover, as our analysis of the examples above also shows, these are films with a deceptive depth of awareness about their own relevance to a larger conversation, as they thematically and stylistically internalise the very confluence of attitudes that makes hit comedy such a locus for how a national industry voices its own throes of adaptation to an increasingly global cultural economy.

NOTES

1. The only book-length accounts on contemporary popular French comedy remain Remi Lanzoni's quite general overview (Lanzoni 2014) and Mary Harrod's *From France with Love*, which offers welcome analysis of how French romantic comedies of the 2000s articulate tropes of gender and identity with respect to a genre that trades heavily on the norms of globalised popular culture (Harrod 2015). Several related contributions include scholarly forays into the increasingly diverse Franco-European star system, which draws heavily on comedy, and features increasing numbers of 'ethnic' performers, including Jamel Debbouze, Omar Sy, Dany Boon, Kad Merad and Gad Elmaleh (Vanderschelden 2005; Vincendeau 2014). Citing the overall paucity of the literature, a recent issue of *Studies in French Cinema*, edited by Powrie and Harrod, begins to fill these gaps with a compelling group of articles by leading scholars in the emergent field.
2. 'Si l'on définit les comédies communautaires comme un état des lieux qui nous permet de cerner, dans le présent immédiat, les limites des communautés lisibles, la question reste donc de savoir comment ces films nous imaginent en tant que public (divisé ou non en communautés) et cherchent à anticiper notre lecture.'.
3. Notable titles include *Taxi* (1998, 2000, 2003, 2007, 2018), *Astérix et Obélix* (1999, 2002, 2008, 2012), *La Verité si je mens!* (1997, 2001, 2012), *Brice de Nice* (2005, 2016), (*Camping* (2006, 2010, 2016), *Babysitting* (2013, 2015), *Papa ou maman* (2015, 2016), *Les Tuche* (2011, 2016, 2018), and *Les Profs* (2013, 2015).

WORKS CITED

Béglé, Jérôme and Albert Sebag (2014), 'Le triomphe de la comédie à la française', *Le Point*, 22 May.

Bouvet, Bruno (2014), 'Cinq millions de rires pour combattre les préjugés', *La Croix*, 7 May.

Buisson, Jean-Christophe (2014), 'Qu'est-ce qu'on a fait au bon dieu? Les raisons d'une triomphe', *Le Figaro*, 13 June, <http://www.lefigaro.fr/cinema/2014/06/13/03002-20140613ARTFIG00131--qu-est-ce-qu-on-a-fait-au-bon-dieu-les-raisons-d-un-trio mphe.php> (last accessed 4 February 2019).

De Lamberterie, Olivia (2016), 'La French Tuche', *Elle*, 26 February, <http://www.elle. fr/Societe/Edito/La-french-Tuche-par-Olivia-de-Lamberterie-3050557> (last accessed 4 February 2019).

Delaporte, Chloé (2017), 'Du stéréotype dans la comédie française contemporaine: autour de Qu'est-ce qu'on a fait au bon dieu?', *Mise au point* 9, 2 May, <https://journals.openedition.org/map/2271#quotation> (last accessed 4 February 2019).

Deleau, Quentin (2016), 'Quels sont les genres du cinéma français qui s'exportent le mieux?', *Unifrance*, 3 February, <https://www.unifrance.org/actualites/14552/quels-sont-les-genres-du-cinema-francais-qui-s-exportent-le-mieux> (last accessed 4 February 2019).

Fairclough, Norman (2006), *Language and Globalization*, London: Routledge.

Ferenczi, Aurélien (2016), 'J'avoue, j'ai ri aux *Tuche 2* (comment ça, je suis viré?)', *Télérama*, 4 February, <https://www.telerama.fr/cinema/j-avoue-j-ai-ri-aux-tuche-2-comment-ca-j-suis-vire,137863.php> (last accessed 4 February 2019).

Ferran, Pascale *et al.* (2008), *Le milieu n'est plus un pont mais une faille: Rapport de synthèse*, Paris: Stock.

Finkielkraut, Alain (2014), 'Pourquoi je n'ai pas aimé *Qu'est-ce qu'on a fait au bon dieu?*', *Le Figaro*, 13 June, <http://www.lefigaro.fr/cinema/2014/06/13/03002-201 40613ARTFIG00144-finkielkraut-pourquoi-je-n-ai-pas-aime-qu-est-ce-qu-on-a-fait-au-bon-dieu.php> (last accessed 4 February 2019).

Fisek, Emine (2018), 'Rethinking *Intouchables*: Race and Performance in Contemporary France', *French Cultural Studies*, 29:2, pp. 190–205.

Forest, Claude (2002), 'Fais-moi mal! Ou l'abandon des genres par les cinémas européens', in Thomas Paris and Jérôme Clement (eds), *Quelle diversité face à Hollywood?*, *CinémAction* (2002), pp. 75–80.

Forest, Claude (ed) (2017), *L'internationalisation des productions cinématographiques et audiovisuelles*, Strasburg: University of Strasburg Press.

Fourny, Marc (2014), 'Qu'est-ce qu'on a fait au bon dieu? trop polémique pour les Etats-Unis!', *Le Point*, 10 October, <https://www.lepoint.fr/culture/qu-est-ce-qu-on-a-fait-au-bon-dieu-trop-polemique-pour-les-etats-unis-10-10-2014-1871073_3.php> (last accessed 4 February 2019).

Granotier, Sylvie (2011), 'J'ai aimé *Intouchables* ... et alors?' *Libération* 5 December 2011.

Harrod, Mary (2015), *From France with Love: Gender and Identity in French Romantic Comedy*, London: I. B. Tauris.

Harrod, Mary and Phil Powrie (2018), 'New directions in contemporary French comedies: from nation, sex and class to ethnicity, community and the vagaries of the post-modern', *Studies in French Cinema*, 18:1, pp. 1–17.

Hutcheon, Linda (2000), *A Theory of Parody: The Teachings of Twentieth Century Art Forms*, 2nd edn, New York: Methuen.

Iacub, Marcela (2011), 'Intouchables la preuve par oeuf', *Libération*, 11 December.

Jäckel, Anne (2013), 'Comedy', in Tim Palmer and Charlie Michael (eds), *Directory of World Cinema: France*, London: Intellect, pp. 243–250.

Jeancolas, Jean-Pierre (1979), *Le cinéma des français: la cinquième république (1958–1978)*, Paris: Broché.

Joudet, Muriel (2017), 'Babysitting 2 et Si j'étais un homme: deux comédies faussement décomplexées', *Le Monde*, 27 February, <https://www.lemonde.fr/cinema/article/2017/02/27/alibi-com-et-si-j-etais-un-homme-deux-comedies-faussement-dec omplexees_5086188_3476.html> (last accessed 4 February 2019).

Jullier, Laurent (2010), 'Politiquement (in)correct: *OSS 117* dans les forums de discussion d'Allociné', *Studies in French Cinema*, 10:3, pp. 289–301.

Jurgensen, Genviève (2014),'La chronique du rabat-joie', *La Croix*, 9 May, <www.lacroix.fr.https://www.la-croix.com/Culture/Cinema/La-chronique-du-rabat-joie-par-Genevieve-Jurgensen-2014-05-09-1147832> (last accessed 4 February 2019).

Kealhofer-Kemp, Leslie (2017), 'Unpacking the Success and Criticisms of *Intouchables* (2011)' in Masha Belensky, Kathryn Kleppinger and Anne O'Neil-Henry (eds), *French Cultural Studies for the 21st Century*, Newark: University of Delaware Press, pp. 155–170.

King, Gemma (2018), 'No Laughing Matter? Navigating Political (In)correctness in *Intouchables*', *Francosphères*, 7:1, pp. 1–14.

Lanzoni, Remi Fournier (2014), *French Comedy On Screen: A Cinematic History*, London: Palgrave Macmillian.

Lefort, Gérard, Didier Perron and Bruno Icher (2011), 'Intouchables – Ben, si . . .', *Libération*, 14 November.

Loison, Guillaume (2018), 'Les Tuche 3: le sommet de nanar populiste', *Le Nouvel Obs*, 31 January, <https://www.nouvelobs.com/cinema/20180131.OBS1540/les-tuche-3-un-sommet-de-nanar-populiste.html> (last accessed 6 February 2019).

Mandelbaum, Jacques (2011), 'Derrière la comédie populaire, une métaphore sociale généreuse', *Le Monde*, 2 November, <https://www.lemonde.fr/cinema/article/2011/11/01/intouchables-derriere-la-comedie-populaire-une-metaphore-socia le-genereuse_1596827_3476.html> (last accessed 4 February 2019).

Mazdon, Lucy (2000), *Encore Hollywood: Remaking French Cinema*, London: British Film Institute.

Michael, Charlie (2014), 'Interpreting *Intouchables*: Competing Transnationalisms in Contemporary French Cinema', *SubStance*, 43:1, pp. 123–137.

Moine, Raphaëlle (2018), 'Stereotypes of class, ethnicity and gender in contemporary popular French comedy: From *Bienvenue Chez les Ch'tis* (2008) and Intouchables (2011) to *Qu'est-ce qu'on a fait au bon dieu?* (2014)', *Studies in French Cinema*, 18:1, pp. 35–51.

Moine, Raphaëlle (2014), 'Contemporary French Comedy as Social Laboratory', in Hilary Radner, Alistair Fox, Michel Marie and Raphaëlle Moine (eds), *A Companion to Contemporary French Cinema*, London: Wiley-Blackwell, pp. 233–255.

Momcilovic, Jérôme (2014), 'Mais Qu'est-ce qu'on a fait au bon dieu?', *ChronicArt*, 20 April, <https://www.chronicart.com/cinema/mais-quest-ce-quon-a-fait-au-bon-dieu/> (last accessed 4 February 2019).

Morain, Jean-Baptiste (2014), 'Qu'est-ce qu'on a fait au bon dieu? Pourquoi ça cartonne', *Les Inrockuptibles*, 21 April, <https://www.lesinrocks.com/2014/04/21/cine ma/quest-ce-quon-fait-au-bon-dieu-pourquoi-ca-cartonne-11499455/> (last accessed 4 February 2019).

Morain, Jean-Baptiste (2016), 'Que vaut le "nouveau carton comique français"?' *Les Inrockuptibles*, 5 February, <https://www.lesinrocks.com/2016/02/05/cinema/les-tuches-2-que-vaut-le-nouveau-carton-comique-national-11803639/> (last accessed 4 February 2019).

Mulholland, Rory (2014), '"Racist" French cinema hit "too politically incorrect" for UK and US audiences', *The Telegraph*, 13 October, <https://www.telegraph.co.uk/news/worldnews/europe/france/11158603/Racist-French-cinema-hit-too-politically-incorrect-for-UK-and-US-audiences.html> (last accessed 4 February 2019).

Nathan, Patrick (2014), 'Qu'est-ce qu'on a fait au bon dieu?', *Témoinage Chrétien*, 18 July.

Pettersen, David (2016), 'Transnational Blackface, Neo-Minselstry and the 'French Eddie Murphy' in *Intouchables*', *Modern & Contemporary France*, 24, pp. 51–69.

Powrie, Phil (1998), 'Heritage, History and New Realism.' *Modern & Contemporary France*, 6:4, pp. 479–491.

'Qu'est-ce qu'on a fait au bon dieu?: Enquête sur un phénomène' (2014), *Marianne*, 9 May.

Regnier, Isabelle (2017), 'Gangsterdam: trois pieds nickelés dans les filets de la pègre', *Le Monde*, 28 March, <https://www.lemonde.fr/cinema/article/2017/03/28/gangsterdam-trois-pieds-nickeles-dans-les-filets-de-la-pegre_5101692_3476.html> (last accessed 4 February 2019).

Rosello, Mireille (2018), 'L'emergence des comédies communautaires dans le cinéma français: ambiguitiés et paradoxes', *Studies in French Cinema*, 18:1: pp. 18–34.

Schatz, Thomas (2003), 'The New Hollywood', in Julian Stringer (ed.), *Movie Blockbusters*, London: Routledge.

Schatz, Thomas (1981), *Hollywood Genres: Formulas, Filmmaking and the Studio*, Philadelphia: Temple University Press.
Vanderschelden, Isabelle (2005), 'Jamel Debbouze: A New Popular French Star?', *Studies in French Cinema* 5, pp. 61–72.
Vincendeau, Ginette (2014), 'From the Margins to the Center: French Stardom and Ethnicity', in Hilary Radner, Alistair Fox, Michel Marie and Raphaëlle Moine (eds), *A Companion to Contemporary French Cinema*, London: Wiley-Blackwell, pp. 547–569.
Weissberg, Jay (2012), 'Review: Untouchable', *Variety*, 29 September. <https://variety.com/2011/film/reviews/untouchable-1117946269/> (last accessed 6 February 2019).

CONCLUSION:
A DISPUTED HERITAGE

At Cannes in 2010, a boisterous, ten-minute standing ovation followed a quiet, mannered film about a group of ill-fated monks (Henning 2011: 77). The fifth feature-length effort from Xavier Beauvois, *Des hommes et des dieux / Of Gods and Men* focuses on the two-year span leading up to the fateful events of 18 May 1996, the day that eight monks from Tibéhirine were beheaded after refusing to abandon their mountain monastery during the Algerian Civil War. Critics raved in the aftermath of the film's *Grand Prix* win, calling it an instant 'classic' (Widemann 2010a), praising its relatable message of faith that 'even non-believers can get' (Frois and Le Fol 2010) and lauding its treatment of the enduring mystery around the tragic murders (later investigations implicated the Algerian army and government rather than the fundamentalists initially blamed) (Broussard 2010). This acclaim was a mere prelude to the following September, when the film also surprisingly dominated the national box office, drawing 300,000 viewers on its opening weekend, and remaining atop the rankings despite the annual autumn parade of Hollywood Oscar contenders onto French screens. Here then, once again, was an individual title whose aesthetic peculiarities and financial success spurred a slew of secondary reflections about the amplitude of contemporary 'popular' French cinema – and its capacity for generating its own form of 'blockbuster' cinema.

By year's end, *Of Gods and Men* was touted as the most unexpected Gallic hit in recent memory. A modestly budgeted (€4 million) auteur venture into 'slow cinema' aesthetics (De Luca and Jorge 2016) that still managed to draw 3.2

million viewers to the cinema, it conjured memories not just of the traumatic events it treated on screen, but also of the recent legacy of heritage cinema – the genre chosen to lead the renewed French charge against Hollywood some thirty years prior (see Chapter 2). In many cases, scholars have also aligned it with the visual and narrative tropes of that genre. Hilary Radner, for instance, argues that the film's combination of visual simplicity and aestheticisation places it in familiar territory, 'aligning [it] with academicism of the heritage film more generally' (Radner 2015: 301). For our purposes here, the varied responses to the atypical success of a slow-paced heritage auteur film also serve to bring us full circle, re-invigorating the sorts of perennial strategic and cultural questions at stake in this book.

OF HERITAGE AND CRITICISM

Ostensibly 'about' the contemporary re-invention of national traditions, the heritage film ranks as one of Europe's more frequent gambits for seducing international audiences while re-captivating domestic ones. Beyond a focus on historical, bio-historical or literary recreation, recent iterations of the genre also resonate with a history of largely unrequited Franco-European ambitions to 'go global'. From the Film Europe 'super productions' of the 1920s (Thompson 1987) to the 'Euro Puddings' of the 1950s and 1960s (Bergfelder 2004) and the Langian blockbusters of the 1990s (Chapter 1), attempts to merge a pan-European global sensibility with popular forms tend to suffer both critically and economically, falling prey to the often deadly combination of universalist designs laced with varying degrees of local authenticity. Yet as Bélen Vidal points out, post-1990s incarnations of the genre in many ways succeeded where previous versions fell short, managing to be 'embraced by international audiences in search of the pleasures of cultural authenticity without the demands of the art film' (Vidal 2012: 53). In the case of France, this analysis is certainly accurate in a general sense, but our coverage of that period also suggests an industrial background that makes it more complicated (see Chapter 1).

Gallic debates about heritage should be seen in light of concurrent trends elsewhere in Europe. In the UK, for instance, Andrew Higson warned in 1993 that despite the 'liberal-humanist' intentions of films like *Chariots of Fire* (Hudson 1981) and *A Room with a View* (Ivory 1985), the films were often submerged by a 'visually spectacular pastiche' that celebrated a photogenic, pastoral – and ideologically suspicious – upper class history (Higson 1993: 109–110). Compared with the more immediate and gritty depictions of contemporary British life in films like *My Beautiful Laundrette* (Frears 1985) the 'heritage space' evoked by the Merchant-Ivory trend made period details of costume and landscape into 'an autonomous attraction' (Higson 1993: 125) that evoked 'pastness' without a genuine concern for its social and material conditions (Higson 1993: 110). A breakthrough moment for the confluence between film theory, cultural studies and concepts of the 'national', the 1990s 'heritage film debate' (later delineated as such by Clare Monk) followed Higson's remarks by reaching beyond his narrowly Thatcherite reflection-ism to affirm the genre's essential plurality, and to filter its visual pleasures through other lenses – popular reception (Monk 2011), feminist readings of genre (Pidduck 2004) and a 'figural' tradition of film theory (Vidal 2012). In a related but wider-ranging study, Rosalind Galt convincingly argues that materialist critiques like the one lodged by Higson and many others reduce the ideological possibilities of the genre's 'decorative image' in a cynical (and quite patriarchal) condemnation of formal beauty common to an entire lineage of film criticism (Galt 2006; Galt 2011).

Since the turn of the century, scholarship on contemporary Gallic variants of heritage cinema has worked to disentangle its features from these signifi-cant cross-channel currents.[1] Though superficially similar to Thatcherite films, post-Lang heritage blockbusters are also their own historical beast – initially a result of a Socialist search for new forms of popular culture that crested with films like *Cyrano* (Rappeneau 1990) and *Germinal* (Berri 1993) (see Chapter 1). Despite these origins, the genre has encountered similar obstacles to cul-tural legitimacy in France. As early as 1992, critic and film scholar Antoine De Baecque expressed broad suspicion of the Lang films, likening them to the infamous 'Tradition of Quality' famously reviled by his predecessors at *Cahiers du cinéma* (De Baecque 1992, referenced in Vidal 2012: 20). Though similar in flavour to Higson's critique, the exceptionalist edge to much recent French film scholarship and criticism often adds local colour to the work on the Gallic heritage film, where scholars often find themselves hashing out their arguments against a backdrop of presumed ideological critique. James F. Austin, for instance, describes the lingering doubt brought to French criticism by a much longer European philosophical tradition, where 'Too much interest in pretty visuals is, in and of itself, suspicious' (Austin 2004: 292) while Dayna Oscherwitz spends an entire chapter of her book defending the remit of the genre beyond costume drama and literary adaptations while pushing it to include films like *Amélie* (Jeunet 2001) and *The Gleaners and I* (Varda 2000), which she claims call for a 'revision and expansion' of the genre to include different types of films (Oscherwitz 2010: 99).

What scholars of French heritage cinema tend to acknowledge less overtly is how the recent trajectory of the genre also dovetails with the industry's quite particular (and ongoing) ambivalence about its relationship to 'globalised' forms of popular culture. Early Langian heritage blockbusters like *Indochine* (Wargnier 1992) at first may have seemed to vindicate the populist repackag-ing of national traditions under Mitterrand, but their ability to draw audiences away from global Hollywood franchises was short-lived (Chapter 1). Even so, as support for the ambitions of that first big-budget cycle dwindled, the funding mechanisms they left behind forged a path for the emergence of a different sort of 'heritage' altogether – the revamped popular films that constitute the primary impetus behind this book. Taking stock of these changes, Gwenaëlle Le Gras shows how recent French films like *La Môme* (Dahan 2008), *Mesrine* (Richet 2008) and *Coco avant Chanel* (Fontaine 2009) use historical takes on the biopic to splice 'serious' historiography with a renewed focus on commercialised stardom – a move that helps them appeal to the audiences of both art and popular cinema, hence remedying the 'ideological fracture that has been aggravated by systems of financial support and modes of production in France' (Le Gras 2015: 323). Here Le Gras is on the same page with heritage genre specialist Vidal, who argues that European heritage films have recently found their 'own niche as part of an international popular film culture that exposes and occasionally interrogates received ideas about national identities' and yet 'also constitutes a belated phase in the rebranding of the national as a strategy for survival in the globalized market' (Vidal 2012: 78).

And it is here, at last, that *Of Gods and Men* re-emerges, offering a stark example of how the paradoxical energies at the heart of an ongoing drive for stylistic 'diversity' remains a generative force behind the cultural posture of the industry more generally. Notwithstanding the generous talents of lead actors Lambert Wilson and Michael Lonsdale, *Of Gods and Men* does not compare readily with other trends in star-driven heritage cinema since the 1990s. If anything, its extended scenes of chanting and daily ritual are far more reminiscent of the German documentary *Into Great Silence* (Gröninger 2007) than any previous post-Langian costume drama. Moreover, it is perhaps also because the aesthetic of the film downplays the mediating commercial moves so typical of other French heritage films of the 2000s that its subsequent success created a platform for debate.

Of Monks and Diversity

If the deliberately 'slow cinema' approach in *Of Gods and Men* isn't abundantly clear from the film's austere marketing campaign or its trailer, numerous sequences of the film verily announce it to the viewer. Here the camera moves over the chanting, hirsute visages of the eight doomed protagonists in such deliberate fashion that it could be read as a stylistic rejoinder to other memorable entries in the French heritage tradition – certainly the bullet-time flamboyance of a *Brotherhood of the Wolf* (Gans 2001), but also the crowded battle sequences of *Germinal* (Berri 1993) or even the more conventional fascination with nostalgic grandeur evoked by *L'Anglaise et le Duc* (Rohmer 2001) or *La Princesse de Montpensier* (Tavernier 2010).

Twin narratives of the film's critical and commercial success began to unfold. In an initial phase quite typical of Cannes coverage, the reception combined rather different rhetorics of authorship and history. Here Beauvois was understandably front and centre, telling the Catholic readership of *La Croix* that his approach to cinematography was inspired by 'the same rigor with which [the monks] lived' (Raspiengeas 2010) even as he pointed the more *cinéphiliac* readers of *Les Inrockuptibles* to its visual resemblance to Leone westerns (Barnett and Morrain 2010). To some extent, a differential approach to publications is to be expected in the marketing of a film. In this case, however, it took on a more pointedly exceptionalist slant as the film opened wide in the autumn.

Of Gods and Men emerged from select screenings for Catholic audiences during the summer to general release on 8 September 2010. Building on the growing buzz since Cannes, mainstream media coverage amplified certain angles of its aesthetics that began with the festival – in many cases emphasising its contrast with various traits of popular cinema. In an interview with *L'Humanité*, for instance, screenwriter Etienne Comar recalls that his original script initially imitated the flashback structure of the American television series *Lost*, but changed when Beauvois demanded that a more commercialised approach be jettisoned for the asceticism more typical of his previous films – and, he argued, more appropriate to the film's subject matter (Widemann 2010b). Meanwhile, interviews with the director and his actors dwelled on a religious angle, with Beauvois (who is elsewhere described as a devout agnostic) pointing out that the deceased monks actually 'spoke to him' about how to approach the film's final shot – convincing him that he should replace an image of their decapitated heads with what became its memorable last frame of their figures walking off and disappearing into falling snow (Carrière 2010). As if on cue, Serge Kaganski of *Libération* extolled the authorial virtues of features like these while also managing to highlight his own erudite knowledge of the history of auteur cinema:

> Even if we forget that we might die some day, we cannot forget that Xavier Beauvois is a self-taught cinéphile, a disciple of great critics like Jean Douchet and Serge Daney, and a fan like them of the most important Christian filmmakers, or should I say mystics, like Rossellini, Dreyer and Bresson. [...] [The film is] a serene painting of a community, illustrated through simple but significant shots, attentive to details of space, free of recourse to affected spectacle, economical in its dialogue, and full of suggestive truths. It's as if Beauvois has scored his film to the patient rhythm of the monastic ethic, or at least to the tempo of the great masters of cinema – we think of course of Renoir, Rossellini or Ford. (Kaganski 2010)

Still known to many as the leader of the charge against *Amélie* a decade prior, Kaganski self-consciously plays here on his own reputation as a devout aesthetic exceptionalist. Yet even without exaggerating the words of a few critics, it is possible to see here how the features of the film came into contact with the different framing tendencies we have been working to identify in this book.

Over the weeks that followed, the film faced down more conventionally 'big' films at the French box office, and its features became readable beyond the narrowly authorial frame suggested earlier. Here journalists from a variety of publications sought to re-frame the film's success as a 'phenomenon' – and to measure its aesthetic features according to various transnational contexts. Two weeks into its run, an exuberant pair of *Libération* critics overtly linked *Of Gods and Men* to the political economic model of French cinema:

> These are the joys and surprises of the French cultural exception: an austere film about a group of ill-fated monks who swallow their last spoonfuls of soup and down their last glasses of wine, trembling, doubting and praying. It's almost like Bernanos or Bresson is outdrawing Ben Affleck (*The Town*) and Angelina Jolie (*Salt*). (Arnaud and Péron 2010)

These words display the measuring stick by which the 'popular' features of French cinema are routinely gauged today. On one hand, the 'joy' and 'surprise' alluded to by the authors resonates with the long-term ideological vantage point of cinéphiles with their own ideas about what the goals of the 'mixed-economy' system should be. On this view, their words might even be read as an implicit riposte against other production strategies – which might be based more on chasing the bottom line; as they reflect at the end of the article, 'the most gratifying part' is that *Of Gods and Men* reveals 'the unpredictable nature of an art form that can never be completely reduced to formula or recipe. In sum, the film is a miracle' (Arnaud and Péron 2010). In other words, properly honouring a national tradition launched by artists like Bernanos and Bresson means embracing a filmmaking heritage that continues to resist the temptations of conforming to market principles.

In the ensuing weeks, a professionalist strain of rhetoric also emerged, complementing the devout exceptionalism already on full display since May. Four days after the spread in *Libération*, *Le Monde* published its own extended exposé on the film's success, reporting on its box office fortunes week-by-week while adopting a longer historical perspective:

> Close to 1.3 million tickets sold in just 19 days! The huge success of *Of Gods and Men* is a surprise. Once in awhile, an unexpected film draws crowds here, as did *Les Choristes* with 8.5 million in 2004. But it is much

more rare for a film on such a tough subject – the monks of Tibéhirine, in Algeria, captured and assassinated in 1996. (Baro and Guerin 2010)

In the same article, readers were also given numerous details about the film's exhibition and distribution. Here a week-by-week account traces the film's journey and measures its ability to compete on the open market against more traditional blockbusters like *Inception* (Nolan 2010) – week one: 468,000 tickets on 252 prints; week two: 481,000 tickets on 424 prints; week three: 336,000 tickets on 442 prints. Allied with this 'neutral' economic account came a pragmatist view of how the film could appeal to multiple audiences. As Eric Libot of *L'Express* put it, 'From the atheist to the minister, the believer to the soccer player, the cinéphile to the buffoon, and Uncle Boonmee to Auntie Georgette, all will find something in this film that speaks directly to their own personal experiences' (Libot 2010).

One month later, as the film eventually lost its top place on the box office rankings, yet another round of analyses emerged, this time consecrating Beauvois and the film as the most recent 'phenomenon' of French popular cinema. On 13 October, *L'Express* reiterated the basic lines of exceptionalism floated by Beauvois and later taken up by Kaganski and *Libération*. This time, however, they explicitly connected the film's deliberate pacing to a form of cultural (and implied cinematic) resistance:

> Xavier Beauvois expresses a form of resistance against contemporary culture that echoes in some ways the militants of today who call for simplicity, for reasoned consumption, for a stately grace for respect for nature's gifts. (Chartier *et al.* 2010)

Three days later, the traditionally right-of-centre staff at *Le Figaro* offered the most thorough retrospective to date, in which they echoed their colleagues from *Le Monde* about the relevance of the film as a 'cultural phenomenon':

> When a film approaches or passes 3 million tickets sold, it enters the category of 'phenomenons' that we try to explain. The reasons are most often sociological (*Bienvenue Chez les Ch'tis*), generational (*Brice de Nice, Inception*), or technological (*Avatar*). That's why *Of Gods and Men* is so intriguing. It doesn't seem to appeal to an explicit part of the population or to a specific age group, and it does not rely on technical prowess. That means that its success comes first and foremost from its cinematographic virtues. (Sevilla and Buisson 2010)

Here again, various types of cinema are listed alongside each other, suggesting that while success is always difficult to predict, a pragmatist embrace of all of the above might be the most prudent option – and offer the most routes to commercial success and cultural viability. Crucially, although the article also conducts a thorough discussion of the other reasons for the film's success (religious audience, distribution and marketing efforts and great performances by the cast), *Le Figaro* also seeks to yank the film away from the public's interest in actual historical events, instead arguing that its success relates not to any relationship to factual history but rather to its enduring aesthetic qualities as a 'little masterpiece' of the cinema (Sevilla and Buisson 2010).

For our purposes here, the rare success of a film like *Of Gods and Men* stands out for how it incited agreement among French publications more traditionally known to occupy different ends of the ideological spectrum. And although they do emphasise different elements of the film in their coverage, diverse outlets managed to arrive at a common reading of the film's unexpected commercial 'bigness'. Whatever slant they adopted – from auteurist (*Les Inrocks*), to Catholic (*Le Croix*), to Marxist (*Libération*), to 'objectively' economic (*Le Monde*), to reservedly nationalist (*Le Figaro*) – critics seemed to agree that this was a specimen that could serve as evidence for the overall particularity – and success – of the film industry as a whole. Moreover that consensus was far from free of blind spots. Amidst the initial excitement around the film's Cannes opening, historian Benjamin Stora cautioned the readers of *L'Express* about embracing the film's view of history, arguing that the ambiguous ending served to obscure the emerging facts about what actually happened (Stora 2010), a point picked up on by *Libération* reviewers when they revisited the 'entirely fantasised' film a year later (Loiseau 2011). Yet both the euphoric rhetoric around the film's success and its notable oversights become more difficult to parse without knowledge of the years of cultural and industrial sedimentation that inform them both.

OF FRANCE AND BLOCKBUSTERS

Despite clear connections to the heritage impulse of the Socialist reformers that began this account, *Of Gods and Men* belongs definitively in its conclusion. There are both chronological and methodological reasons for this. In the opening sections of this book, we saw the longer-term evidence for how the French film industry has worked to change its international profile by remaking itself as the source of aggressively commercial filmmaking practices to go along with a renowned legacy of auteur cinema. From this perspective, the rise of a modestly budgeted auteur title from a venue like Cannes to the 'blockbuster' echelon of national success (3.2 million tickets) could be used to suggest that any strategy for competing with Hollywood 'toe to toe' – from within its economic and aesthetic lures – is foolhardy at best. Not only that, but the unprecedented success of a contemplative, ambiguous, slow-paced work about the everyday lives of monks seems to offer aesthetic ammunition for the most vociferous critics of Lang's legacy. So if *Of Gods and Men* generated a new 'conversation' in the French public sphere, it was one that actually seemed to confirm what exceptionalist critics of 'French blockbusters' have been arguing for years – that French cinema is at its strongest when it seeks to embrace truly alternative types of filmmaking that, were it not for Hollywood hegemony, might flourish in France.

Yet although the rousing success story of a film like this in 2010 might seem to offer a rebuttal of the strategic wisdom of the tradition traced in the past few chapters of this book, its reception also reinforces their central claim. As the series of case studies that follow this book's opening contextual canvasses suggest in different ways, 'globalised' French cinema of the current era cannot be reduced to one strategy or aesthetic 'program' alone (Frodon 1999: 692). Rather, since the advent of Canal Plus and the various 'mixed market' strategies it engendered, the Gallic film industry has become remarkable for an often unruly amalgam of quite different philosophical tendencies and practices that find expression in a conjoined ethos about how to seek success – despite manifest disagreements on how to define what that word means. And in almost every case, the films that actually emerge from this current state of affairs are far from univocal about their cultural and political-economic bearing. Rather, what most characterises the contemporary cultural phenomena I am designating the 'French blockbuster' is its status as a site of struggle manifested in the sphere of French cultural politics by brief flurries of rhetorical energy that cut across discursive fields, and wherein the sheer spread of opinions exposes the ideological conflicts that remain very much alive within a community that produces and consumes them. Despite the historical efforts by Lang and his cohort, and notwithstanding the recent incursions by companies like EuropaCorp and StudioCanal, the production of a sustainable form of Francoglobal franchise filmmaking remains an elusive goal at best. Yet the account offered in these pages remains less concerned with any putative generic form than with historicising the cluster of hopes and fears that hovers around the engaging possibility of finding one.

One of our other primary suggestions in this book has been that responses to the seeming paradox of its title are also conditioned by what role the reader envisions for the French media industries in an era where uneven exchange with global Hollywood has become quotidian reality. Rather than any univocal response to this initial query, this account proposes a way to think through the entwined generative factors and explanatory frameworks that impinge on that very question. Reasonable people can come to address these dilemmas in different ways, and each time a French-made film breaks – or seeks to break – the mold, it sets off a parallel conversation about cultural ownership and legitimacy that has important historical dimensions of its own. From this perspective, each of the chapters in this book constitutes a small step towards accumulating an alternative view of contemporary French cinema as an industry engaged in a persistent and ongoing dalliance with what Raphaelle Moine would term the 'genericity' (*généricité*) of the 'big' film (Moine 2009: 9).

By seeking to balance the explanatory weight of the quite different views that exist on this issue within the current industry and cultural establishment, we see how ambitious and/or successful commercialised cinema becomes a site for a Gallic staging and re-staging an ongoing quandary about the remit of localised culture in a global age. The first chapter began with an excavation of the Socialist reform movement of the 1980s, in which we find a historical record that offers thirty-plus years of new 'mixed economy' strategies intended to encourage commercialised entrepreneurship in the Hexagon. Viewed against this backdrop, recent trends in popular French cinema start to look much less like a post- national 'erasure' (Danan 2006: 177) or a disreputable form of 'globalised' film practices (Hjort 2009: 15) than a series of tentative, mixed transnational parries from the culture industry that has long housed different mindsets about how to best address the challenges of 'going global'. To better capture these vexed dynamics, we therefore proposed a concentric model for viewing three concomitant ways that one industry works to produce – but also to describe and to understand – its own relationship to globalised cinema (Chapter 2). Each of the following four chapters then shows how these concurrent views rise to the surface in a localised politics of readability surrounding the features of the films themselves. In some cases, we see those tendencies emerge in the collective assessments of individual films – especially those that seem to inspire or challenge the definitions of what French filmmaking can be – an *Amélie* (Chapter 3) or a *Valerian* (Chapter 4). In other cases, we find that these ideological affiliations inform longer-term industrial patterns of change, be they the incipient forms of 'global' articulation in fast-cut action sequences (Chapter 5) or the 'double-voiced' appeals of recent 'politically incorrect' comedy hits (Chapter 6).

Finally, perhaps the most daunting challenge – and provocation – of proposing an account like this one remains the intellectual obstacles to adopting a multi-perspectival approach to the narrativisation of recent French film history. On one level, the various topics related to popular cinema covered in these chapters all circulate in the push-pull of an inveterately localised dialogue occurring among French-language articles and media coverage. However, news of these internal debates rarely if ever travel, and when they do – as with the '*Amélie* effect' (Chapter 3) or the recent Cannes-Netflix conflict (Chapter 1) – their nuances do not translate easily to other shores. As Jonathan Buchsbaum shows, the scant media coverage of the French film industry in North America only continues to replicate fundamental misunderstandings about what terms like 'cultural exception' and 'cultural diversity' even mean

– let alone how France's labyrinthine set of cultural policies actually play out on the ground (Buchsbaum 2016: xix–xxvii). To Buchsbaum's breathtaking account of cultural policy since Lang, I would therefore simply like to add a measured proviso. For if the general neglect of the French film industry in North American media coverage does create the potential for broad misunderstanding among the general public, that same knowledge vacuum also tends to create a kind of perverse echo in academic circles, which instead tends to embrace narratives of resistance in a far less scrutinised way than those advanced in the pages of a book like *Exception Taken*. From this perspective, the different strands of what we have been calling the professionalist discourse are frequently shrugged off as self-serving manoeuvres of the powerful, while the concurrent, pragmatist search for consensus and problem solving offers far too blunt an instrument for fighting against it.

And this is where I hope the tripartite discursive model proposed here – with its three concomitant viewpoints on transnationalism – can stake a claim. With due respect to all they have contributed to the history of cinema, I would wager that unexamined exceptionalist framings of contemporary French cinema also skew our perspective of what the Gallic industry is actually doing these days – much less what it has been up to for the past three decades. French sociologist Olivier Alexandre expresses similar sentiments in the opening salvo of his recent book *La règle de l'exception*:

> In the eyes of the world, the country of the Lumière brothers remains the embodiment of all that opposes Hollywood hegemony and of the liberal-ised initiatives of the European Commission. [. . .] The legacy of the New Wave continues, and with it the concept of the *auteur*, not just as a way to organize how films are made, but also to determine how we think about them. This book instead seeks to analyze foundations, to understand how this system actually works and to reveal the contradictions that lie beneath this 'exceptional' state of affairs [*régime de l'exception*] [. . .] To carry this project out, we must therefore reverse the perspective that most people are used to taking on the subject. While the public and the media most often concentrate on the films, we are interested in the very system that makes them possible. (Alexandre 2015: 14)

The role of the present account, I hope, will be to complement ground breaking work like Alexandre's, offering a developed case study of how the ideological fault lines in contemporary French film culture tend to colour how various players in the industry and cultural establishment read a disputed recent heritage of 'going global'.

If national film studies are to become truly transnational, I would wager, they must reach not only for a plurality of methods beyond national containers, but also for the historically determined ways that localised discourses of 'transnationalism' develop over time, in many cases in a push-and-pull dynamic with the same political-economic and aesthetic traditions they aim to transcend. In the process, as we have seen in this extended case study of France's blockbuster ambitions, the various discursive traces of those exchanges intermittently rise to the surface of visual culture itself, reflecting in and refracting from the ambivalent features of popular films that continue to animate the disputed frontiers of what it still means to make (or see) a 'French' film today.

NOTE

1. Contributions to this literature include Moine and Beylot 2009; Vincendeau 2001; Oscherwitz 2010; Radner 2015; and Le Gras 2015.

WORKS CITED

Alexandre, Olivier (2015), *La règle de l'exception: Ecologie du cinéma français*, Paris: Editions EHSS.

Arnaud, Didier and Didier Péron (2010), 'La France chauffée aux moines', *Libération*, 25 September, <https://next.liberation.fr/cinema/2010/09/25/la-france-chauffee-aux-moines_681587> (last accessed 4 February 2019).

Austin, James F. (2004), 'Digitizing Frenchness in 2001: On a 'Historic' Moment in French Cinema', *French Cultural Studies*, 15:3, pp. 281–299.

Barnett, Emily and Jean-Baptiste Morain (2010), 'Xavier Beauvois, Réalisateur Des hommes et des dieux', *Les Inrockuptibles*, 26 May.

Baro, Romain and Michel Guerin (2010), 'Des hommes et des dieux, quel succès', *Le Monde*, 28 September, <https://www.lemonde.fr/cinema/article/2010/09/28/des-hommes-et-des-dieux-quel-succes_1417054_3476.html> (last accessed 4 February 2019).

Bergfelder, Tim (2004), *International Adventures: German Popular Cinema and Co-Productions in the 1960s*, New York: Berghahn Books.

Broussard, Philippe (2010), 'Une drame, trois thèses', *L'Express*, 1 September 2010.

Buchsbaum, Jonathan (2016), *Exception Taken: How France has Defied Hollywood's New World Order*, New York: Columbia University Press.

Chartier, Claire, Christophe Carrière and Kevin Louargant (2010), 'Des hommes et des dieux, du film au phenomène', *L'Express*, 13 October.Carrière, Christophe (2010), 'Il était une foi', *L'Express*, 1 September.Danan, Martine (2006), 'National and Postnational French Cinema', in Paul Willeman and Valentina Vitali (eds), *Theorising National Cinema*, London: British Film Institute, pp. 172–186.

De Luca, Tiago and Nuno Barradas Jorge (eds), (2015), *Slow Cinema*, Edinburgh: Edinburgh University Press.

Frodon, Jean-Michel (1999). *L'âge moderne du cinéma français: de la nouvelle vague à nos jours*. Paris; Flammarion.

Frois, Emmanuelle et Sébastien Le Fol (2010), 'Profession: conseiller monastique', *Le Figaro*, May 19, <http://www.lefigaro.fr/festival-de-cannes/2010/05/18/03011-20100518ARTFIG00647-profession-conseiller-monastique.php> (last accessed 4 February 2019).

Galt, Rosalind (2006), *The New European Cinema: Redrawing the Map*, New York: Columbia University Press.

Galt, Rosalind (2011), *Pretty: Film and the Decorative Image*, New York: Columbia University Press.

Greene, Naomi (1999), *Landscapes of Loss: The National Past in Post-War French Cinema*, Princeton: Princeton University Press.

Henning, Christophe (2011), 'Des hommes et des dieux: retour sur les raisons d'un succès', *Etudes*, 415: pp. 77–88.

Higson, Andrew (1993), 'Re-presenting the national past: nostalgia and pastiche in the heritage film', in Lester Friedman (ed.), *Fires Were Started: British Cinema and Thatcherism*, Minneapolis: University of Minnesota Press, pp. 109–129.

Hjort, Mette (2009), 'On the Plurality of Cinematic Transnationalism', in Kathleen Newman and Natasa Durovicova (eds), *World Cinema, Transnational Perspectives*, London: Routledge, pp. 12–33.

Kaganski, Serge (2010), 'Des hommes et des dieux, le film de la grâce'. *Les Inrockuptibles*, 8 September, <https://www.lesinrocks.com/cinema/films-a-l-affiche/des-hommes-et-des-dieux-le-film-de-la-grace/> (last accessed 4 February 2019).

Le Gras, Gwanaelle (2015), 'Major Stars, the Heritage Film and Patrimonial Values in Contemporary French Cinema', in Hilary Radner, Alistair Fox, Michel Marie and Raphaëlle Moine (eds), *A Companion to Contemporary French Cinema*, pp. 314–332.

Libot, Eric (2010), 'A hauteur d'hommes', *L'Express*, 8 September.

Loiseau, Sylvain (2011), 'Retour sur *Des hommes et des dieux*', *Libération*, 27 April, <https://next.liberation.fr/culture/2011/04/27/retour-sur-des-hommes-et-des-dieux_731640> (last accessed 4 February 2019).

Moine, Raphaëlle (2009), 'Film, genre et interprétation', *Le Français Aujourd'hui*, 165, pp. 9–16.

Moine, Raphaëlle and Pierre Beylot (eds) (2009), *Fictions patrimoniales sur grand et petit écran: Contours et enjeux d'un genre intermédiatique*, Paris: Broché.

Monk, Clare (2011), *Heritage Film Audiences: Period Films and Contemporary Film Audiences in the UK*, Edinburgh: Edinburgh University Press.

Oscherwitz, Dayna (2010), *Past Forward: French Cinema and the Post-Colonial Heritage*, Carbondale: Southern Illinois University Press.

Pidduck, Julianne (2004), *Contemporary Costume Film: Space, Place and the Past*, London: British Film Institute.

Radner, Hilary (2015), 'The Historical Film and Contemporary French Cinema: Representing the Past in the Present', in Hilary Radner, Raphëlle Moine, Alistair Fox and Michel Marie (eds), *Companion to Contemporary French Cinema*, London: Wiley-Blackwell.

Raspiengeas, Jean-Claude (2010), 'Entretien avec Xavier Beauvois', *La Croix*, 10 May.

Sevilla, Jean and Jean-Christophe Buisson (2010), '*Des hommes et des dieux*: Cinq grands raisons l'expliquent', *Le Figaro Magazine*, 16 October.

Stora, Benjamin (2010), 'L'Algérie comme un décor', *L'Express*, 13 September.

Thompson, Kristin (1987), 'The End of the "Film Europe" Movement', in Tom O'Regan and Brian Shoesmith (eds), *History on/and/in Film*, Perth: History & Film Association of Australia, pp. 45–56.

Vidal, Bélen (2012), *Heritage Film: Nation, Genre and Representation*, London: Wallflower.

Vincendeau, Ginette (2001), 'Introduction', *Film/Literature/Heritage: A Sight & Sound Reader*, London: British Film Institute.

Widemann, Dominique (2010a), 'Dieu dit: vous mourez comme des hommes', *L'Humanité*, May 19.

Widemann, Dominique (2010b), 'Dire la fraternité dont témoignent les moines: Entretien Etienne Comar', *L'Humanité*, 7 September.

INDEX

Note: *italic* signifies illustration; n signifies note; t signifies table